AGILITY

AGILITY

Competing and Winning in a Tech-Savvy Marketplace

MARK MUELLER-EBERSTEIN

John Wiley & Sons, Inc.

Published by John Wiley & Sons, Inc., Hoboken, New Jersey.
Published simultaneously in Canada.

For general information on our other products and services or for technical support, please contact our Customer Care Department within the United States at (800) 762-2974, outside the United States at (317) 572-3993 or fax (317) 572-4002.

Wiley also publishes its books in a variety of electronic formats. Some content that appears in print may not be available in electronic books. For more information about Wiley products, visit our web site at www.wiley.com.

Library of Congress Cataloging-in-Publication Data:

Mueller-Eberstein, Mark, 1970-
Agility : competing and winning in a tech-savvy marketplace / Mark Mueller-Eberstein.
p. cm.—(Microsoft executive leadership series ; 21)
Includes index.
ISBN 978-0-470-63544-5; ISBN 978-0-470-91250-8(ebk);
ISBN 978-0-470-91251-5 (ebk); ISBN 978-0-470-91252-2(ebk)
1. Information technology—Management. 2. Creative ability in business. 3. Success in business. I. Title.
HD30.2.M873 2010
658.4'01—dc22

2010021350

Printed in the United States of America

10 9 8 7 6 5 4 3 2 1

ABOUT THE EXECUTIVE LEADERSHIP SERIES

The Microsoft Executive Leadership Series is pleased to present independent perspectives from some of today's leading thinkers on the ways that IT innovations are transforming how organizations operate and how people work. The role of information technology in business, society, and our lives continues to increase, creating new challenges and opportunities for organizations of all types. The titles in this series are aimed at business leaders, policy makers, and anyone interested in the larger strategic questions that arise from the convergence of people, communication media, business process, and software.

Microsoft is supporting this series to promote richer discussions around technology and business issues. We hope that each title in the series contributes to a greater understanding of the complex uncertainties facing organizations operating in a fast-changing and deeply connected new world of work, and is useful in the internal dialogues that every business conducts as it plans for the future. It remains our privilege and our commitment to be part of those conversations.

Titles in the Executive Leadership Series:

The Think Factory: Managing Today's Most Precious Resource: People! by Susan D. Conway, 2006

Rules to Break and Laws to Follow: How Your Business Can Beat the Crisis of Short-Termism by Don Peppers and Martha Rogers, 2008

Generation Blend: Managing Across the Technology Age Gap by Rob Salkowitz, 2008

Uniting the Virtual Workforce by Karen Sobel Lojeski and Richard Reilly, 2008

Drive Business Performance: Enabling a Culture of Intelligent Execution by Bruno Aziza and Joey Fitts, 2008

Listening to the Future: Why It's Everybody's Business by Daniel W. Rasmus with Rob Salkowitz, 2008

Business Agility: Sustainable Prosperity in a Relentlessly Competitive World by Michael Hugos, 2009

Strategic Project Portfolio Management: Enabling a Productive Organization by Simon Moore, 2009

Leading the Virtual Workforce by Karen Sobel Lojeski and Richard Reilly, 2009

Young World Rising: How Youth Technology and Entrepreneurship Are Changing the World from the Bottom Up by Rob Salkowitz, 2010

My Parents & Melanie, you rock!

Patcha, Maximilian and Annalisa:
Thanks for all the happiness—
thanks for being you.

CONTENTS

PREFACE

It is said that "You are who you are with." I have had the great fortune to meet and learn from many smart people around the world—all with different experiences. I feel extremely thankful for the mentoring and guidance I have received and am enjoying giving back as much as I can. This book covers many of the lessons I have learned over the past years helping organizations use technology solutions to increase their agility in their business sector. The experience combined a lot of using the latest technologies with airplane and conference room conversations in far-flung places. I've had the opportunity to watch companies evolve from basic users of information technology to dynamic forces leading their industries by unlocking knowledge and potential.

This book is particularly aimed at:

- Business leaders who want to understand how technology can help them be fundamentally more successful and how they can evaluate and prioritize IT projects based on business impact.
- CIOs who are challenged with running an efficient and effective IT organization that empowers core businesses.

- IT leaders who want to move from being a cost center to a business driver and who want to articulate the current and potential value of their work and infrastructure to the business.
- Anybody who wants to become a leader in an organizations by tapping into the power of an optimized IT infrastructure.

Why is a company like Microsoft so interested in helping customers realize their potential? Why would a software vendor invest in helping customers realize as much value as possible from their products and their IT infrastructure overall instead of simply selling an additional product? In short, the more successful the customers' organizations are, the more value is generated and can be shared over the long run.

Over the last decade, enterprise software companies have developed a licensing model—organizations make a purchase decision for a specific product once and then move into a subscription or maintenance model. They pay an annual fee and receive updates to the software, often coupled with additional services, support, and so forth. For the software companies, this is a very predictable and profitable business model, allowing them to continually reinvest licensing fees into further innovation and development. And it works well for all if the software companies continue to improve the products and customers actually are continuing to upgrade and leverage the subsequent versions of the products they originally procured. Where this cycle doesn't happen, customers realize only a fraction of the value from their purchase and ultimately do not renew their maintenance agreements.

In 2005 I was looking for a new challenge within Microsoft. After spending four very, very interesting years discussing intellectual property challenges and product strategy—usually thinking a few product versions and market transformations ahead—I wanted a role that took me closer to our customers and partners again.

After looking at several groups, I received some mentoring advice from Microsoft Vice President Takeshi Numoto. It was simple; he said, "Join the Office team." I had worked in the Windows organization, with embedded devices (later became the phone business), and the Server team, so learning about the other "Big Business" of Microsoft made perfect sense for my next career steps.

For five years, my team and I were responsible for understanding and addressing the challenges in this cycle. And while, in the spirit of full disclosure, I am kind of a geek and find technology usually pretty cool, at the end of the day, it is the value for a customer and society the tools deliver that determine the technology's ultimate value. That holds true for software, as it does for most other areas—if you are developing new cars, new medication, new materials for new or familiar uses, a new breakfast cereal, or changing how processes work.

Little did I know how the experience of owning the topic of helping customers deploy Microsoft technology earlier would transform not only the company or how academics think about the impact of technology on business success but also myself. I got to meet and work with people who were passionate about the potential and customers elated to talk about their great experiences with technology and how it changed their businesses.

During those years, we had the opportunity to gain insights into thousands of organizations. Through the global Microsoft sales organization, we collected data on customers' affinity to adopt technologies, and we had an unknown number of discussions with IT and business decision makers. To all of you: Thanks for your insights; they were invaluable.

It didn't take long to realize that many customers did not actually use the latest technology but were several versions behind. They paid for the upgrades through software maintenance agreements so they had purchased the latest versions. But the innovation and enhancements weren't used and the software became "shelfware," collecting dust. The organizations often waited for years before actually making an upgrade or moving to a new platform.

I found it especially interesting to ask customers who had moved early: "Why?" Why did they not go the safe route? Why did they decide to be on the bleeding edge? And what was their experience? Sometimes the reasons for the move were simply that their old stuff was too old. Compatibility with the rest of the infrastructure made an upgrade impossible. But most often business changes were the triggers—usually from the core business function as well as from the business leader of the IT organization.

Changes rarely were initiated from within the "lower levels" of the IT departments. This surprised me. Aren't these the folks who know the technologies best and read the right papers, sites, and blogs? Why did they not help their business colleagues to understand what the technologies could do for them?

More often than not, the same IT people had trouble explaining to their business colleagues why an upgrade with all the cost and hassle associated would be necessary or even desirable. Wasn't there a saying "Never disturb a running system"? Was the investment worth it? What is the return on investment (ROI)?

There seemed to be this huge gap of understanding between the potential (and limitations) of technology known to the tech wizards and the colleagues who were just trying to run the actual business. I sometimes asked myself, "Does software really matter?" And after some eye-opening anecdotes, I had to ask, "Is there a correlation between customers who move quickly to adopt a new technology and their ultimate success in their business?"

Fortunately, some very smart people from institutions such as the Massachusetts Institute of Technology and Boston University as well as colleagues from our consulting and partner organizations asked themselves the same questions. While Microsoft had the data, our partners and consultants had the real customer stories and the university folks had the academic background and interest to really dive deep into the existing data and insights. They asked critical questions and developed new models of thinking.

What we found out was interesting—sometimes surprising—and it confirmed the general hypothesis that the speed of technology adoption *does* matter. We also learned that companies that are adopting technology faster are usually faster in adapting their processes, products, and workforce faster as well. And those same organizations are very often the current or upcoming leaders in their industry. We called them the "Agile organizations." And we could use them as benchmarks to compare with the majority and laggards in specific segments and areas.

Most organizational leaders want their organizations to be agile but often don't know how to identify which investment areas bring in the biggest returns. They also don't know how to leverage the technical competency that often already exists somewhere in the bowels of their organizations. Fortunately, the Microsoft ecosystem of solution partners and service organization developed and used a variety of approaches to help those leaders not only to prioritize but also to implement technical and organizational changes. Discussions about the business value of IT for specific challenges became the best and most helpful exchanges for our combined teams.

The literature over the last years has focused on the role of the chief information officer—the head of the IT business unit—to bridge this gap. This book will build on the experience and insights to provide a framework, common language, and better understanding for all of our roles and responsibilities. It will help the IT teams that need to make it happen show why and how they can help their business colleagues. And yes, it will help explain what those IT capabilities are and how they can help to run the business. It will help business owners ask the IT teams and providers the right questions about the capabilities they need to run the business better.

This book exists because of the huge business impact I have seen organizations achieve by adopting technology fast and right. It is the summary of our collective and empirical findings. It provides actual guidance on tackling the challenges of your business and how to fully leverage the potential of technology.

Many customers wanted to continue our dialog as technology and business needs evolved. This book starts the conversations. For those of you who want to discuss the ideas in this book or how you can personalize the concepts for your organization, I have founded a consulting organization (www.adgetec.com) through which my colleagues and I can be engaged. And yes, we are on Facebook, LinkedIn, and Twitter. I am personally looking forward to hearing from you at markme@adgetec.com. We can exchange, teach, and learn together.

ACKNOWLEDGMENTS

This book would not have been possible without the help of very special people. They have given their best. Credit belongs to them; any omissions or imperfections in this work are mine.

People say what they like best about working in Microsoft are the people with whom they work. It has been an extraordinary privilege to work on *Agility* with and on contributions of real leaders like Paul Lidbetter, Kyle Langenbach, Stephen Gordon, Ilco van der Bie, Tim Rowe, Roland Zeitler, and many others. Thanks for sharing your insights and experiences as well as providing invaluable contributions and feedback. Also thanks to Bob McDowell and Dan Rasmus, who inspired this project.

The infrastructure optimization team within Microsoft has been essential in developing the customer-focused approach as well as helping me in this process; especially Samm and Lisa, who supported the project to completion. Thanks to Samm DiStasio's leadership, Lisa Downey's invaluable coaching and guidance, Yoav Land's material, and last but not least Mathias Wunderer, who was instrumental in our analysis and insight generation of the IO data.

I am also indebted to the curiosity and dedication of the Boston University team of the Institute for Global Work, which includes

Kathleen F. Curley, Stephanie Watts, Andy Corbett, Zachary Halloran, and especially Professor John C. Henderson, whose intellectual and analytic capabilities helped me to find better and better angles to tackle the challenges.

Our Business Strategy consultants Simone Ruppertz-Rausch and Meinrad Lay generously shared their insights and experience the impact of their work for their clients business every day.

Liz Ngo allowed me the knowledge into new levels of technology value and introduced me to the team at Bloomberg L.P. (Pam Snook, Andre Paris, Stefanos Daskalakis) and Intuit (Alex Chriss).

It was uplifting to get insight on the impact technology makes on saving people's lives from Claire Bonilla and her Disaster Response team. Their work is an inspiration and cannot be overvalued.

To my other colleagues at Microsoft who introduced me to customers and partners, thanks for letting me stand on your shoulders and experiences; through you, I was able to gain the knowledge and understanding and build the content.

And of course I am indebted to the many IT and business leaders who took their time to explain their challenges and share their thoughts.

While storytelling and presenting and discussing insights has always been an interest of mine, writing a book to reach more people has been an interesting and humbling challenge. Fortunately, I was able to count on the phenomenal help of my editors, Bettijean Collins and Julie Bick, who helped me through this process and kept me going and accountable. Nor can I forget my agent and manager of the series, Jan Shanahan, whose guidance and encouragement were instrumental in getting the project going and finished. Some authors say that working with publishers is hard for them. Based on my experience with John Wiley & Sons, I have no idea what they are talking about. Sheck Cho and the Wiley team were fantastic and patient partners every step of the way. Thanks to you for sharing the enthusiasm about this project and excellence in managing the process.

Finally, family and friends are what gives our lives love, and what we do to make the world happier is our legacy.

This book is dedicated to you. Thanks! Danke!

Your love and encouragement are making this a great world every day. Especially my parents, Bernd and Rosemarie, and my sisters, Melanie and Malina: I am glad to be able to call you and my relatives "my family." Your nurturing and patience allowed me to grow, make mistakes, and learn and always be welcomed back and supported.

True friends are a very rare find. Those of you who have granted me your friendship over the years mean more to me than you might ever know.

My children, whose presence brighten my life. You can be so proud of your accomplishments and who you are.

True love is hard to find and truly priceless. Patcha, I am thankful for every hour I have with you. Your confidence, patience, and support are invaluable and give me happiness I didn't know was possible.

AGILITY

CHAPTER 1

LEADING INTO THE FUTURE

"Lead with the future, not with the past" is a favorite mantra of Microsoft's chief operating officer, Kevin Turner. Today, sticking with the tried and true won't keep a company in the lead for long. Technology has changed the landscape. Its powerful impact on business performance ensures that companies that do not know how to take advantage of new tools will lose their competitive edge.

Collaboration, customer communication, and product development are just three of the myriad areas where business strategy and technology intersect and go right to the bottom line. Companies that know how to efficiently choose, roll out, and measure the effect of new technology have shown themselves to be winners in today's marketplace. Whether it's reductions in energy use or a quicker time to market with a new product, companies like BMW and Del Monte have used technology to gain a competitive advantage. These are today's Agile companies.

CURRENT LANDSCAPE

In this book, you'll see the many ways technology agility impacts business performance and how you can get your company ready for and apply new technology. This is true whether your job is to define business strategy, manage facilities or sales accounts, or oversee technology and its management. Any and every part of your company can and will be transformed.

Often it is easier to recognize impact if observed through a magnifying glass, and economic shifts and crises can function as such. The financial, automotive, and healthcare industries are in the middle of radical change, and will take center stage in this book. They are both exciting and relevant, impacting most of our lives directly. At the same time, the insights crystallized here illustrate the impact of business and information technology (IT) agility or lack thereof and apply to business and IT decision makers in any industry.

Excellent technology by itself, though, cannot make an organization innovative or Agile. The nuts and bolts of a new technology are of course critical, but there's another set of factors that are equally important when it comes to creating an Agile company. It is essential to understand that a complete framework needs to be in place. This includes rules and processes as well as the organization's and individuals' attitudes toward change. Establishing a culture that welcomes and encourages change will go a long way to making your company Agile. Employees who embrace change look at new technology adoption as a way to improve their jobs and their performance. These tech-savvy workers are not only comfortable with new technologies, such as social networking, mobile access to information, and virtual workplaces, but they often already use them to do their work and expect them to be supported and provided by the organization they work for and interact with. In contrast, other employees may view change and new ways of doing things as obstacles or even threats, additional burdens to their workload, or even something to rally against. We address these challenges for the Agile leader as well and discuss new roles regarding employee education and motivation. Many employees bring technology they are experiencing in their private lives into their workplace. The chapters ahead also explore the impact of consumerization of IT and the ease of use of technology.

We are leveraging the largest structured data set on organizations' IT capabilities and share the insights in these pages. Here you will find correlations between organizations that have embraced technology and those that are moving more slowly. Examples and discussions of trends are based on work with hundreds of decision makers over the last 15 years, data and experiences from thousands of documented Microsoft engagements with customers and best practices, and also deviated Infrastructure Optimization (IO) Models and research from leading universities.

The companies highlighted in this book no longer just *use* their technology—they *own* it. They have learned that the new digital divide is between those who view technology as a competitive asset and optimize it versus those who merely have the technology.

We look at how BMW Rationalized its IT environment and became a benchmark for its industry and how system integrator Tieto reduced employee travel by 25 percent while keeping up its relationships with partners. We drill into how AT Kearney managed to complete six months of client's work in 8 hours and how Procter & Gamble (P&G) improved productivity by an average of 14 minutes each day for each of its 130,000 employees. It's as if P&G suddenly added 3,800 more people to its team without changing payroll or facility costs. These companies own and leverage technology for their businesses and, in doing so, have become leaders in the Agile company race.

There are four key stages of technology adoption:

1. Spot trends.
2. Maximize current IT investments.
3. Implement strategy.
4. Gauge impact.

View these stages as a road map to go from simply using technology to owning it. The stages are not just chronological, they are also cyclical. They need to become a constant in your company's ongoing business strategy. In this book, we use an IT IO Model to guide you through these stages and point you to insights, examples, best practices, and resources along the way.

Maximizing current IT investments and continually looking at evolving the technology to fit new trends help establish the two pillars responsible for all companies' economic success: lower cost and maximum value.

This strategy not only helps your company weather an economic downturn; it also positions you to quickly capitalize on recovery as it materializes and win in competitive markets. Nothing clarifies a situation like crises—and we surely have had enough of those in recent years. In addition, crises are fertile ground to reexamine the business-as-usual scenario in order to bring about needed change.

KEY FORECAST OF IT TRENDS AND SPENDS

This book delves into the "what" and "how" behind leveraging IT investments. As you read it, keep these key IT trends and spends in mind. The top IT trends forecasted by International Data Corporation (IDC) are:[1]

- Growth is returning to the IT industry in 2010; forecasted 3.2 percent growth for the year, returning to 2008 industry spending levels of about $1.5 trillion.
- Improved growth and stability in worldwide telecommunications market; worldwide spending projected to increase 3 percent.
- Emerging markets will lead IT recovery; BRIC countries (Brazil, Russia, India, and China) forecast to grow 8 to 13 percent.
- Cloud computing will expand and mature as a strategic battle for cloud platform leadership pushes the technology forward.
- There will be an increase in mobile devices as strategic platforms for commercial and enterprise developers as over 1 billion access the Internet, iPhone apps triple, Android apps quintuple, and penetration of Apple's iPad and Amazon's Kindle grows.
- Public networks will continue aggressive evolution to fiber and 3G and 4G wireless. 4G will be overhyped, more wireless networks will become "invisible," and the Federal Communications Commission (FCC) will regulate over-the-top VoIP (Voice over Internet Protocol).
- Business applications will undergo a fundamental transformation—fusing business applications with social/collaboration software and analytics into a new generation of "socialytic" apps, challenging current market leaders.

- Rising energy costs and pressure from the Copenhagen Climate Change Conference will make sustainability a source of renewed opportunity for the IT industry in 2010.
- Other industries will come out of the recession with a transformation agenda and look to IT as an increasingly important lever for these initiatives. Smart meters and electronic medical records will hit important adoption levels.
- IT industry's transformations will drive a frenetic pace of merger and acquisition activity.

That looks like a lot of change to come, but likely it is only the tip of the iceberg. Nearly every forecast from the past has been surpassed by reality. And if the past teaches us one thing . . . the future will have much change and opportunity for those who are willing to embrace it and to build on it.

LEADING BY EXAMPLE

The Microsoft Infrastructure Optimization Model and customer case studies illustrate infrastructure maturity concepts throughout this book. The customers encompass a wide range of industries—from manufacturing, to entertainment, to the financial sector. Some companies are privately owned, and some are government agencies. But one of the best examples of how a company infuses technology across the breadth and depth of its business practices is Microsoft itself. Microsoft's chief information officer and his team are among the most sought-after and valued speakers in customer engagement. Instead of you coming to Redmond, Washington, we will share some of the Microsoft findings in this book too. Granted, the company does have a certain expertise in using technology tools. However, if we look at some of the business practices Microsoft uses, we see powerful examples of owning technology versus just using it.

How does the actual IT environment contribute to the largest software provider's business? Although Microsoft has had solid growth with popular products, its profitability also depends on keeping costs as low as possible while maximizing impact. The company is not immune to everyday business tasks such as ordering supplies, printing pay stubs, processing expense reports, and connecting colleagues across a geologically diverse company landscape.

For example, the procurement process at Microsoft was once so manual and error prone that the average cost to order anything from pencils to servers was more than $60 per order. Do you or your executives know what your organization's costs are? Multiply this over a workforce of thousands of employees (for Microsoft, about 50,000 at the time) and you see the problem. Let's look at something as simple as ordering business cards. When using paper forms, it is easy to enter the contact information incorrectly. The resulting printed cards are useless—lost time and money. Chances are high that the approving managers' contact information or the department code that should be charged for the order was entered wrong as well. More delays, and correction costs add up.

To reduce the error rate, entry time, and cycle time, Microsoft automated the procurement process for business cards and just about everything else the business would need. Six people took four months to design and build a new database server and Web server to link the email, Human Resources, and electronic document exchange systems together.

After automation, all ordering was done online using an always-current form. Common information was queried and prepopulated from the corporate database, significantly reducing errors. Since the Human Resources system was integrated into the solution, approval, billing, and shipping information entry was automatic. Although information could be overridden, the system usually was accurate and better than the employee's memory or typing skills.

Email integration ensured automatic approval notifications on any type of order. In addition, the electronic exchange integration enabled staff to see a vendor's stock levels at the time of order. It also created error-free transaction hand-offs between companies.

After the new order system MS Market launched, the per-order cost went from $60 to less than $5, saving Microsoft over $15 million annually. The total cost of the project was $250,000.

At the same time, Microsoft standardized on fewer vendors and products. The company was able to negotiate lower prices for higher volumes of consolidated orders. It created simple solutions, such as buying a package of ten computer servers instead of one server for each of ten different departments. The receiving department used the system to route each item to the correct team.

As needs and platforms change, the systems are updated, continually reducing complexity while maximizing employee productivity with the latest capabilities. The software solution increased agility, reduced cost, and increased the time available to employees to do impactful work by reducing their administrative load.

The ability to automate processes and connect employees directly to information was developed in other areas of the company. Each year, Microsoft spent $650,000 just to print and mail paper pay stubs. It was a huge bill that contributed nothing to the company's bottom line. Creating a secure online system was less expensive to operate, more flexible, and saved time. Employees are able to view their personal salary details online on demand. Information is available 24/7 to verify deposit details and transaction history for years. When people need a paper copy, they can securely print as many as they need. The system has been saving money and paper for 11 years.

Another unnecessarily complicated process was the expense reporting system. Before Microsoft automated the process, it used paper forms, as most commercial companies do. When the decision was made to eliminate the paper form, the team thought it would be a simple matter of replicating the existing one online.

However, they learned that some steps of the process were unnecessary. For example, the prevailing wisdom of the time was that all receipts over $25 needed to be submitted by employees and retained by the finance department for tax purposes. In fact, the Internal Revenue Service revealed that it was confused why commercial companies took such great pains to keep all those receipts. The IRS had no such requirement. The final automated process raised the limit for mandatory receipt submission to $75.

To keep the initial transition as smooth as possible, the first phase kept the standard expense Excel workbook form that was used for many years, but the workflow was automated. That allowed the approval process to route submitted reports to managers wherever they happened to be. It also bypassed approvers who were on vacation or otherwise unavailable, to ensure a speedy review. Too often people had sent paper forms by Express Mail to traveling managers to get them approved in time to avoid or reduce late filing fees.

These initial changes alone saved the company $250,000 annually in printing and routing costs. Later phases converted the form to an online tool that exchanges information directly with the preferred credit company. As a result, employees no longer float expenses waiting for reimbursement. Instead, they categorize and approve charges so the companies can settle the transaction directly. The software-automated process that saved the company money also increased employee satisfaction and convenience.

As the Internet became more pervasive and robust, it created an opportunity for Microsoft to reduce operations costs and increase convenience in another area. The unified communications environment now serving employees ensures that all communication is accessible easily from anywhere at any time. New collaboration tools have reduced travel costs as well as the need for office space. Vendors and employees working for the company can work from anywhere, from home offices, in all time zones. Since their contact information follows them, they can work with their teams from anywhere. If you call employees' offices in Redmond or Munich, their cell phone or laptop PC may ring on their business trip in Sweden or Singapore. Converting from the standard telephone to an Office Communication Server environment saves the company more than $90 million annually. In addition to the reduced communication charges, it also simplified the IT environment as it allowed the company to retire its expensive voice conferencing system.

Increasingly even corporate headquarters meetings are going online, eliminating the travel time that would otherwise require a participant to miss part of another meeting. Nor is participation limited by room size any longer. International calling either from or to the employee's home country is simpler and cheaper. Reaching a colleague no longer requires a complicated set of dialing codes. Now it's a simple matter of finding them in the corporate online address book. The system can even report their availability status (called Presence) so no more missed calls or busy signals.

Every day Microsoft is launching new systems to simplify and streamline the way it operates. With nearly 100,000 worldwide employees, the impact on the company is massive. Does this mean you need to be at a Fortune 500 company to make a difference with technology? Simply put, the answer is no. Organizations large and small can and do achieve the same or even better impact with software. Companies of any size can move from using technology to owning it. Darwin had it right when he said: "It is not the strongest of the species that survives, nor the most intelligent that survives. It is the one that is the most adaptable to change."

NOTE

1. Frank Gens, *IDC Predictions 2010: Recovery and Transformation*, IDC Predictions Team (December 2009).

CHAPTER 2

MAXIMUM RIDE: OWNING TECHNOLOGY VERSUS JUST USING IT

When we buy a car, we expect to drive it—usually on a daily basis. Sure, there are a few people—like comedian and car lover Jay Leno—who buy cars, put them into a garage, and sometimes never use or even look at them again. But most of us look at our needs, add a few "wants," and come up with a car package that is going to get us where we need to go safely, securely, and maybe with a bit of style.

So why do companies act more like Jay, the car collector, than the regular Joe when it comes to IT purchases? Just about every company has acquired and deployed software and hardware that sits on or under someone's desk and is never used. Somebody thought it was a good idea at some point. Somebody bought it. And now it sits, taking up valuable real estate and maybe some valuable IT time.

When I met with the Kimberly-Clark team in 2004 to discuss its then recent and early Office 2003 migration, I really wanted to know why the company made the upgrade. What was its driving factor? Headquartered in Dallas, Texas, Kimberly-Clark has nearly 56,000 employees worldwide and operations in 35 countries. Its global brands are sold in more than 150 countries. Every day, 1.3 billion people use Kimberly-Clark products, such as Kleenex, Scott, Andrex, Huggies, Pull-Ups, and Kotex. This is not a small operation. And the answer to my questions was definitely interesting.

The customers' IT team did a beautiful job of repeating Microsoft's marketing message of "higher end-user productivity." However, the CIO had a different story, which he made perfectly clear. He grumbled that Kimberly-Clark had five different directory systems, multiple webcast and communication clients, and countless IT infrastructure management tools. When managers started to drill down and tried to inventory their resources, they realized many of their currently licensed—and often under expensive maintenance contracts—software tools were repetitive at best or obsolete at worst.

If we ask the right questions, answers are often similar across companies. Although paper production and car manufacturing have their individual challenges, their optimization potential is in common. For example, BMW's thought leaders had similar insights. When analyzing their environment, the BMW team realized that the same capabilities were delivered often by five or more different tools that were purchased and often repurchased over and over again. There are, of course, many reasons that this happens, but it often looks like IT decisions are made as if the tools were free. Unfortunately even if the acquisition is, the maintenance and follow-up costs can be scarily expensive.

This is a prime example of "using" technology. Yes, a company knows it is there. Yes, it is sometimes a great tool for employees and other times not so great. Yes, people either learn to use it or learn to work around it. But they don't "own" the technology. Research over the past 30 years shows that companies that truly own their IT infrastructure not only gain a competitive advantage in their sector—they continue to maintain it even as the world changes around them.

HOW THE WORLD IS CHANGING

If you are a baby boomer, you remember rotary dial phones and electric typewriters. If you are a Gen Xer, you grew up on MTV and fell in love with your first PC. If you are a Millennial, you are the digital natives—connected and wired wherever you go—and the rest of the world are just digital immigrants.

Technology changes faster than any of us ever believed it could. How a company uses technology now determines if it is going to fail or succeed in the global market. A business needs to offer a great product or service for customers, but every component that goes into that product of service affects the bottom line. High-quality manufacturing reduces waste and therefore reduces costs. Coordinated managers reduce work overlap. Marketing helps the business reach targeted customers with its message. Smart inventory management makes sure the popular items don't run out and the not-so-popular aren't stuck in the warehouse. The list is endless. Every part of your business, if managed better, can increase sales, decrease costs, free up workers to think creative thoughts, or otherwise affect your bottom line. What may be less obvious is how every single one of those factors—the levers you pull or adjust in business—can be improved with technology.

That is certainly the strategy at Wet Seal, a 500-store specialty retailer of clothing, mainly for teenage girls. Wet Seal is a so-called fast-fashion retailer, meaning that trends in its market change quickly and the company needs little time—as few as three weeks—to put its clothes, shoes, and accessories into stores after its buyers make their decisions. Staying in tune with the shifting tastes among young women is crucial, said Edmond S. Thomas, the chief executive officer.

Wet Seal's stores account for more than 80 percent of the company's sales, but its presence on the Web is growing, using its site as a source of market insights as well as revenue. In 2009 Wet Seal introduced a Web feature called Outfitter, which allows users to put together their own outfits online. The virtual outfits are posted, and users can browse through them, comment, and exchange recommendations. So far, more than 300,000 user-generated outfits have been designed, generating millions of page views.

"We can get a read on where our customer is headed faster than ever before," Thomas said. In October, Wet Seal created its own iPhone application, called iRunway. With it, a customer in a store can tap in an item's ticket number—bar code recognition comes later this year—and see how it has been used in outfits that other customers have created online. The user-generated product selections and recommendations, combined with mobile phone access, will build a community of customers that should increase sales, Thomas predicts. "We're at the very initial stages, but that will be the wave of the future in fashion retailing."[1]

New technologies are coming quickly, and each needs to be evaluated to see how or if it could help your business. Communication tools are a prime example. After all, the last 20 years brought more changes in how people communicate than thousands of years prior.

Written language and eventually a mail system allowed somewhat regular means of communication over distances. The invention of the telephone and its broad adoption within private and business life gave us the opportunity for "real-time" communication and collaboration over geographical distances. Until the Telex and fax came along, written and asynchronous communication was still snail mail based.

Over the last few years, this changed dramatically. As recently as only ten years ago, "progressive" business decision makers were buying PC-to-fax solutions as their anticipated primary form of PC-based communication. But over the same ten years, completely new forms of communication have emerged and quickly reached broad adoption in the consumer and the business world. Email is everywhere, and billions of messages are sent around the globe daily.

But email wasn't portable enough, so another electronic form of communication emerged rapidly. Instant messaging (IM), initially with TCQ (Tagged Command Queuing) and AOL Messenger, became a new way of maintaining contact over distances. Soon the other Internet companies offered their own IM platforms. MSN Messenger and Yahoo! Messenger took over more of this growing user base. Soon the IM clients became more and more powerful, adding features like voice chat and cameras that transmit and record video. Today, most laptops now have built-in Webcams.

People may now have any kind of combination of email, instant messaging, video calls, and video conferencing along with fax, phone, and voicemail system—often using different numbers for work, home, and cellular phone. Just managing, let alone optimizing, these communication platforms and their ongoing tidal wave of information is a challenge (and opportunity) for most of us.

The concept of "unified communication" (UC) has entered our vernacular. UC provides one unified experience for all the different information sources. Microsoft Outlook is a great example to show what UC looks like in the work world.

Here at Microsoft, my email inbox is also the inbox—thanks to Microsoft Exchange—for my voicemail and faxes as well as for text messages sent to my mobile phone. My Outlook-powered inbox contains my task list and calendar information as well as all my contact information.

With Voice over Internet Protocol (VoIP) and the integration with the Outlook and Communicator clients, I do not have an actual telephone in my office. I have a device that looks like a phone. It's not plugged into a jack on wall. It is connected to my PC via a USB connection, which in turn connects to the corporate data network. In truth, the device that looks like a phone is a glorified PC speaker and microphone. It can be replaced when traveling or working from home with a simple headset connected to my PC, or I can simply use my laptop's built-in microphone and speakers.

This technology change completely altered the understanding of what a workplace is. For the last several years, the actual physical place of where I am at a given time becomes more and more irrelevant. When I am out of the (actual) office, I can forward incoming work calls to my cell phone or pick them up on my computer—even if I am sitting in a hotel in Munich or at a beach bar in Bali.

The technology leaders in the corporate space are not the only ones utilizing these technologies. Many small businesses are embracing the flexibility that these technologies deliver. I have met small business owners with "local" phone numbers for customers to call for their "subsidiaries" in Chile, California, or Seattle: all routed to their cell phone. For many of these entrepreneurs, the easiest way to tap into this potential is a cloud or services-based solution like Skype or instant messaging. Independent of my organization's size, I can but do not need to build these capabilities myself and inside my own infrastructure anymore. I have more and more choices simply to subscribe to an IT capability though a hosted environment or a cloud service through the Internet.

Using UC has become part of everyday life. Demonstrating this technology to customers and partners has been a highlight in my recent travels around the globe. Feeling a little like a magician, I need only my laptop and an Internet connection to demonstrate my work environment.

In 2009 I showed this to the IT leadership of the Asia Development Bank (ADB). ADB is an international development finance institution whose mission is to help its developing member countries reduce poverty and improve the quality of life of their people. Headquartered in Manila, and established in 1966, ADB is owned and financed by its 67 members, of which 48 are from the region and 19 are from other parts of the globe. ADB's main partners are governments, the private sector, nongovernment organizations, development agencies, community-based organizations, and foundations.

The IT leaders were passionate about the organization's mission. And that is probably why the theoretical discussion on technologies moved quickly to the problems ADB employees across the region were facing. ADB supports projects in agriculture and natural resources, energy, finance, industry and nonfuel minerals, social infrastructure, and transport and communications. More than half of ADB's assistance has gone into building infrastructure: roads, airports, power plants, and water and sanitation facilities. Such infrastructure helps make essential services accessible to the poor. ADB employees go in before the infrastructure. PC connectivity is not a given and is often slow. Phone and cell phone connections are also sketchy.

Quickly the discussion turned to Groove, a peer-to-peer file sharing infrastructure that Microsoft had acquired a few years earlier and integrated into the Office suite. Groove lets users create workspaces on their PC and then share them with others without worrying about networks or servers. An ADB employee had a trial account. He and I created a shared workspace between his PC and mine across our various firewalls and infrastructure difference in seconds. This technology could revolutionize how field employees stay in touch with each other, as well as with their headquarters.

Word spread pretty quickly through text messages from one colleague to another, and soon the room was beginning to overflow. With so many cell phones in the room, I couldn't resist showing the telephone capability of the Unified Messaging software. After demonstrating the instant messaging capabilities, I explained that my PC is actually also my office phone. One of the participants of the now-significant crowd inside and outside the room gave me her cell phone number. I typed it into my PC and, seconds later, her phone rang, showing my U.S. phone number on the display of her Philippines' phone and allowing us to have a conversation through the crowd of people. We didn't have time to talk about social networking and how that adds another flow of information through status updates, RSS, and Twitter feeds.

We have been talking about PCs so far. Now let's add the mobile experience that has dramatically transformed our lives—and our kids' lives—in the last decade. A mobile phone used to be a nice-to-have item. Now it is an integral part of life. As they have become more prevalent, mobile phones have become more and more powerful.

"Smartphone" devices like Apple's iPhone, RIM's Blackberry, Google's Android devices, and Windows Mobile–powered phones are one of the fastest-growing markets in the communications sector. All of these little wonder machines are more powerful and more connected than most PCs were less than a decade ago. And not surprisingly, people use them much like they use their PCs today.

While it is a cliché to say that technology is changing our world, there is no denying that it is true. But every change comes with downsides. The Romans revolutionized their world by building amazing roads. Barbarian hordes used the same roads—and not for friendly commerce. Early technology adopters may struggle with the downside of being beta testers, but they are also in the position to overcome challenges faster. Those slow to adopt new technologies fall farther and farther behind. It all comes back down to owning versus just using technology. And a body of research highlights that just using technology instead of owning it may relegate a company to the scrap heap.

CURRENT RESEARCH IN ENTERPRISE ARCHITECTURE

"Companies that manage their IT investments most successfully generate returns as much as 40 percent higher than those of their competitors." The people behind that statistic are Jeanne W. Ross and Peter Weill of the Center for Information Systems Research (CISR) at the Sloan School of Management of the Massachusetts Institute of Technology (MIT). CISR has been studying how companies generate value from information technology for over 30 years. Some of their landmark research into enterprise architecture came from their work with Johnson & Johnson. In 1995 Johnson & Johnson worked to develop shared infrastructure services for subsets of its 170 autonomous business units. CISR found that the IT infrastructure had been developed to support the way Johnson & Johnson traditionally had done business, *not the way it wanted to do business in the future.* Johnson & Johnson was the first but not the last to take this approach to technology. Every company CISR studied faced the same problem. The business could not function as it wanted to unless IT created new capabilities, but IT could not implement those capabilities until and unless the business changed.[2]

MIT's Enterprise Architecture Map

The research of Ross and Weill developed a model that showed how organizations and IT mature and the associated best practices. The model has four stages, Business Silos, Standardized Technology, Optimized Core and Business Modularity, each of which has the investment components of local applications, enterprise systems, shared infrastructure, and shared data.[3]

At low maturity, the business and IT operate as investment business silos that support local business needs but that do not have established technical standards. This creates high costs to support local and often customized applications to support ongoing specific tailored needs as well as support of heterogeneous technologies and associated infrastructure. This level of maturity does provide local flexibility as each investment is linked to the local business/silo need. However, such flexibility can also be a barrier to becoming more efficient.

Eventually complexity increases to a point where costs and risk escalate with a decreasing agility to meet local and wider business needs. Hence the next level of maturity is about IT efficiency and consolidation on to standardized technology with lower investments in local and custom applications, increasing investment in common enterprise solutions for example and associated IT cost reduction. Indeed, many organizations remain at this level and have traded reduced flexibility for lower operating costs and have started to reduce the number of systems and duplication.

To gain increasing value from IT, change must be driven from the business, which requires data visibility and a focus on processes across the business based on the organizational operational model. At this level of operational efficiency, much of the original local flexibility has been removed, but overall business agility is increasing. The organization can implement business change faster, lowering IT costs based on enterprise-wide solutions and processes with increasing levels of shared data.

The final stage of maturity provides strategic choices based on business modularity and reusable modules, such as Web services, for example, thereby increasing speed to market and impacting business performance. Although this stage may come at increasing IT costs, the costs are no longer an issue based on the higher leverage of value for the business.

The Microsoft Infrastructure Optimization (IO) was developed to reflect a similar approach but has focused more on the IT capabilities across core platforms, business productivity, and applications with associated maturity levels moving from Basic, through Standardized and Rationalized, before reaching a Dynamic level. This model is described in more detail in Chapter 3.

Boston University

The Boston University (BU) School of Management prides itself on fusing the art, science, and technology of business. John Henderson and Lloyd Baird, both professors at BU, are experts on the organizational impact of process and technology usage in the business sector. Microsoft took notice of BU's research as various teams at Microsoft pushed to quantify "productivity improvements" in the office environment.

Ongoing discussions led to a joint research project. BU had a research team focused on team productivity and organizational results, and Microsoft had the only wide and comprehensive data set of capability maturity by industry and customer. The concept, analytics, and data coupled with in-depth interviews of individual teams across a variety of business sectors combined to form a picture of what BU calls "networked teams." Networked teams are units of individuals, working together on joint tasks in environments of knowledge complexity and different levels of collaboration strategy maturity.

The BU researchers identified a fundamental shift from "design-based collaboration"—structured work flow, also known as "routine," that companies had used for decades—to more ad hoc work and projects. This so-called emergent collaboration strategy is used today in 30 to 50 percent of all office work.

One common strategy used by most firms to cope with this paradox has been to increase the role of teams. Over the past several decades, the use of teams as a core building block of organization design has increased. Traditional designs that emphasized hierarchy and functional specialization have been tempered by the increased use of teams to integrate across the boundaries of discipline, organization, and geography. The changing nature of high-performing teams raised the importance for business leaders and the academic world to better understand the guiding factors of what makes and keeps those teams successful.

This increasing focus on the role of teams in organizations motivated development and widespread adoption of new tools, processes, and strategies designed to increase team performance. The maturation of our understanding of the factors that enhance team performance, coupled with our increased ability to successfully deploy these key enablers, served to accelerate the use of teams as a primary structure to organization and execute work processes.

A key component of the research was knowledge—documented, with an individual or with a team, or hidden in unstructured data—that is present in an organization. Organizational or technical barriers often prevent this knowledge being fully used. Unanticipated events coupled with increasingly complex organizations means that individuals are forced to make decisions out of context and with incomplete information. The bottom line for BU is that organizations cannot be effective if they lack access to organizational knowledge when and where it is needed. BU refers to an organization's capability to access data, adjust plans, and select the most efficient collaboration environment as Agile Collaboration Strategy.

An advanced Agile Collaboration Strategy allows an organization to drive innovation. Paul Carlile (formerly at MIT, now at BU) studies how infrastructures for innovation across a variety of organization settings are and can be created. Based on his model of the Innovation Sweet Spot, the capacity to access and distribute relevant knowledge combined with the ability to interpret and act on this knowledge is the key determining factor for an organization's ability to identify novelty and to address its consequences for the organization and the market. In a world of massive amounts of available information and distributed expertise, tools and technologies to manage the data become a critical foundation to foster—or hamper—this process. Excellent technology by itself, though, cannot make an organization innovative or Agile. It is essential to understand that a complete framework needs to be in place, which includes rules and processes for:

- Formal and informal processes
- Administrative coordination
- Expertise coordination, including leveraging communities and crowd sourcing
- Peer synchronization, from water cooler, over blogs, wikis, social networks, to localization of concepts and content to regional or language-specific requirements
- Ease of knowledge sharing
- Flow of the knowledge, where routine processes, formal hand-offs, and choice of technology can make huge differences
- Technology environment that is the enabler and indicator for processes and work/information flow

While all of these are critical, the technology environment determines the quality of the interactions, the speed of finding and accessing knowledge, and the reach and available links and network of an individual and team. Today, the availability and variety of tools is exponential and growing. Organizations must understand their collaboration needs of today *and* tomorrow to design and enable the use of the tools and processes most beneficial for their business goals.

In a world of increasing complexity, more and more problems are novel, and the solutions must be innovative. If the solutions and related behaviors are novel, the value potential can increase dramatically. Groups that share knowledge effectively will win the competition. Carlile argues that when faced with novel problems, groups that develop effective knowledge-sharing mechanisms will outperform those that do not.

The insights generated support the hypothesis that collaboration technology affects performance not as a direct driver but as a moderator. A performance moderator may impede or enhance the impact of other factors but cannot by itself drive performance. The key premise here is that collaboration technology does not do work; people or intelligent applications (agents) do the work. The collaboration tools aid or detract from this work process by enabling the individuals or agents to better share information and knowledge relevant to task goals.

How the technical capabilities and tools are delivered to teams is another question the IT and the business teams must consider carefully. Both on-premise and hosted or cloud models—either alone or in combination—are readily available for many capabilities and many users and usage scenarios. With the rapid evolution of technology, an organization needs to look at architectural flexibility and simple extensibility not only for today's needs but also for the evolution going forward to stay on the cutting edge.

MAKING QUANTUM LEAPS AND NOT JUST INCREMENTAL CHANGES

Why is the alignment of the business and IT leadership so vital for organizations? We have seen, too often, that companies without a sound IT strategy can only dream of success. Think of it this way: You are on the right road going in the wrong direction if your organization has not carefully thought through how IT infrastructure contributes to—and, more and more often—determines business outcomes. For years, customers, researchers, and analysts tried to find a way to map business priorities to strategic IT investments, allowing them to prioritize and align resources. In the 1990s, the PC and the client-server architecture became prevalent in most organizations. A company could not function without it, but often neither the strategy nor the technologies were mature enough to allow a centralized management or strategy. This changed in the early 2000s with a strong push to standardization and manageability of the IT infrastructure. However, standardization argument often stifled new technologies coming into the workplace. Researchers, customers, consultants, and analysts were trying to define recommendations that allowed new capabilities while maintaining a secure and well-managed IT environment. Everyone wanted the most business bang for the IT buck.

Like every good model, simplicity wins—as long as differentiation and individualization are possible. In 2002, the Gartner Group published the first version of its Infrastructure Maturity Model. The Gartner model was based on work Marianne Broadbent did with

Peter Weill of MIT and allowed organizations to map people, processes, and IT capabilities to "maturity stages." Once a company has this information, it can build a road map that prioritizes business goals and the technology implementation that will take it to its goals. As a company's IT infrastructure matures, it becomes a key strategic asset that supports and drives innovation, profitability, and customer satisfaction.

Gartner's Infrastructure Maturity Model, introduced in 2004 and updated in 2007, identifies six levels of infrastructure maturity that can be seen in Figure 2.1.

Obviously, the goal of a company is to move quickly out of IT survival mode and work its way to a point where IT is considered a valuable business partner within a company.

This idea dovetailed into a phenomenon that Microsoft had been seeing. Through the Microsoft licensing model of Enterprise agreement and Software Assurance, customers owned many of the latest Microsoft technologies but often only realized a fraction of their value. Companies had the technology to use their IT infrastructure as a business asset but often were simply in IT survival mode. Every year Microsoft invests more than $5 billion into the development of their products—adding functionality as well as simplifying their use and management. However, there is often a disconnect when a company is deciding when and how the products impact its business goals. How does a company choose which of five already licensed and utilized products to use for one purpose? Layered on top of this issue are IT

SURVIVAL	AWARENESS	COMMITTED	PROACTIVE	SERVICE ALIGNED	BUSINESS PARTNERSHIP
Little to no focus on IT infrastructure and operations	Realization; beginning to gain operational control and visibility	Moving to managed environment	Gaining efficiencies and service quality through standardization, policy development, governance structures, and proactive processes	Managing IT like a business;. focused on customer; proven competitive	Trusted partner to the business for increasing value and competitiveness of business processes

Figure 2.1 Gartner's Infrastructure Maturity Model

Source: Thomas J. Bittman, Gartner Introduces the Infrastructure Maturity Model, Gartner, Inc., November 19, 2002. Donna Scott, Jay Pultz, Ed Holub, Thomas Bittman, Paul McGuckin, *Introducing the Gartner IT Infrastructure and Operations Maturity Model,* Gartner, Inc. October 1st, 2007.

complexity and organizational politics. The IT picture is too big and overwhelming.

Based on the experiences of enterprise-focused customers and *very* clear customer feedback—often made directly to Microsoft executives—a Windows Server team under Samm DiStasio analyzed the existing guidance and models. In 2005 this team introduced a customer- and capability-focused model on how to be more strategic with IT infrastructures. Together with experts, the team compiled and tested with customers key questions differentiating capability maturity steps. To reach scale and allow more customers and partners to leverage the questionnaire and model, they developed a Web-based self-assessment tool. The team assessed every customer connected to a Microsoft salesperson that agreed to share self-assessment results. All in all, the team collected data sets for tens of thousands of organizations. The team fine-tuned the model, capability definitions, and questionnaire to make them more accurate and actionable for customers and partners. The wealth of data also provided an additional and unique opportunity to analyze correlations between capabilities, their maturity, and other factors, such as an organization's business success. Together with leading research organizations, Microsoft embarked on major studies to help businesses figure out how IT affects their success and how IT can better drive business success.

MICROSOFT'S STRUCTURED APPROACH

Helping a company break out of IT survival mode became a major focus for Microsoft. By combining its own experiences with those of its enterprise customers, the key findings represented by Gartner's Infrastructure Maturity Model, and some of MIT's Architecture Maturity Model research, Microsoft developed the Microsoft Infrastructure Optimization Mode.

The Microsoft Infrastructure Optimization (IO) Model helps customers understand and subsequently improve the state of their IT infrastructure and reap benefits in terms of cost, security risk, and operational agility. Dramatic cost savings can be realized by moving from a basic unmanaged environment toward a dynamic environment. Security improves from highly vulnerable in a basic infrastructure, to dynamically proactive in a more mature infrastructure. IT Infrastructure

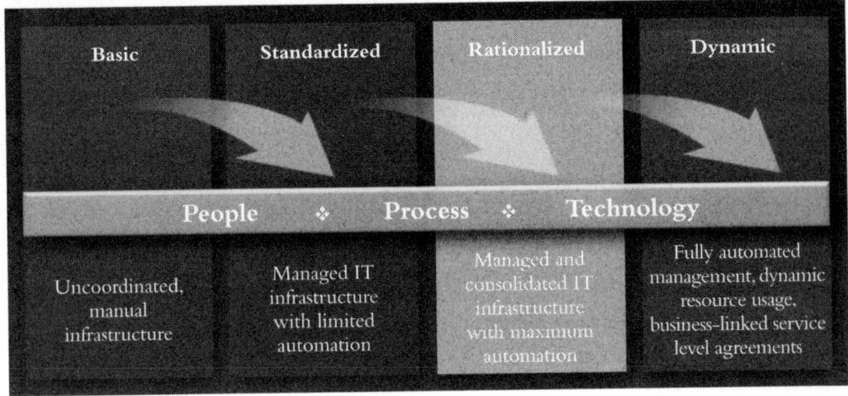

Figure 2.2 Infrastructure Optimization

Management changes from highly manual and reactive to highly automated and proactive. Infrastructure Optimization, which is shown in Figure 2.2, is a structured, systematic process of assessing maturity across IT capabilities, then prioritizing projects to progress toward a more dynamic state.

At the heart of the Infrastructure Maturity Model are sectors that focus on key aspects or capabilities of an organization's IT environment. Figure 2.3 shows the Core Infrastructure sector (including desktops,

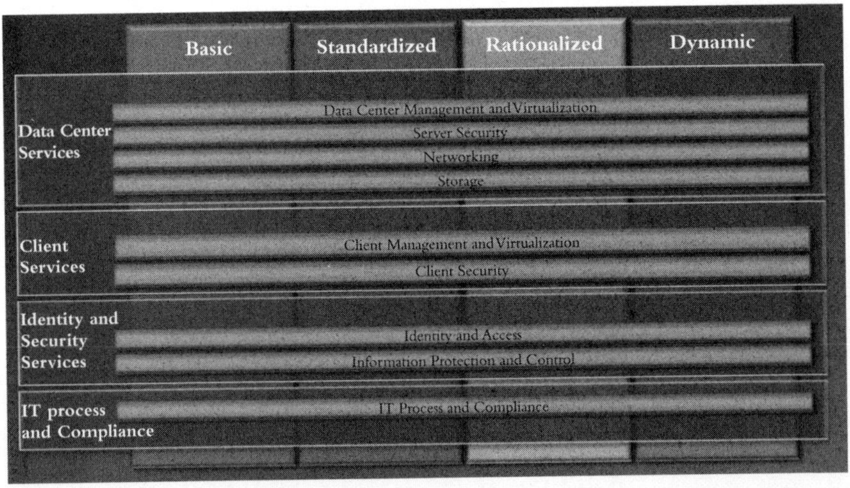

Figure 2.3 Core Infrastructure Model

devices, and servers), and Figure 2.4 shows the Business Productivity Infrastructure sector (including productivity, collaboration, and communication tools).

For our analysis, it was critical to have the broadest possible organizational coverage of data. Over the five years of data collection, we were fortunate to have updated information for over 15,000 organizations on capability maturity for the Core Infrastructure and the Business Productivity Infrastructure assessments. This allows us to compare individual organizations against each other, their markets, and across industries by these capabilities:

Core Infrastructure

- Data center services
- Client services
- Identity and security services
- IT process and compliance

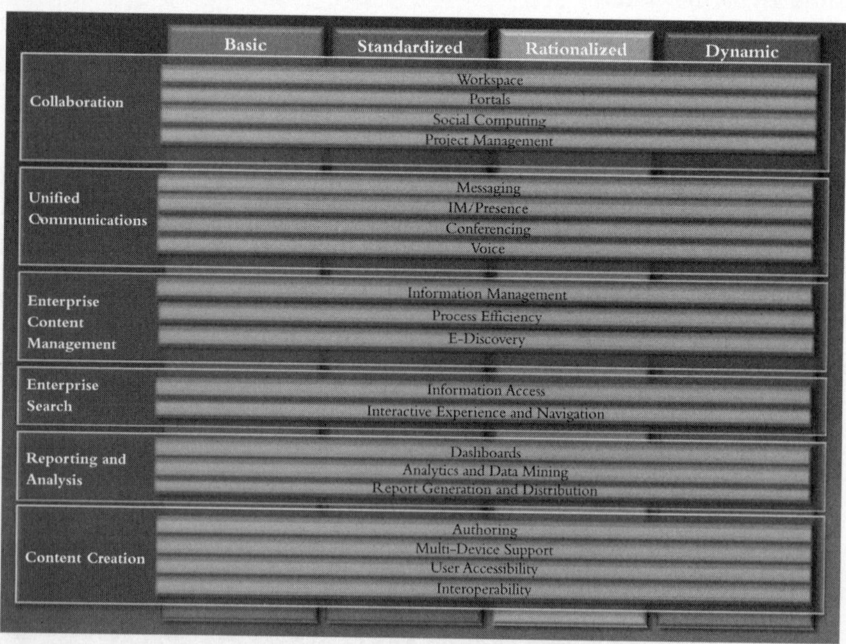

Figure 2.4 Business Productivity Infrastructure Model

Business Productivity

- Collaboration
- Unified communications
- Enterprise content management
- Enterprise search
- Reporting and analysis
- Content creation

Now, we know the IT people love all this focus on their infrastructure, but what does it really mean to a company's bottom line? Does IT matter? By improving and maturing IT capabilities, will a company see improvements in business performance? By investing resources and time to move through the Standardized, Rationalized, and Dynamic levels of maturity, can an organization create both change and higher business performance?

INFRASTRUCTURE MATURITY AND THE IMPACT ON CORE BUSINESS PERFORMANCE

Across research, anecdotal evidence, and the analyzed customer and segment data, the answer to these questions is a resounding *yes*. In an ever-changing global marketplace, companies are looking for every opportunity to gain a competitive advantage and simultaneously grow revenue, profits, and customer loyalty. Meanwhile, new regulatory requirements, competitive pressures brought on by an increasingly connected global economy, and technologies that level the playing field for companies of all sizes are making it more difficult for them to stay ahead.

As a company moves away from basic IT infrastructure to a more dynamic and rationalized infrastructure, business benefits *increase* and IT costs *decrease*. Organizations can accelerate this value by leveraging best practices with their current technology and/or by leveraging innovative opportunities provided by new technology that accelerates and drives new ways of working. The role of IT is rapidly becoming a key strategic asset to support and *drive innovation*, profitability, and customer satisfaction. Figure 2.5 recaps some of the findings published in "Enterprise IT Capabilities and Business Performance."[4]

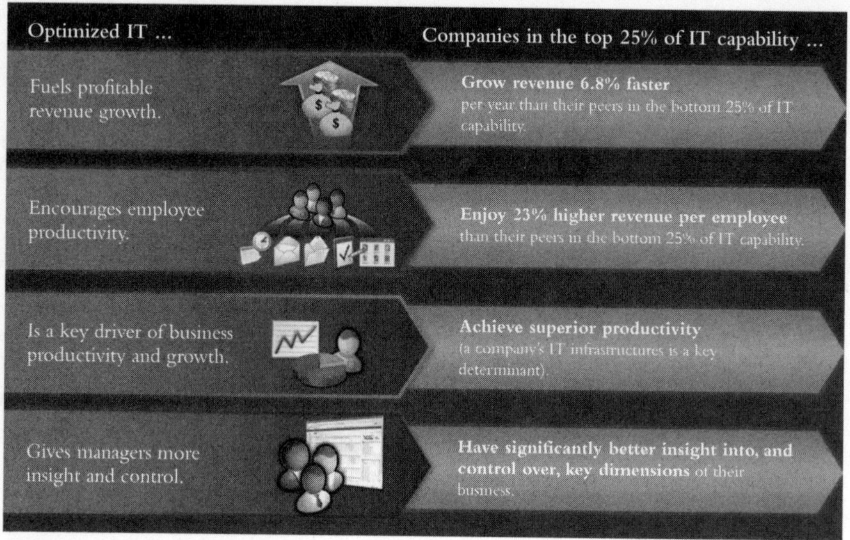

Figure 2.5 IT Drives Business Performance

More recent data continues to confirm why infrastructure optimization matters to any organization. By 2009 a wealth of data was available for scientific analysis. Using the CISR methodologies, best practices, and sector-wide advice, a Microsoft research team analyzed worldwide IT infrastructure optimization data across multiple industries. The analysis used the Core Infrastructure and Business Productivity Infrastructure Optimization maturity data and correlated this to business performance metrics compiled and purchased from Standard & Poor's.

The research focused on the possible relationships between IT Capability maturities and measured affects on business efficiency and effectiveness performance metrics. Researchers looked for interdependencies between IT and company performance that could inform investment priorities for IT capabilities.

To better understand the business and collaboration capability impact, academic research collaboration utilized the data set in different studies, one with guidance from MIT as part of a patron relationship and the other led by the research team at BU both under strict compliance with privacy practices. This data provided the backbone of the extremely deep analysis on business impact of technology capability maturity. The BU project identified success metrics for organizations and mapped the data sets from the IO assessment against those performance indicators and the competitive position of organizations and teams. Microsoft now had a more scientific way to figure out which products and capabilities matched customers' needs.

TRENDS

Figure 2.6 provides a high-level summary of the average results for business productivity metrics. The move between Basic to Standardized provides gains in both Profit/Employee and Revenue/Employee, with Return on Assets also increasing. Between Standardized to Rationalized/Dynamic, the improvement is more significant for all metrics. The dollar figures show the absolute change but are of course relevant to the sample average, but the percent figures provide the generic performance improvements. How could these improvements impact your business?

What technical capabilities drive the business productivity impact? Business Intelligence and Search—how and where an organization stores its knowledge and data—had the strongest impact on Profit and Revenue, indicating that these capabilities drive *business growth*. However, UC—how your organization communicates and collaborates—had a larger impact on Profit but less on Revenue, indicating an increasing impact on

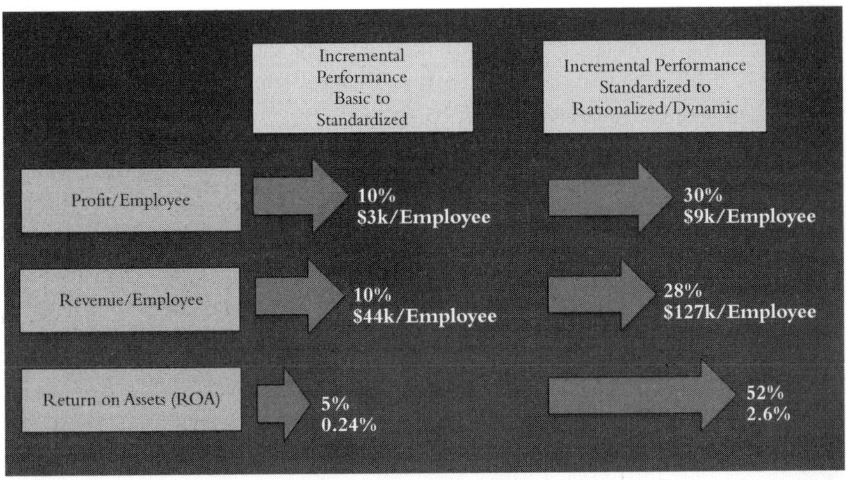

Figure 2.6 Infrastructure Maturity Impact on Business Productivity

business costs. For example, in order to cut travel costs, Microsoft recently analyzed a company program aimed at increasing the IT capability for UC. To date, some $93 million savings in travel costs and $3.1 million savings in audio conferencing costs have been reported. In addition, the value based on productivity equates to over 6 percent average/employee productivity gain. This won't show up in revenue numbers at the end of the year, but the cost savings certainly will be noted in the overall revenue figures.

What does this theory look like in practice? Do companies get lucky with their IT maturity decisions, or is it strategic focus? Let's look at an example. A large manufacturing organization—as part of its product development processes—needed to certify that the product could meet customer and various legal criteria before acceptance. As business grew, the number of certifications increased, and the requests become more ad hoc. The communication and collaboration breakdown increased time to market, and the sales numbers showed a loss of tenders and market share, which, in turn, impacted plans for further company growth. Business productivity was definitely at a Basic maturity level. The company invested in work flow, e-forms, collaboration, and content management that enabled a more structured work flow, avoiding lost time creating and searching test results and analysis. All this improved certification cycle time and impacted the bottom line by about $300,000.

A large book publisher in the United Kingdom faced a different challenge. The company needed to increase sales in specific market segments. The organization invested in enterprise content management technology—reported as part of the Business Productivity Infrastructure sector—that managed Web content and enabled social networking. The technology allowed authors and customers to interact, making books more accessible for younger, computer- and social networking–minded customers. The company also needed an effective business intelligence capability—also part of the Business Productivity Infrastructure sector—to analyze and report performance trends to help it make quicker decisions in its fast-paced sales environment. Increased contact with customers enabled the company to offer related products and increase cross-selling. Also the authors, who are a publisher's raw material, gained value from increased visibility and feedback on their work and, of course, royalties. Without these capabilities, the company would have lost customers, authors, and future market share.

These two examples come from very different business sectors, but both show that by moving IT infrastructure out of basic survival mode, a company improves business performance with quantifiable results. That is the good news. The bad news is their competitors may be focusing on the same IT optimizations. If this is the case, how does a company optimize for innovation and agility to stay ahead? Henry Ford once said, "It has been my observation that most people get ahead during the time that others waste." Is your organization wasting time?

NOTE ABOUT CASE STUDIES AND THE INFRASTRUCTURE OPTIMIZATION MODEL

The Infrastructure Optimization Model described in this book was originally developed by Microsoft. The many tools customers and partners can use today to leverage the model for their own analysis and solution prioritization and implementation planning were also designed by Microsoft. The optimization tool is not proprietary and can be found on Microsoft's public Web site.

It is important to understand that the model is purely capability based—it describes what an organization is capable of doing in a certain defined area. It does not require a customer to buy specific technologies from any one company to gain or demonstrate technology capabilities.

A company can achieve a certain infrastructure maturity level as much with IBM's Lotus products as they can with Microsoft's Exchange and SharePoint products. It can leverage Oracle's Database programs as well as Microsoft's SQL software. And there are several different hosting offerings in addition to Microsoft's that allow customers to switch on a capability like collaboration or UC through software as a service without having to install the components all in their own data centers. With the exception of Microsoft's Active Directory as a centralized authentication mechanism—something nearly every organization has at least partly today—there is no requirement to purchase or use a specific Microsoft product to gain specific capabilities.

The key message of this book is that organizations that use advanced technologies and embrace them in their business processes are more successful in the mid and long term. Companies gain more powerful technology capabilities through integration and standardized interfaces. Many software vendors are embracing the concept and are delivering solutions that are integrated with and build on general platform technologies.

If there is independence, why so much focus on Microsoft's customer stories and their technologies in this book? This focus serves as a guide to the improvement process to leverage technology in business. I can give you the theory, but I think some of the best learning is done by talking about real companies that have designed real solutions. Using the best available data and direct long-term customer insights was a higher priority for me in this book than trying to appear vendor neutral.

As a former long-term Microsoft employee, most of my customer interactions in the last ten years centered on the use of Microsoft technologies. For this book, I decided to leverage the examples and customer stories my colleagues and I had directly seen—from problem identification to solution results—rather than trying to identify specific end-to-end stories from other technology vendors. The insights we have gained and the models we are using generate similar business and organizational value with technologies that are not from Microsoft. I personally did not have the opportunity to monitor those projects and therefore cannot include them in my book. However, if other vendors in the industry are willing to share their insights on their customer experiences, my academic colleagues and I would be delighted to engage with them for another research and publication project.

NOTES

1. Steve Lohr, "A Data Explosion Remakes Retailing," *New York Times*, January 2, 2010.
2. Galen Gruman, "The Four Stages of Enterprise Architecture," *CIO*, February 7, 2007.
3. Jeanne Ross, Peter Weill, and David C. Robertson, *Enterprise Architecture as Strategy* (Boston: Harvard Business School Press, 2006).
4. Marco Iansiti and George Favaloro, "Enterprise IT Capabilities and Business Performance," Keystone Strategy (March 2006).

CHAPTER 3

OPTIMIZING FOR AGILITY: A DIFFERENT WAY TO VIEW YOUR BUSINESS

The right plan, the right people, the right data, and the right tools are all components of a successful business. All of these factors organized in the right way allow a company to optimize for agility. The IT infrastructure and the capabilities it delivers play a major part in how the pieces come together. IT can either help or seriously hinder any organization.

The IT team has arguably a tough balancing act. It needs to deliver a strategic, coordinated, mobile, and flexible data-crunching beast of an infrastructure to an organization—oh yes, it also needs to be easy to use for the business organization it supports—while facing its own intense pressures in managing cost, resources, and complexity.

As IT teams develop infrastructure plans, regardless of business sector and organization size, several trends impact their work:

- **There is a stronger emphasis on teamwork**. Better decisions and results come from sharing expertise, but technology often has been a barrier in helping people work together efficiently. Geographical, organizational, or technical boundaries limit the ability to build or self-organize into teams. Collaboration and communication tools on the PC have revolutionized how people work together.
- **The new social networking tools take teamwork to a whole new level**. The Millennials or Gen Y'ers who are now entering the workforce grew up with technology and an Internet connection. They connect and collaborate constantly.
- **The nature of teamwork has changed**. One individual or team doesn't complete a piece of a plan and pass it on to the next in line anymore. Teams work on deliverables at the same time so tools need to track who is working on what and manage the data and changes seamlessly.
- **Teams are more global**. Economies are entwined on a global level. IT teams need to overcome geographic and time zone obstacles.
- **People are more mobile**. Teams are more productive, regardless of the location of their members at any given time. Most mobile workers travel with a laptop but also expect to stay informed and productive by using their phone while waiting in line at the airport, checking into a hotel, traveling between meetings, or even lying by the side of the pool while "on vacation."
- **Data has taken on a life of its own**. We've entered a truly digital age, where the challenge has shifted from digging to find information to managing large volumes of information to find the right insights and present it in a meaningful way.
- **Everyone demands faster response times**. People expect to have access to the information they need no matter where they are—no excuses or exceptions allowed.
- **There is a shift toward digital content**. Media looks and feels very different. For instance, YouTube is an amazing business tool.

- **Software as a service and the cloud**. These allow an organization of any size to leverage capabilities that a few years ago only the most up-to-date innovation leaders had to their disposal.
- **Information and knowledge are the key assets for organizations**. The security of that information and knowledge determines the organizations' current and future competitiveness.
- **The diversity of the workforce is changing on many dimensions**. Organizations need to compete globally for talent at the higher end of qualification and motivation but also need to find ways to utilize and leverage motivated or Agile employees to contribute consistently to the organizational success.

But all of these trends are external factors. IT has its own set of internal challenges that also impact infrastructure planning and execution.

- **IT has to empower people with the right tools to be productive**. It's not only the creative types looking for cutting-edge multimedia who need specific tools of the craft. So does the number-crunching, lone data analyst.
- **Tools need to accommodate a variety of work styles**. Often they must balance how to introduce new capabilities to meet the needs of some while maintaining continuity and familiarity for others.
- **User adoption can affect the return on investment (ROI) of software investments**. If employees don't want to use the new tools, the investment becomes a huge liability—especially the next time IT submits a budget.
- **IT has to provide users with more freedom to work from more locations and devices**. But data must remain safe and secure. Intellectual property is golden, both for a company *and* for its competitors.
- **IT must balance control with providing self-service capabilities to end employees**. Employees don't rely just on one computer to get things done. They want hardware and software that works at work, at home, and on the road. IT ends up supporting more devices in far more locations.

Touching all of these factors is the simple truth that both businesses and IT teams need to do more with less. In the current economic climate, people often are forced to look for ways to be more efficient. The existing workforce has taken on more responsibilities but often after being reduced and restructured. Everyone is looking for ways to save on operating expenses wherever possible—from avoiding the need for specialized or duplicative applications to reducing the amount of paper used. As I said, IT never had it easy, but today it has an even tougher balancing act to master.

INDIVIDUAL, ORGANIZATION, OR INFORMATION TECHNOLOGY: WHERE DO YOU START?

While today's economic environment is driving the focus toward cutting costs, it also presents a unique opportunity for leaders to step back and evaluate whether their systems and business processes are driving the right results for their company. Through an infrastructure that increases business capability while still saving money, it's possible for companies to reinvent themselves rather than simply reducing costs. It is an opportunity to improve their overall business intelligence and get ready for the next generation of the technology wave while also achieving immediate cost savings.

Three areas can produce results. Alone, any one of these areas will drive value, but together, the results can transform a company.

1. **Individual impact** can drive down costs in a very immediate way.
2. **Organizational agility** comes from connecting teams and managing information and utilizing knowledge. The results hit all aspects of an organization.
3. **IT efficiency** affects everything from the cost of doing business to the speed a product gets to market. It determines if the IT resources are busy maintaining the status quo or can focus on delivering business impact and results.

Individual Impact

When given the right tools to do a job, an individual can impact the cost of doing business. Often individual impact is influenced simply by the way people can communicate. For example, *Tieto Digital Innovations* is an international IT services company headquartered in Helsinki, Finland. One of Europe's largest IT services providers, Tieto has offices in 26 countries and employs nearly 17,000 people.[1] The organization delivers software solutions and consulting services to enterprises in the public administration, finance, telecommunications, and forest industries and others. Its largest customers are located in northern Europe, Germany, and Russia.

A major challenge for Tieto was getting its employees to work together effectively despite the geographic distance between offices. "Even though many of our employees are based in different competency centers in locations all over the world, they need to work in virtual teams," says Michael Wittwer, Vice President of Business Development. "We need to combine the best expertise and competences from all of those offices into virtual teams to provide the best possible solutions to our global customers." In other words, putting people on planes to go to meetings is expensive, time consuming, and disruptive and not in line with Tieto's strategy to become the leading IT services provider in northern Europe.

In January 2008 Tieto looked at various unified communications (UC) solutions. After comparing different alternatives, the Tieto team implemented Microsoft's Office Communications Server with full Voice over Internet Protocol (VoIP) functionality, along with Exchange Server Unified Messaging. Using these tools, employees could communicate quickly with colleagues in other offices through instant messaging, email, or voice—all from their computers. And they could launch audio or video conferences whenever they needed to. It meant no more planes, complicated global conference calls, or long rounds of phone tag. Tieto significantly reduced its costs related to long-distance calling and off-site meetings. "We have already reduced travel by 25 percent, and we have reduced total travel costs by 15 percent company wide," says Wittwer. But the impact is not limited to Teito's bottom line alone. Teito decided to offer its solution experience to its own customers as well. "We did a detailed assessment for a customer that will use a solution including Office Communications 2007 that we're helping to implement," remarks Wittwer. An ROI study Teito oversaw showed that this one customer alone can reduce its travel costs by €12 million ($15.7 million) annually. That is a reduction of more than 20 percent, and the customer is providing increased communication capability to its employees too. Interestingly enough, while the organizations are saving, most employees actually report an increase in their own productivity after the migration. You can think of this as individual impact on steroids.

Other leading companies have also used improved communications and collaboration infrastructures to increase individual impact within their organization. *BMW* has 100,000 employees spread across 24 production sites in 13 countries. With increased competition and the need to develop and deliver more specialist products for niche markets, BMW understood that development, production planning, marketing, and sales functions needed to be far more effective. Realizing that an outdated infrastructure was holding back the employees' potential and seeking to optimize the strength of its workforce, BMW needed to go from a Basic technology infrastructure to a more Dynamic one. BMW looked holistically at its hardware devices, communications options, employee locations, and vendors. Like most Basic infrastructures, its hardware used multiple platforms, communication was not easy, and the multitude of vendors supporting communication could not easily plug into BMW's systems. A dynamic model—one of the key indicators of company agility—needs to be fully automated, customizable, manageable, and easy for everyone to access and use.

In about 2005, BMW deployed a communications and collaboration solution from a large networking hardware company. The upfront cost was small, which made it an easy sell to decision makers. However, it took a lot of expensive engineering to make it work in a way that was acceptable against original specifications and for the IT team. After the original solution was set up, the system was still hard for employees to use and did not integrate well with BMW's widely used Microsoft Office tools, something most people around the world are familiar with.

In round two of going from a Basic to a Dynamic infrastructure, BMW switched to Office Communications Server and Office Live Communications Server. This combination provided a unified approach to communications and collaboration. Employees now had instant messaging, presence monitoring, voice communications as well as audio, video, and Web conferencing that plugged into current workplace tools. Engineers were particularly happy with some of the new security levels, which let them share designs without the risk of losing confidential or proprietary information.

For BMW, the results have been outstanding on many fronts. Reduced conferencing and communications costs, faster project completion times, reduced IT issues, and reduced IT management costs were all realized in short time. Designers, engineers, and manufacturing sites are now in constant effective communication regardless of their location across the globe. Innovations don't sit on a drafting table in Munich when they need to be in South Carolina, South Africa, or Kuala Lumpur. This move from a Basic infrastructure to a Dynamic one gets better BMWs to market faster and enables the firm to continue to lead in every automotive class in which it offers a model. But the competition is not asleep either. Some other automakers are now benchmarking themselves against BMW. Whether they can catch up or not remains to be seen.

For another company, individual impact based on innovative communications and collaboration tools combined with improved business intelligence netted wins for both the company and all of its clients. *A.T. Kearney*, based in Chicago, Illinois, is a leading management consultancy that serves clients in all major industries as well as government agencies.[2] It has more than 2,500 employees worldwide. "The consulting market has dramatically shifted over the past few years," says Hugo Evans, Chief Information Officer for A.T. Kearney Procurement and Analytic Solutions. "Clients want innovative technology solutions that play a more substantive role in the procurement and knowledge capture and transfer process to increase their return on investment by several orders of magnitude."

To meet clients' repeated demands, Evans and his team looked at technologies that would facilitate active collaboration of consultants with clients. The team established key parameters quickly. The target solution needed all of the capabilities generally required for intranet collaboration, including a central location to store documents as well as the ability to create virtual workspaces and gather information easily. It had to be easy to use and manage for individual consultants and for the IT team. More important, it had to meet enterprise requirements for efficiency and security. The unit also had to consider clients' firewalls, which could block any solution A.T. Kearney developed.

A.T. Kearney adopted a client extranet based on the Microsoft Office system as well as Extranet Collaboration Manager for SharePoint. With this change, clients gained 24-hour-a-day access to their information, and the information was more intuitive and comprehensive. Clients loved it, and their public kudos boosted A.T. Kearney's competitiveness in the market. Internally the impact was also impressive: quantum leaps in time to deliver results to customers. "We have financial systems, people systems, and legal systems from which we've taken all the data outputs and connected these to our business intelligence dashboard in Office SharePoint Server," says Michael Chovan, Business Technology Senior Manager, A.T. Kearney Procurement and Analytic Solutions. "Now we can take six months' worth of client work and give it to the client in a day." I surely would call that a competitive advantage.

Organizational Agility

Organizational agility allows a business to be flexible, adaptable, coordinated, and cost efficient in its product and service delivery. IT infrastructure is front and center in Agile organizations. From manufacturing, to financial services, to nonprofits, to healthcare, the solutions may look very different but the results are the same: A company must be able to adapt and change more quickly than the competition.

Ampacet is an excellent example of a manufacturing company that used its IT infrastructure as a competitive resource to gain agility in the market.[3] Ampacet is a specialty chemical manufacturer. It has five major research and development (R&D) facilities and 17 manufacturing sites in multiple locations worldwide. Business leadership recognized that the company lacked a consistent approach to process and track projects across facilities, limiting its ability to introduce new products. The company needed a way to accelerate product development through better collaboration, to increase process automation, and to implement more consistent work flows. The IT department was tasked with making it so.

Ampacet automated its product development process by implementing an infrastructure that blended business intelligence, enterprise content management, and collaboration tools. The solution was based on Microsoft Office SharePoint Server in combination with the familiar Microsoft Office client as the interface for the end user. The company's willingness to take a critical look and to make the changes paid off handsomely. Over a three-year period, Ampacet estimates that it developed 12 to 15 additional new products for additional revenues of $60 million. And it also is well on the way to reduce R&D costs and increase customers' satisfaction.

In a very different business sector is *Sasfin Bank*, a South African bank providing financial services for entrepreneurs.[4] We are looking into the financial sector in more detail later, but agility and speed are critical here. Competitors move very fast and utilize knowledge and insights to their advantage. Sasfin had no single view of its customer. Customer information on balances, financial reports, and activity was stored in disparate databases, and each business unit used separate transaction processing systems. For these reasons, it was difficult to create a consolidated, up-to-date view of customer information and balances and of relevant credit exposures in all areas of the bank's business. Data storage created a host of difficulties; users had to manually capture information, which resulted in delays in lead generation, limited cross-selling, and slowing down of credit processing. The manual capture of information caused "double work," which increased the potential for errors. Sasfin's IT architecture made risk analysis and compliance reporting time consuming and difficult. For Sasfin and many other organizations today, professional data warehousing is necessary. If the data can be utilized for the business, it becomes a potential competitive asset. Lizande Vermeulen, manager at Sasfin, summed the situation up nicely: "We had to redesign the way we look at customer information and needed a mechanism to consolidate information and create an overall view of the client to build reports."

Sasfin deployed an enterprise content management and business intelligence solution that included the latest versions of Microsoft Office and Microsoft SharePoint Server shortly after they were released. The results were a single complete view of customer and risk data. What does this outcome mean for the business? The time to create compliance reports was reduced by 10 days, and errors in such reports and in the credit data systems were reduced by 80 percent. In any business sector, these are impressive numbers. In the banking world, this type of improvement is essential for success.

Not all industries move as quickly as the financial sector. Manufacturing, by nature or tradition, can be slow, yet consumers are constantly looking for new products and experiences. With more than 3,400 products, *Del Monte Foods* is one of the largest U.S. manufacturers and distributors of branded canned fruit, vegetable, tomato, tuna, and pet products.[5] Del Monte Foods wanted to improve one division's product lines, introduce new products, and maintain quality by streamlining its formula-change process. In the past, that process relied on manual routing, approval, tracking, filing, and archiving of documents related to development of new products. It was a time-consuming and error-prone process.

The company hoped to streamline the process and transform it into one that could serve as a model for new product development companywide. By customizing standard off-the-shelf products, Del Monte rapidly implemented enterprise content management capabilities, again leveraging standard components from the Office System to build a scalable and quick-to-deploy environment. The new solution provided a fully automated document management and approval work flow that simplified the initiation and monitoring of change requests, provided a library for managing and archiving related documents, and reduced the formula-change process from 15 days down to 10. Reducing development time by a third and reducing time to market meant this IT solution created a distinct market advantage. But quality also improved dramatically because the solution reduced risk errors. The right technologies and processes meant saving money and time in the product development cycle.

IT Efficiency

I've talked about individual impact and organizational agility, but IT infrastructure and efficiency is the foundation on which the others rest. How a company builds and deploys its IT infrastructure directly impacts people, dollars, and its ability to innovate in the future. Take, for example, *EMC*, a provider of information-infrastructure solutions that help organizations effectively manage their information throughout its life cycle.[6] I was fortunate to help establish the first collaboration agreement between EMC and Microsoft. Today EMC has nearly 33,000 employees worldwide. By rolling out a new IT infrastructure in 2007, the company calculated that it would save $19 million in four years just in management costs and equipment alone. The investment paid off nicely. By maturing their infrastructure solution, EMC created an IT cost reduction of up to $500 per employee.

What about communication costs? On an individual level, we are experiencing the increase over the years. The days of only one landline per household are over. Multiple mobile phone lines, data connections, and information channels are not only the norm at home, but rising communication costs are also a fact for many organizations. *Royal Dutch Shell*, the global group of energy and petrochemical companies, is active in more than 130 countries and territories and employs 108,000 people.[7] Like all companies in the oil business, the challenges for the IT organization are tremendous. In addition to the typical business roadblocks, difficulties, and pitfalls, topics like security, safety, and limited Internet bandwidth or even connections are impacting the day-to-day business on much deeper levels. I have been working with Shell since 2005 when I met its Malaysian-based desktop management team for the first time. Shell's global organization looked at its voice communication infrastructure as an area to gain additional IT efficiencies. A combination of hardware and software improved communications throughout the company and has allowed it to reduce communications cost and retire hardware without impacting business processes.

The IT team at *Intel*, the world's largest semiconductor chip maker, is always looking to give the company's 86,000 employees the best possible computing experience and still drive down costs.[8] The team saw great value in creating efficiency in how employees "talked" to each other. Again, using a combination of hardware and software solutions, the IT department was able to reduce administrative costs and infrastructure while also cutting conferencing costs. As Donald Clark, Intel's Technical Services Manager, stated, "As we scale out the deployment, we expect to save 20 percent or more from our audio conferencing expense. When you conference a million minutes a day, that is significant."

Lionbridge, a leading provider of language, content, and technology outsourcing services, is much smaller than Intel.[9] However, it also has to think globally. The company is headquartered in Waltham, Massachusetts, and has 4,600 employees across 26 countries, including 1,600 skilled professionals in India, the People's Republic of China, and Eastern Europe. Through its translation and globalization service offerings, Lionbridge adapts client software products, applications, and Web content to meet the linguistic, technical, and cultural requirements of users worldwide.

As you can imagine, communication and collaboration of its employees across geographical boundaries is critical for Lionbridge. The company wanted to simplify the way employees communicated with each other while reducing the costs associated with external conferencing and telephony providers. Lionbridge implemented Microsoft Office Communications Server and Exchange as its communication infrastructure and Office Communicator on the client PCs to unlock user capability. The complete experience gave every employee access to integrated VoIP, Web conferencing, presence, instant messaging, email, and voicemail—independent of where they were working. Lionbridge realized quickly the benefits and continued leveraging technology improvements as they became available. It also added integrated audio conferencing and improved voice connectivity options by upgrading to new versions of the Communications Server soon after their release. The results have been impressive. Lionbridge reduced its conferencing costs, saving $1.3 million a year, by relying on Web and audio conferencing capabilities. It also has seen an 80 percent reduction in telephony connection charges, and long-distance charges have been reduced by 25 percent.

Communication is critical for individuals and organizations. Ensuring that we provide the essential capability to our employees in the most efficient way is a responsibility we can take on. As the examples have shown, technology actually can help to save tremendously here by providing more for less.

ROLE OF PLACE, PEOPLE, AND TECHNOLOGY

"Going to work" has always meant commuting to an office, a factory or store. Even for workers in the technology world, work was where they had their computer, access to the information, and the communication tools they needed. These tools were usually found on a cluttered desk in small, windowless cubicles.

However, in the last decade, use of the Internet has completely changed the concept of "going to work." If you have Internet access, you have an office. A coffee shop or a client's lobby replaces the desk and cubicle. For more and more people, "going to work" means they walk from their living room into their home office, close the door, turn on the computer, and log on. A new generation of workers is growing up thinking this is as natural as riding a bike.

For those of us who are a little older, it is helpful to have a mental framework to understand how this shift in where and how you work affects us now and in the future. Research of user behavior and market trends can be grouped into a few areas.

- **Insights to impact**. Collecting information alone is not sufficient. The insights derived from information and how effectively they are shared are a key for organizational success.
- **Teamwork makes the dream work**. Effective collaboration across boundaries is also essential. Tools need to be engineered for the diversity of people working in diverse location with diverse types of data.
- **The office is everywhere**. Working with and through a PC, a smart phone, or a browser each has its own advantages and disadvantages. However, all are needed and used by individuals and organizations.
- **Complexity will continue to increase. Managing it is essential**. The business and IT world are not getting less complicated. Given trends toward consumerization of IT, where people have preferences regarding the types of hardware and software they want to use both at home and at work, IT is challenged to support more devices. Ensuring that the complex environment is manageable allows security, compliance, and cost controls.

Most people are familiar with models and strategy recommendations based on a worldview of People, Processes, and Technologies. For the next section, I would like to invite you, the reader, to try on a model that sees formal and informal processes underlying every environment we drill into. Understanding and managing *processes* is critical in our solution design approach.

In our work within Microsoft and with our customers, we find it critical to look at three overlapping environments in an integral way (see Figure 3.1).

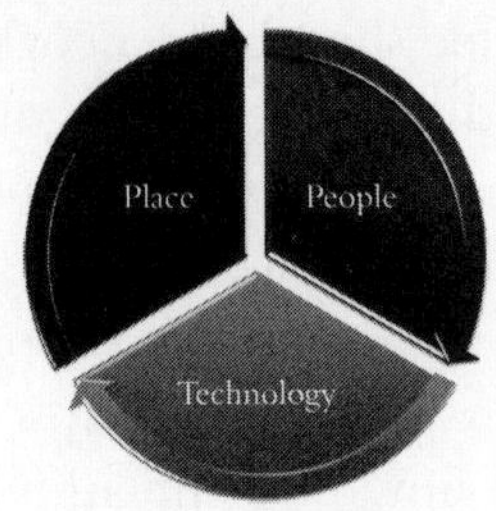

Figure 3.1 Sectors of Influence

Place is where you work. It could be at home, on the road, the office—really anywhere. *People* represent workers *and* the culture in which they operate. Finally, *Technology* represents the hardware, software, and cloudware that are used, plus the actual end user experience.

In the following sections, I'll discuss each of these areas in depth. Keep in mind that there are many variables and processes behind these areas. These days, clear linear relations between actions and benefits are rare. Multidependencies, such as those listed next, complicate matters within our complex systems:

- Benefits are relative and depend on the starting situation.
- Benefits depend on the length and depth of the implementation process.
- Benefit results depend on the definition of the measurement and when and how they are measured.

In the past few years, several large and complex projects—during challenging economic times—have allowed Microsoft to analyze the cost/benefit scenarios in an immediate way. New offices in the Netherlands and the challenges of bringing a collection of new high-rise office buildings in downtown Bellevue, Washington, online gave us insights that we were able to combine with findings from a large number of customers as well.

Across all these different and diverse projects, the biggest consistently measureable gains are found in:

- People productivity (People)
- Office space (Place)
- Cost of collaboration and communication (Technology)

Different organizations have different ownership and measurements for these factors, but across all of them, the potential impact on the bottom line is highly significant. In the same projects, we were also able to crystallize the key risk factors that block or slow IT projects, reducing overall business agility:

- Cost and control of technology
- Cost and control of collaboration and communication
- Level and speed with which people adopt the change of work style

In our project work across industries and geographies—and through our research cooperation with Massachusetts Institute of Technology (MIT) and Boston University (BU)—it became clear that organizations embracing and driving technology infrastructure changes are realizing the benefits. And those of their competitors that cannot embrace these change quickly fall behind not only in capturing market share but in attracting critical, new talent as well.

Place and the Impact of Office Space and Travel

No longer is the physical work environment the central office location. No longer is work confined to a desk and a stationary PC or a single conference room. People work from home, in transit, in satellite offices, at customer sites, or even in the middle of a disaster zone. Organizations are gradually realizing the challenges and also the opportunities these changes can bring.

Often an existing office layout, setup, and even location can be adapted to the changing work environment; at other times, opening up a new location provides the opportunity to do things differently. For example, in the Microsoft headquarters in Redmond, every employee had his or her own individual office. Like the free soda and coffee, this arrangement was just a part of the Microsoft culture. As the workforce grew, the older buildings couldn't accommodate more employees and definitely didn't accommodate a more collaborative and connected work environment. Newer buildings now look nothing like the original campus, and the individual offices are gone. The buildings have far more open and flexible layouts. With ever-increasing cost per square foot for prime real estate, the cost-saving potential is tremendous.

Microsoft's Dutch subsidiary had the chance to truly do things differently when it ran into the challenge of office space shortages. The organization took the concept of mobile work without any assigned workspaces to a new level. The changes came after a long and detailed review process.

When asked what he liked and did not like about Microsoft Netherlands' existing office space, General Manager Theo Rinsema said: "There is nothing that I like about this office or the way we work. Every day people enter the office, occupy the same desks, work on their notebooks, go to meetings, return to their desks, pack their notebooks, and go home. I don't see 'anytime, anyplace, any device' here. And they have to sell our vision? First we need to *live* our vision."

These are pretty harsh words. But Rinsema heads up Microsoft Netherlands and has firsthand experience. Although Microsoft's Dutch subsidiary had sustained spectacular growth for almost 10 years, the office space no longer worked. The organization simply needed more room. At the time, the leased floor area per person was 16.4 square meters (176 square feet), and only 25 percent of employees shared desks. Rather than simply move to a larger location, the project team developed an office plan to accommodate more employees but use less space.

The new building, which opened in April 2008, got rid of any assigned desks—not even the country manager there has an individual office—and requires only 8.82 square meters (95 square feet) per person. Each employee can work anywhere in the office by using a laptop, headset, Webcam, or Windows-based smart phone and connecting to the network either wirelessly or by plugging in at a desk. On paper it sounds good, but not everyone was happy. As Toby Wilson, Microsoft Netherlands Finance director, diplomatically put it, "Not everyone on my team was enthusiastic about the idea of not having a private office, but I volunteered because I really believed in the concept." The overall space design saved the organization more than $640,000 per year.

But Rinsema will tell you it goes beyond just the dollar benefits. "It is all about reputation, and reputation starts internally. At Microsoft Netherlands we use the expression 'eat your own dog food,' which means that we ourselves always use our own technology first, so we will understand what our customers will be using later on. With our new office design, we have taken this concept to a new level. We are 'eating' our new way of working vision."

And even if some employees did not enthusiastically embrace the change in the beginning, the experience of living in and benefiting from the new environment won over most of the doubters over the next two years. Two studies attest to the improvements in work quality and employee satisfaction following the initiative. Microsoft Netherlands was honored as the "best employer" in the Netherlands, scoring 92 out of 100 in an employee survey that measured credibility, camaraderie, and other factors that make for a vital workplace. The subsidiary also topped all other companies in the survey in terms of "employee pride." The study, conducted by the Rotterdam School of Management, Erasmus University, showed that employees' satisfaction regarding their workplace improved significantly after moving to the new building.

People and the Impact of Productivity, Sick Leave, and Retention

Today, almost any decision maker will agree that whatever measure you take in striving for business success, the most important factor you have to deal with are people. They can be employees, customers, shareholders, consumers, partners, family, or any other role that we all play from time to time. For organizations that are able to positively motivate these groups of individuals, nearly anything is possible.

Let's look at Microsoft Netherlands again. People are at the heart of the organization. Company leaders wanted to create a work culture that empowered its employees when they began their office reengineering. Part of the design focused solely on employee work styles and patterns. For instance, workers were surveyed on how much time they spend sending and receiving email messages and attending meetings. Thirty percent of the workforce completed questionnaires about how they were *expected* to do tasks versus how they *actually* did these tasks. Why? The subsidiary realized that "personal discovery"—which encourages employees to engage with tools, space, and other people in ways that are comfortable and productive for them as individuals—gave them an ownership stake in the initiative. Ownership often leads to successful change.

Successful change within an organization relies heavily on culture and leadership, diversification, office facilities, technology, and infrastructure. The "people" part of the equation is tightly linked to culture and leadership. Finding the right strategy and culture for an organization has impressive and measurable results. A leadership team that focuses on people when designing business processes can:

- Increase the individual's as well as the team's productivity.
- Attract and retain the right people.
- Reduce sick leave and other costs of nonproductivity.

Technology and infrastructure have a direct impact on employee satisfaction and productivity. If employees aren't happy, they aren't giving you their best and brightest work. If employees don't like the tools, they don't use them. Simplicity and familiarity often beat features and functionalities.

Let's look deeper again into the Microsoft Netherlands experience. The subsidiary tried to implement a new hospitality management system, which called for employees to plan their own meetings with external visitors—including reserving meeting rooms and organizing beverages, lunch, and parking spaces. This self-service concept was implemented with an internal tool that did not meet employee "expectations." The debate over whether it was too complicated to learn or simply unfamiliar has not been settled, but, nevertheless, many employees refused to use the tool and planned their meetings the old-fashioned way: by walking to the reception area and arranging meetings through the receptionists. But the receptionists didn't like the new processes either, and the results were a contentious mess.

This impasse was resolved by taking one step backward, away from the sophisticated point solution. The subsidiary simplified the self-service process by shelving the new tool and using technology that workers were already familiar with in their daily work flow from expense reports to performance evaluations—Microsoft Office InfoPath, the information-gathering program in Office that easily creates XML-based data forms. With Office InfoPath, employees fill out the forms on an intranet site and then send them to the hospitality team, which handles the request within 24 hours. The organization is quick to make changes because it continually sees that empowering employees and teams to choose the way they work leads to higher accountability, increased innovation and inspiration, and overall better morale and attitude for the complete location.

Technology and Understanding the Total Cost of Workplace, Communication, and Collaboration

When assessing the costs and benefits of an integrated communication and collaboration environment, it is important to look holistically across functions, locations, and budgets as well as realized and potentially not realized results.

Getting a lot of smart people in a room to work together only enhances the result, if they can actually communicate with each other. Spreading them across vast geographic areas and asking them to solve complex financial issues at lightning speeds seems laughable. But this is exactly what many leading financial institutions ask of their employees, and they rely on the IT specialists to provide a secure and accessible communication system that integrates with a company's client and transaction databases.

Without a UC strategy, a company is powerless to stay competitive in today's business climate. And with ever-evolving communications tools, a company needs a messaging system that works now and will work five years from now.

Bank of America has more than 18,000 ATMs and nearly 3 million active online banking users. It serves one in two households in the United States, and its retail footprint covers 80 percent of the U.S. population. It also serves 59 million consumer and small business clients. In 2008, with the acquisition of Countrywide and Merrill Lynch, Bank of America grew to over 300,000 employees. Email is the communication channel not only within the company but with their customers as well. After the mergers, it was crystal clear that the bank's aging and heterogeneous messaging infrastructure could not handle the communication flow. In addition, federal regulators require Bank of America to archive roughly 100,000 of its 320,000 email accounts located across five data centers in the United States. Market pressures and budgetary constraints further complicate the communications issue.

NASDAQ OMX, the world's largest exchange company, delivers trading, exchange technology, and public company services across six continents. Like Bank of America, email is the vital communications channel. "Next to our trading systems, email is one of the most critical systems to our business," explains Carl-Magnus Hallberg, Senior Vice President of Global IT Services. When NASDAQ and OMX merged, both companies were using an older version of Microsoft's Exchange Server as their core messaging platform. Both companies agreed that they could consolidate and reduce the number of data centers and of servers by migrating to the latest available version of Exchange. Again, this solved many issues of the merger, but the new NASDAQ OXM group felt even more could be done to consolidate parts of its messaging system and simplify the overall IT architecture. The driving force behind these decisions was the commitment to technology to keep an edge over competitors.

The two companies faced two very different communications challenges. Bank of America was dealing with an aging infrastructure while NASDAQ OMX wanted to continually push the envelope on messaging solutions because cutting-edge technology is a driving force in its culture. Interestingly enough, both companies solved these issues by developing solutions based on the latest technology just becoming available at that time, the Microsoft communication platform of Exchange Server 2010, Communication Server, and Microsoft Office. NASDAQ OMX also used the opportunity to modernize the underlying PC platform and added Microsoft Windows 7 Enterprise to the mix, creating an easily manageable platform for further innovation when updated components become available.

Throughout human history, tools and technology advances have made the difference. In today's world of knowledge management and sophisticated production and logistics, the most important tool people use is information technology. It is hard to imagine how people, organizations, or society would function without that toolset and infrastructure. Information technologies enable people to align their skills and ambitions and to ally that with the goals of the organizations for which they work. It is challenging to get technology "right" in the capabilities it provides, to make the investments efficient, and to ensure that the resulting infrastructure is flexible and manageable. But we are seeing and experiencing every day that the rewards are well worth the pain. As you will see in the following chapters, the type of technology and how it is implemented directly impact an organization's bottom line.

Infrastructure	Diversification	Culture	Non-Office	EU Guidance	Standardization
• IT investments are relatively easy to predict and control. • The time from investment to experienced results is short to midterm. • Biggest cost factor is the replacement of vintage technologies.	• Diversification and creating work style–specific offerings normally fall into existing investment planes. • Risk is two sided: (1) the risk that the end user rejects the offering (so a negative result is gained); (2) too much diversification leads to uncontrollable costs.	• Investment in changing a culture is high and has a high risk. • Approximately 30%–50% of the total investment. • This investment however is key and is a make (or break) factor. • Effects are experienced in mid to long term. • Biggest hurdle: middle-management layer.	• Investments in work-at-home, mobility, etc., are often less than 5%. • Biggest part of this investment is in education and risk-reduction (liabilities). • Time until effect is visible is very short, but old habits die slowly.	• End user guidance (education, knowledge, change work style) is absolute key. • Relative low investment: 5%–10%. • Biggest challenges are to change current patterns and replace them with new ones. • Identify and "seduce" the right groups of change agents.	• To control cost of IT and facilities, large-scale standardization is necessary. • Investments are completely dependent on the starting situation. • Effects are visible in short term but... • Expect learning curves and (temporary) fallbacks.

Figure 3.2 Factors Impacting Cost, Time, and Resources

The total cost of workplace and the cost of communication and collaboration is complex and multidimensional. The framework shown in Figure 3.2 has helped many organizations to facilitate the process, ensuring key aspects weren't overlooked.

Figure 3.2 shows a few of the areas that factor into cost equations and the impact they have on time and resources. I suggest using a framework like this to facilitate the discussion in your own organization. Ensure that area experts are included and that their expertise is leveraged through the process, which traditionally is dominated by IT.

INFRASTRUCTURE OPTIMIZATION

As discussed previously, the key measureable factors for business agility are:

- People productivity
- Office space
- Cost of collaboration and communication

- Cost and control of technology
- Cost and control of collaboration and communication

But we have also looked at the complexity and interdependencies of business processes that affect these factors. Putting an infrastructure in place that supports these factors is a complicated, challenging, and *necessary* puzzle. As Jeanne W. Ross of MIT states: "Business agility is becoming a strategic necessity. Greater globalization, increasing regulation, and faster cycle times all demand an ability to quickly change organizational processes."[10] And the only way to achieve and maintain this agility in our times is through a dynamic and mature IT infrastructure.

Information technology is a key strategic asset that supports and drives innovation, profitability, and customer satisfaction. The importance that IT plays in the modern corporate world is highlighted by the escalating IT investment companies are making. In the early 1980s, 15 percent of the capital expenditures of U.S. companies went to information technology; by the end of the 1990s, it had hit nearly 50 percent.[11] In some organizations, a lot of this money is spent on keeping an infrastructure running that is outdated and not ready for the future. But in more and more environments, the funds are seen and managed as business investments for future growth and competitiveness. IT has become a defining factor for success. Gartner's Mahoney and Berg predict that "by 2012, IT contribution will be cited in the top three success factors by at least half of top-performing businesses; and IT barriers will be cited in the top three failure factors by at least half of the lowest performers."[12]

Based on the engagement with researchers, analysts, partners, and customers, we have developed a vision for what an Agile business looks like. These businesses have IT infrastructures that help enhance the dynamic capability of their people, process, and infrastructure and platform through technology. IT groups become a capability advisor instead of just an infrastructure services provider. Before we go any further into infrastructure optimization, it is important to understand what a dynamic or mature IT shop provides to an organization.

- **People are empowered with access to information when they need it**. Integration between users and data, desktops and servers, and collaboration between users and departments is pervasive. Mobile users have nearly on-site levels of service and capabilities regardless of location.

- **Processes are automated and aligned to business goals**. People work smoothly with processes that are automated, often incorporated into the technology itself, allowing IT to be aligned and managed according to business needs. Additional investments in technology yield specific, rapid, and measurable benefits to the company.
- **The business can control and manage security compliance issues**. Self-provisioning software and other technologies important for data retention and auditing enable improved reliability, lowered costs, and increased service levels.
- **IT services can be adapted easily to changing business needs**. Service management is implemented for all critical issues with service-level agreements and operational reviews established. The business is more aware of the strategic value of its dynamic systems infrastructure in running its operations efficiently and staying ahead of its competitors. The business can adopt more technology faster and with less risk. Costs are more controlled.

So why can't a company just buy the latest and greatest software and roll it out companywide to great fanfare and success? Because if it is not done well, an IT infrastructure investment can turn out to be an expensive disaster. However, optimizing the IT infrastructure along clearly defined capabilities has demonstrated core value. A company that is unable to use its IT capabilities to respond to the latest competitive threat or to take advantage of a strategic business opportunity risks becoming obsolete.

The Microsoft Infrastructure Optimization Model provides a road map across capabilities to take on the journey through the maturity steps from Basic, Standardized, Rationalized, to Dynamic and unlocks organizational and individual potential and shows cost and manageability improvements every step of the way.

Benefits of the IT Infrastructure Optimization

Figure 3.3 shows the benefits of IT optimization on costs, service levels, and agility as organizations move from Basic to Dynamic maturity.

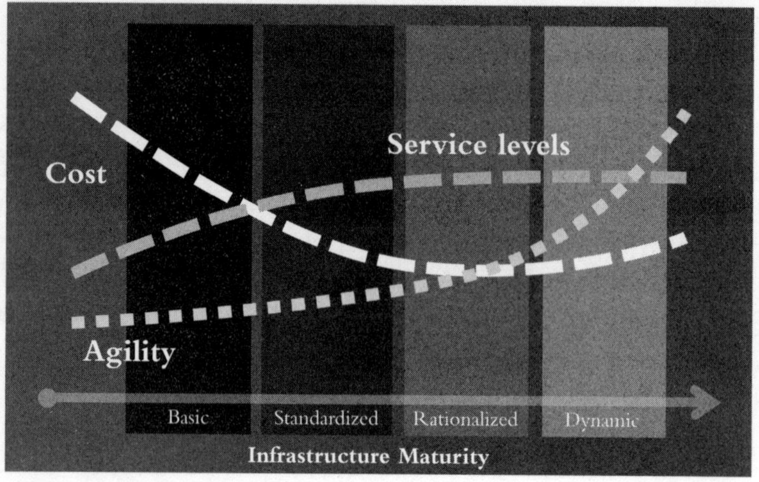

Figure 3.3 Benefits of IT Optimization

- **Control costs**. Simplify, automate, and centralize IT operations to optimize resource utilization.
- **Improve service levels**. Integrate management and security tools to maximize system uptime.
- **Drive agility**. Adapt the IT infrastructure rapidly according to business needs.

The cost for maintaining and managing the IT environment decreases while processes and tools improve. On average, companies that have a Standardized level of Core Infrastructure Optimization have an IT cost structure (per PC per year) that is 56 percent lower than companies at a Basic level. Companies at a Rationalized level have an IT cost structure that is 60 percent lower than companies at a Standardized level and 83 percent lower than companies at a Basic level.[13] At the same time, the end user experience increases through improved capabilities and service level. The results are significantly reduced service desk calls per PC per year. Improved IT infrastructure also improves security of information and the organization's business intelligence. The most significant improvements come when an organization transitions to a Rationalized level and when it does it before its competitors.

Fortunately, there are models and resources to help an organization assess its strengths and weaknesses. Microsoft developed a tool that does this and goes on to create a long-term strategy for continued infrastructure optimization. I touched on it briefly in Chapter 2. The model uses industry best practices and Microsoft's own experiences with its enterprise customers, and incorporates elements of Gartner's Infrastructure Maturity Model and MIT's Architecture Maturity Model. Microsoft's Infrastructure Optimization Model (see Figure 3.4) is a simple way to use a maturity framework that is flexible and can easily be used as the benchmark for technical capability and business value.

The models also provide an actionable road map to help an organization transition from one optimization level to the next. They also provide customers, technology partners, and Microsoft with a common terminology to coordinate efforts to help customers improve their level of IT optimization.

Tony Scott, Corporate Vice President, CIO of IT Strategy and Planning at Microsoft, explains how and why Microsoft uses the model: "Microsoft IT uses the Infrastructure Optimization framework for planning, as a way to identify improvements, and as a tool to communicate to management. As an organization, IT is focused on moving from the Standardized to Rationalized phase. The framework

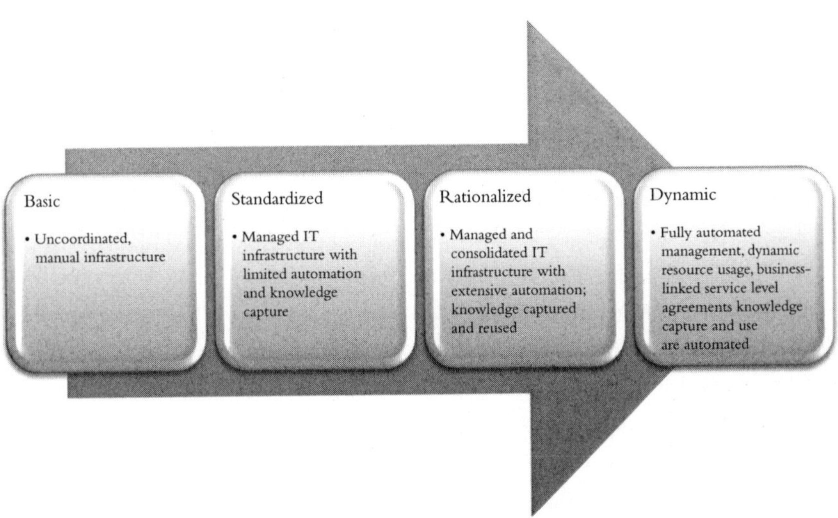

Figure 3.4 Microsoft's Infrastructure Optimization Model

Source: "Taking the Lead: Gaining a Competitive Advantage Through Infrastructure and Platform Optimization", Microsoft, 2008.

has been helpful in identifying areas that offer the most opportunity for improvement and to help develop a road map for key next steps."

The first step in using the model is to evaluate what maturity level you are at. Once you have established the current maturity level, the next step is to use the model to develop a plan on how to progress through each maturity level in order to reach the target level needed for maximum business benefit.

Level 1: Basic

This is the bargain basement of IT infrastructure. It is characterized by manual, localized processes; minimal central control; and nonexistent or unenforced IT policies regarding security, backup, image management and deployment, compliance, and other common IT standards. There is a general lack of knowledge regarding details of the infrastructure or which tactics will have the greatest impact to improve on it. Overall health of applications and services is unknown due to a lack of tools and resources. There is no vehicle for sharing accumulated knowledge across IT. Customers with Basic infrastructure find their environments extremely hard to control, have very high desktop and server management costs, are generally very reactive to security threats, and have very little positive impact on the ability of the business to benefit from IT. Think of it as the Wild West of infrastructure.

Level 2: Standardized

Businesses sitting at Level 2 probably won't win any awards, but they have a better handle on what they have and how the IT tools can be used than businesses at Level 1. The Standardized infrastructure introduces standards and policies to manage desktops and servers, how machines are introduced to the network, the use of Active Directory to manage resources, security policies, and access control. Companies at this level have realized the value of Basic standards and policies but are still quite reactive. Generally all patches, software deployments, and desktop service are provided through medium IT touches with medium to high company costs. However, these organizations have a reasonable inventory of hardware and software and are beginning to manage licenses. Security measures are improved but not ironclad. Often an individual's PC is locked down to prevent security, IT, licensing, or intellectual property issues; this also limits the user's ability to use productivity tools and resources outside of cubicle walls.

Level 3: Rationalized

At the Rationalized stage, IT has moved beyond being a cost center to being a business asset. Costs involved in managing desktops and servers are at their lowest, and processes and policies have matured to begin playing a large role in supporting and expanding the business. Security is very proactive, and response to threats and challenges is rapid and controlled. The use of Zero-Touch software deployment minimizes cost, time to deploy and technical challenges. These companies have a clear inventory of hardware and software and purchase only those licenses and computers they need. Security is extremely proactive with strict policies and control from desktop, to server, to firewall, to extranet. Responding to business demands by deploying updated software or additional tools (like a corporate instant messaging client) is easy, and business benefits are immediate.

Level 4: Dynamic

Customers with a Dynamic infrastructure are fully aware of the strategic value their infrastructure provides in helping them run their business efficiently and staying ahead of competitors. Costs are fully controlled; integration between users and data, desktops and servers, and collaboration between users and departments is pervasive; mobile users have nearly on-site levels of service and capabilities regardless of location. Processes are fully automated, often incorporated into the technology itself, allowing IT to be aligned and managed according to business needs. Additional investments in technology yield specific, rapid, measurable benefits for the business.

CAPABILITIES: THE AREAS OF OPTIMIZATION

By using this model as a framework, an enterprise can quickly understand strategic value and business benefits in moving from a Basic maturity level (where the IT infrastructure is generally considered a cost center) toward a more Dynamic use, where the business value of the IT infrastructure is clearly understood and the IT infrastructure is viewed as a strategic business asset and business enabler.

Although the initial Core IO model was based on Gartner's model, Microsoft has expanded some important dimensions for each aspect of an organization's infrastructure and platform as well as model-specific capabilities. The result is two customized models that are continuing to evolve as technologies and insights change.

1. **Core Infrastructure Optimization (Core IO)**. Core IO covers the management of servers, desktops, mobile devices, and applications. Efficient use of these resources helps companies eliminate unnecessary costs and complexity, ensures that their business is always up and running, and establishes a responsive infrastructure. Core IO has these specific capabilities:
   - Data center services, including management, virtualization, networking, and storage
   - Client services, including desktop or client management and virtualization
   - Identity and security services including access management
   - IT process and compliance
2. **Business Productivity Infrastructure Optimization (BPIO)**. BPIO includes a complete set of technologies that helps streamline the management and control of content, data, and processes across all areas of a business. For business productivity, capabilities include:
   - Collaboration
   - Unified communications
   - Enterprise content management
   - Enterprise search
   - Reporting and analysis
   - Content creation

Figure 3.5 summarizes the characteristics for just one section of the BPIO capabilities at each maturity level—Enterprise Search. Microsoft's Optimization Self-Assessment tool—which you can access online at www.microsoft.com/optimization/tools/overview.mspx—provides a personalized Optimization score, peer comparison, and value

		Basic	Standardized	Rationalized	Dynamic
Enterprise Search	Definition	No search technology standards. Search typically deployed in silos (both desktop and server). It could indude complex or specialized search applications deployed in a siloed way for a limited number of users.	Standards for both desktop and server search. Standardized approach to provisioning data sources across the organization. Buisness drivers typically based on cost savings and enhanced productivity.	Search as a strategic enabler for the business. Search integrated with one or more Business Productivity Infrastructure investments Enterprise Content Management Portal, Collaboration, Line-of-Business applications). Standardized approach to provisioning integration to Line-of-Business applications.	Search as the unified information access infrastructure across all enterprise information and devices.
	Enterprise Search	Desktop and/or server search capability with no IT standardization.	Simple, text-based query refinement by property and scope (for example all intranet, people, HR site).	Unified search experience across desktop, server, and Internet search.	A single way to access all information across the organization, structure or unstructured.
		Simple keyword search for desktop and server search, with query refinement by standard property (for example, documents, email).	Single index across multiple data sources implemented in a standardized approach including standardized desktop search infrastructure.	Combination of indexing and federation infrastructure.	Search user interface is consistent and contextual in applications. Users can leverage a search box (explicit) or the search can data navigation (implicit).
		Primary search focus is on Web sites, email, and documents stored in desktops and file servers, focusing predominantly on unstructured data.	Primary search sources are Web sites, content management repositories, email, databases, and simple people search capabilities.	Primary search sources are Web sites, file servers, collaborative and content-managed data stores, database, and Line-of-Business applications.	Unified taxonomy exists for all key business data.

Figure 3.5 Enterprise Search Capabilities across Maturity Levels

assessment for your organization. The tool generates a comprehensive report that outlines steps for optimizing your IT infrastructure.

NOTES

1. Microsoft, "IT Services Firm Uses Integrated Voice Solution to Build New Applications, Cut Costs," 2009.
2. Microsoft, "Global Management Consultancy Boosts Client Service, Competitiveness, with Extranet," 2008.
3. Microsoft, "Global Manufacturer Expects $60 Million of New Revenue from Product Innovation," 2007.

4. Microsoft, "Bank Improves Risk Analysis and Efficiency with an Intelligent Single View of Customer," 2007.
5. Microsoft, "Del Monte Foods Automates Formula Change Process to Reduce Cycle Time by 33 Percent," 2007.
6. Microsoft, "EMC Saves Millions with Enhanced Productivity and Communication Tools," 2007.
7. Microsoft, "Royal Dutch Shell Envisions Improved Working Environment with Unified Communications," 2010.
8. Microsoft, "Intel Expects Twenty Percent Reduction in Audio Conferencing Costs with Unified Communications," 2009.
9. Microsoft, "Leading Content Provider Saves $3 Million on Telephony Management and Conferencing," 2009.
10. Jeanne Ross, Peter Weill, and David C. Robertson, *Enterprise Architecture as Strategy* (Boston: Harvard Business School Press, 2006).
11. Nicholas Carr, "IT Doesn't Matter," *Harvard Business Review* (May 2003).
12. John Mahoney and Tom Berg, "The Period to 2012 Will Be Years of Transition for IT Organizations and IT Management," Gartner, Inc., December 7, 2006.
13. IDC white paper, "Optimizing Infrastructure: The Relationship between IT Labor Costs and Best Practices for Managing the Windows Desktop," 2006. http://download.microsoft.com/download/f/4/8/f4876338-b998-44b5-9928-300207288ac0/IDC_Server_WP.pdf.

CHAPTER 4

TECHNOLOGY AS THE COMPETITIVE EDGE

In the previous chapters we have seen the impact IT capabilities are having on business results and how we have developed models and guidance to assess and work through the infrastructure optimization process. Next we take those insights and combine them with the research findings from profiling data of thousands of customers and drilling deep into actual customer experiences.

One lesson some leaders have already painfully experienced and other organizations could benefit from: Don't think that "cool technologies" provide you with a competitive edge if you are part of the majority of adopters. Moving after the others have already experimented, to avoid their mistakes often robs an organization of the opportunity to learn and adapt to the change early enough. If your organization is not part of the cutting edge, you are simply keeping up with the Joneses. The lessons are clear: Organizations that are identifying new capabilities and—as important—identifying how to use them for their business will outperform their competition tomorrow.

WHY BENCHMARKING?

Are there days when you would rather scrap your "organically grown" IT infrastructure than own, maintain, support, and manage it? It's okay to admit it. You are not alone. Many feel that the hardware, software, licenses, patches, and support headaches put land mines and speed traps all over their IT infrastructure plans. What would you do if you could throw it all out and start over with a clean slate? One of the world's largest construction companies did just that. *Bechtel*, an engineering, construction, and project management giant, was named by *Engineering News-Record* the top U.S. construction contractor for 11 straight years.[1] The privately owned company, based in San Francisco, has 49,000 employees worldwide and had revenues of $30.8 billion in 2009. "Bechtel's New Benchmarks" from *CIO* magazine tells the story of Bechtel. In 2005 Geir Ramleth, Chief Information Officer, of Bechtel, oversaw the transformation of its old-school IT infrastructure into one that rivaled that of the leading Internet companies.

The transformation began with a benchmarking exercise for IT capabilities, agility, and cost structure. Bechtel didn't look to its direct competitors for benchmarks; instead it chose to look at the most aggressive and advanced users of IT technologies—companies like Amazon.com, Google, Salesforce.com, and YouTube. While these companies have vastly different business models, they were the ones using the latest in network design and server and storage virtualization and management. The benchmark data was incredible:[2]

- YouTube paid $10 to $15 per megabit for its wide-area network. Bechtel paid $500 per megabit.
- Google employed one systems administrator for about 20,000 servers. Bechtel employed one systems administrator per 100 servers.
- Amazon sold storage to external customers for 15 cents per gigabit per month (estimated). Bechtel's internal storage costs were $3.75 per gigabit per month.
- Salesforce.com provided one version of one application for 1 million users with upgrades four times per year with minimal downtime or training. Bechtel ran 230 applications, up to five versions of each—nearly 800 different application versions

altogether. Upgrades and training were constant, and there was no version or software life cycle management.

It was an eye-opening experience, and the findings revolutionized Bechtel's approach to IT infrastructure. Benchmarking is used by many organizations to provide a baseline comparison of parameters against industry performance, trends, and best practices. Such benchmarks can provide direction for investments and change programs for both process and business performance improvements. Benchmarks provide:

- Reference or measurement standards for comparing processes, people, business units, and the like against defined, consistent, and recognized standards.
- Ways to monitor improvements, both within the organization and to external references, such as competitors and/or established best practices.
- Ways to establish best practice and maintain leadership.
- Ways to kick-start organizational change.

In every benchmarking exercise, the most critical step after an honest self-assessment is the selection of whom to benchmark against. Often only direct competitors are considered instead of potential competitors or leaders in other industries. Bechtel went outside of its industry standards for its analysis and to learn about best practices. The exercise made it clear that quantum leaps were possible in all IT areas. And it helped the business leaders gain the necessary support for radical changes.

The Bechtel team eventually retired a host of applications, some of which had been introduced for millions of dollars only a few years ago, and standardized, consolidated, and created a dynamic and wildly successful IT infrastructure. Despite the initial high investment cost, the originally calculated return on investment was extremely positive and, as far as we know, more than realized. The team at Bechtel wisely looked at organizations that fully embraced new technologies and learned from their insights.

Bechtel had to forge many of its own roads. The newer IT infrastructure maturity models and tools allow organizations of any size or sectors not only analyze their infrastructure maturity but tools—like

Microsoft's Core IT Infrastructure model and the Business Productivity Infrastructure (BPI) IT capability maturity model—provide industry-based benchmarking capabilities. Like Bechtel's experience, the information is often eye opening for both the IT group and the business leadership.

Benchmarking answers some of these questions:

- How does your BPI capability compare with that of industry, peer groups, business units, and social trends?
- Are you investing in BPI capabilities that support the overall IT strategy and business model, or are you wasting resources?
- Do different parts of the organization need to invest in the same BPI capabilities, and can duplicate investments be avoided? A good benchmark to know is that once you invest in one business scenario, you probably already have 60 to 70 percent of the capability in place to serve other business needs and divisions.
- How has your BPI maturity changed over time, and have you made progress? Benchmarking isn't a one-time process. Agile organizations continually benchmark as they implement new processes and technologies.

Figure 4.1 shows how the BPI subcapabilities can be grouped visually to indicate where there are unbalanced investments across and within BPI capabilities. The BPI subcapabilities—business intelligence (BI), unified communications (UC), and enterprise content management (ECM)—are represented by the shaded circles. The dotted line shows where a company has or has not invested. The black line shows industry standards. By looking at this chart, a company can quickly assess where it is possibly leading or probably falling behind.

For example, the organization (dotted line) invested in Business Intelligence for Reporting and Analysis and Data Warehousing. However, it has not invested in Performance Management, which would improve overall BI maturity. This would improve its ability to measure and manage business performance—and put it ahead of the industry. It is definitely a hole in the company's BI. Perhaps management has identified other priorities to pursue or there are internal barriers to adoption. Or managers may not realize how a small incremental investment allows them to create scorecards and key

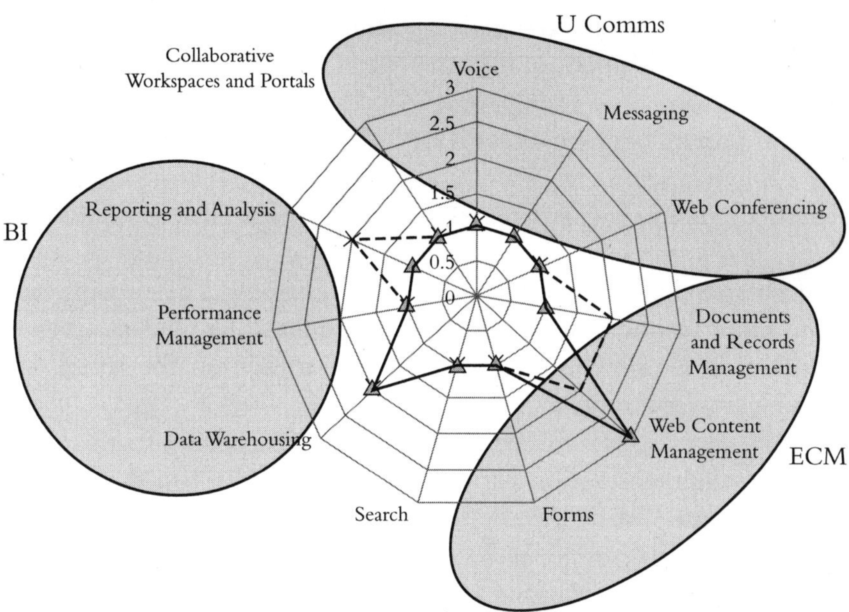

Figure 4.1 Spheres of Investment by Organization and Industry

performance indicator dashboards based on monthly performance that leverage the most recent company data analytics.

The example also shows that the players in the overall industry (black line) are investing heavily in enterprise content management capability—especially in Web content management. However, this specific company does not have competitive maturity in this capability. With this knowledge, the team can decide and make a conscious decision if and how critical such a disadvantage might be for the organization's business model.[3]

While benchmarking may be a one-off event, it is most effective as a continuous process. Capabilities that can provide an important competitive advantage today may be just that—important today but old news and a commodity in your industry two years from now. Benchmarking lets organizations continually seek to challenge their practices and investments. It gives an organization constant information about best practices specific to its industry, allowing it to either catch up or continue to lead. It is important to note that the capabilities in the Infrastructure Optimization (IO) model are designed to stand the test of time and technology churn. Those organizations with mature infrastructures have flexibility and extensibility built in.

As important benchmarking is for business capabilities, it also should play a role in assessing an organization's underlying IT management and process capabilities. For example, a major financial organization in France was struggling with managing the timely and efficient development and deployment of business applications. The organization made huge technology and people investments across a number of countries in Europe and the Middle East to address the issues, but results were very limited.

The leadership was forced to step back to assess the situation. As a first step, the organization reviewed its IO model across the business units. It wanted to define the IT capability maturity gaps that were preventing the organization from delivering more Agile development and deployment applications across all of its subsidiaries. It used the IO assessment tool and identified capability gaps against benchmarks from other leading organizations.

The review process identified duplicate projects for identity management and application development running at the same time. These projects were not only redundant but actually hindered the rollout process. After identifying the challenge, taking the right steps was relatively easy. The organization consolidated and standardized the conflicting projects and got rid of a key blocker and redundancies. Leadership invested funds to close other IT capability gaps identified in the review process.

It can also be interesting to benchmark IT infrastructure maturity and its impact on the total cost of ownership. For many organizations, a Basic IT Core Infrastructure is still common. All studies (e.g., from IDC) show that that is the most expensive place to be. The Rationalized or even the Dynamic IT infrastructure is becoming the new standard, even if only for the simple reason that these infrastructures allow far faster and cheaper deployment and adoption of business applications and capabilities. Organizations in Basic Core IO spend their IT resources on keeping the lights on; Dynamic organizations spend only a small fraction of the IT budget on maintenance. In our Agile organizations, the Core Infrastructure is in a Rationalized or Dynamic maturity state, and the majority of IT budgets for these companies are invested in supporting and growing the IT infrastructure for the business needs and impact of the organization.

AUTO, FINANCE, HEALTHCARE, PUBLIC SECTOR VIEW COMPARISON

We can take the insights and data across industries and geographies along with the ability to cross-reference benchmarking results against organization performance to go a few steps deeper. For confidentiality reasons, we are not able to share explicit maturity data of specific companies. However, we can share with you the insights gleaned from the information.

Having a data set of nearly 20,000 organizations allowed us to look at the maturity level across a broad range of sectors. It also allowed us to identify what sets the leaders in an industry apart from their competitors. We wanted to know if and how IT maturity correlates to an organization's success. There are many ranking mechanisms—from Forbes to net-present-value calculators for the return on investment. Regardless of the evaluation system or methodology, the ranking of organizations in a segment is relatively consistent. Of course, you can also do a gut check against that scientific list. My gut check concerning the future potential of a company is asking "Would I invest my personal money if I had to invest in a specific segment and leave the funds there for five or more years? Which companies would grow my investment faster than their competitors? And which companies might not even be around in a decade?"

We identified the leading organizations across a variety of industries and tested our hypothesis that IT maturity correlates to an organization's current and future potential. Across segments and industries, the results clearly supported the hypothesis. We also learned that there are significant maturity gaps between industries.

When we compared leaders in a specific industry, we found that the majority of IT capabilities were relatively similar. However, the true industry leaders showed infrastructure maturity in a few IT capabilities that separated them from the rest of the pack. The capabilities varied depending on the industry—for some industries, it was BI; others excelled in UC or integrated platform strategies; still others used server security to set themselves apart. The common factor was that the outstanding business opportunities came to those companies through their use of technology.

What does this mean for organizations that find themselves stuck in the middle or even behind their competitors in their industries? These companies can use benchmarking to assess what investments are necessary to keep up and to identify best practices outside of their core markets that they could leverage to leapfrog over their direct competition. In this chapter we look at several industries where the analytical results were crystal clear and you, as the reader, can get a feel for how you can use benchmarking in your own infrastructure plans.

As I said, there are definite gaps in infrastructure maturity between industries. I think it is interesting to look at the actual IT maturity levels in the financial sector and compare them with the maturity levels in the automotive and healthcare sectors. Figure 4.2 shows how the three industries compare and how leaders in each sector differentiate themselves from their competition and the general market.

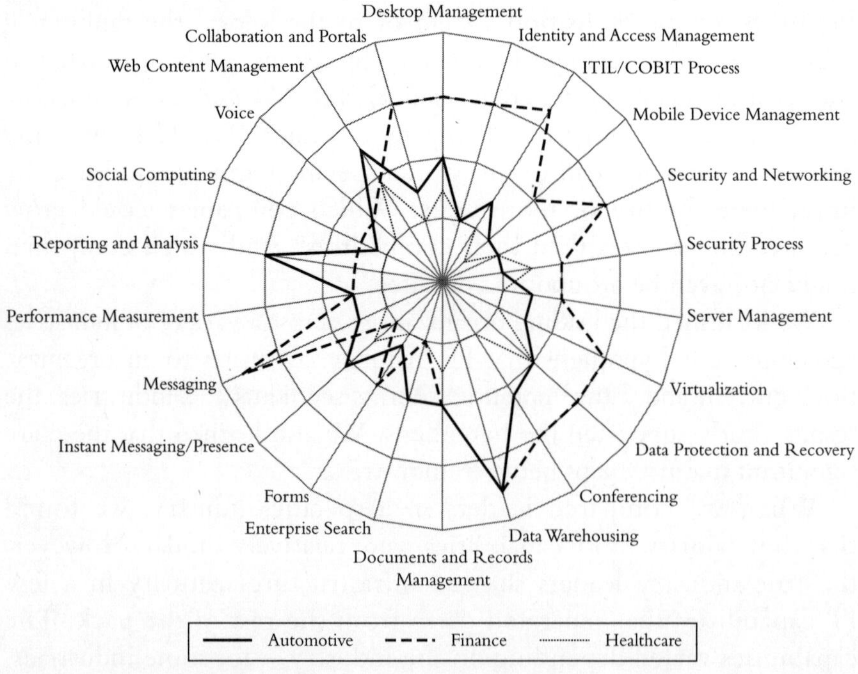

Figure 4.2 Infrastructure Optimization Maturity by Industry

As an industry, automotive manufacturers live in the Basic to Standardized region—even the industry leaders. However, the finance sector claims more Standardized to Rationalized territory, and we will find some outstanding examples of technology used to impact business results here. As I said earlier, "good-enough" technology and infrastructure is often not good enough to succeed, much less survive. Good enough in the financial industry means Standardized, and sometimes Rationalized, as the starting maturity level. Anything less is unacceptable in this industry. As you will see later in this chapter, while many financial organizations invested into data warehousing and analytic capabilities, some were total laggards. I'll tell you a cautionary tale of what happens to these technology laggards.

From Figure 4.2, you can easily see that the financial industry as a whole leverages technology capabilities for its business. The leaders in the automotive industry are leveraging some of these capabilities today too, but they have been focusing on data warehousing and report and analysis capabilities. However, they are not big on security yet nor have they made big investments in Core IO capabilities. In all industries, there is a great deal of potential growth around social computing, voice and instant messaging (UC), and performance management. Savvy organizations see this as a great place to build a competitive advantage.

Now, for the most eye-opening analysis, let's look at healthcare. Considering the importance of this sector for all of us and the amount of money societies spend on it, the leading organizations *barely* use technology in their businesses. The ongoing political discussion highlights some of these points. From our analytical focus, the cost savings and productivity improvement potential—not to mention the lives that could be saved or improved—is staggering. If healthcare organizations implement only a fraction of the insights from other industries, they could make massive improvements in care delivery and patient management. Think of it. The automotive industry makes the healthcare sector look like it is still in the technological dark ages.

Technology in the Auto Industry

This is not your father's Oldsmobile. And today's car companies look nothing like they did 20 years ago, 10 years ago, or even 5 years ago.

Technology, new markets, and the push for green transportation solutions have transformed how cars are conceived, designed, manufactured, and delivered.

But before technology innovations helped transform business practices in the automotive industry, the market stepped in to shake things up. The fundamental shake-up of 2008 to 2010 surfaced the underlying challenges many manufactures had faced and only partly addressed over the last decade. In 2000, GM and Chrysler were still icons of the U.S. industry, but by spring 2010 they had gone through bankruptcy and survived only through government subsidies in unprecedented amounts. When the market stabilized, Toyota, the can-do-no-wrong company in the industry, got hit hard with a quality and public relations nightmare of unintended acceleration and stuck floor mats. Its market leadership—built on quality and reliability—evaporated almost overnight.

Nearly a decade prior to this, Ford struggled with safety issues. The high rate of tire failures on the Ford Explorer caused horrible rollover accidents. The Explorer, which had dominated the lucrative SUV market, lost the market to the up-and-coming Japanese competition.

In 2007 a total of 71.9 million new automobiles were sold worldwide: 22.9 million in Europe, 21.4 million in Asia-Pacific, 19.4 million in North America, and 4.4 million in Latin America.[4] For a billion-dollar business, those numbers represent a really big pie. Everyone wants a piece of it, with the truly Agile automakers getting the big slice.

IT Maturity in the Automotive Sector

The recent crisis in the automotive market affected all of the automakers, but we can look at IT maturity and predict who is most likely to survive and flourish in this very competitive industry. There are a few things to understand about IT maturity in this sector:

- Standardized is the de facto standard in enterprises today. Companies with Basic maturity are falling behind in the market and will end up as road kill.
- IT maturity in the automotive industry is significantly behind that in other sectors, especially the financial sector.
- All automotive companies have similar maturity ratings in data warehousing capabilities. Because of this, data warehousing has

become less of a competitive advantage and more of a fundamental necessity in the industry.

- Automakers have a Dynamic handling of data, but their analytic, reporting, and search capabilities of the data are usually in the Basic stage. They may have the data but lack the means to do anything with it. This is one area that is a potential competitive advantage.
- Management of the Core IT infrastructure—desktops, devices, and servers—in the automotive market is far behind other (even manufacturing) industries. This area also shows a lot of optimization potential across the board and potential competitive advantage for fast movers.

There are many rankings of automotive companies out there. The rankings look at sales volume, customer satisfaction, initial quality, or direct product comparisons. How would you personally rank Audi, BMW, Chrysler, Daimler, Ford, General Motors, Honda, Toyota, and Volkswagen? More important, what is your confidence in the ability of those companies to lead their markets going forward?

Figure 4.3 illustrates how automakers stack up when you look at Core Infrastructure and business productivity infrastructure maturity. We have not listed the names of companies for privacy reasons, but these are true assessments done by IT departments.

Company A has definitely put resources into developing its IT infrastructure to support business processes. It has focused particularly on developing sound BI capabilities. Company B is working to move away from Basic to Standard maturity overall and have put some resources into improving its data management. Companies C and D are just plain behind in their use of technology.

Think about this as you consider your rankings. Ford cars employ sophisticated software that is above and beyond other cars—no matter what car class they are in. BMW gets innovative products and services to the market faster than ever before by linking engineers, project managers, production teams, and key decision makers located around the globe. BMW's agility comes from a combination of hardware and software that its 100,000 member workforce relies on regardless of their location. Volvo Truck North America went from off the grid on customer support to off the charts in showing how technology

Core Infrastructure – Automotive					
Capability	**Sub Capability**	**Basic**	**Standardized**	**Rationalized**	**Dynamic**
Identity and Access Management	Identity and access management	● ◆ ○	■		
Desktop, Devices and Server Management	Desktop management	●	■ ◆ ○		
	Mobile device management	■ ● ◆ ○			
	Server management	● ◆	■ ○		
	Virtualization	◆ ○	■ ●		
Security and Networking	Security and networking	■ ● ◆ ○			
Data Protection and Recovery	Data protection and recovery		■ ● ◆ ○		
Security Process	Security process	◆	● ○	■	
ITIL/COBIT-Based Management Process	ITIL/COBIT-Based management process		■ ◆ ○	●	
Business Productivity – Automotive					
Collaboration	Collaborative workspace and portals	◆	■ ● ○		
	Social computing	■ ● ◆ ○			
Enterprise Content Management	Document and records management	◆ ○	■ ●		
	Forms	■ ○	● ◆		
	Web content management		■ ◆	●	○
Business Intelligence	Performance measurement	■ ○	●	◆	
	Reporting and analysis		● ○	◆	■
	Data warehousing		◆	● ○	■
Unified Communications	Messaging	■ ● ◆	○		
	Instant messaging/presence	◆ ○	●	■	
	Conferencing	○	■ ◆	■ ●	
	Voice	●	■ ◆ ○		
Enterprise Search	Enterprise search	● ○	■	◆	

Company A ■ Company B ● Company C ◆ Company D ○

Figure 4.3 Automotive Infrastructure Maturity Comparisons

transforms customer relationships. These companies have shown that innovation and agility are part of their DNA. These are the companies we are betting on.

My Car Is Smarter than Yours

If you were born between 1981 and 2000—the "Millennial generation"—how you think and work will shape how automakers think about developing cars. And technology won't be an add-on. It will be an integral part of every car. The Millennials expect connectivity and smart technology. They don't want yesterday's solutions, they want tomorrow's innovations—and they want them now.

Ford understands this and has reshaped how it thinks about using technology. Ford SYNC is the factory-installed, fully-integrated in-car communications and entertainment system. The system takes hands-free, voice-activated control to a new level by connecting phones, media players, and USB devices to the car and to the growing data on driving conditions, traffic reports, weather, sports, news, and business information.

Ford, and many of the other automakers, did not to get to this current spot without some proverbial bumps in the road. Several years ago, Ford was trailing the other companies in sales, development, and manufacturing. Instead of focusing on innovating, it froze everything and went at cost cutting with a vengeance. Every area of the company cut back to the very basics. Technology was hit particularly hard. Hardware requirements were set so low, no one could buy a PC with more than 512 MBs of memory. It was cheaper to keep the old PCs since by the early 2000s, no one was making a PC with this small amount of memory.

While Ford struggled with costs, other companies were forging ahead with new technologies—sort of. Chrysler's 2003 300 series vehicles introduced new technologies: Sirius Satellite Radio and an optional stereo with DVD-based global positioning system navigation. This was cutting edge for the time, but all other technology was based on the 300 that came out in 1994 and that was designed and developed starting in 1986. Although the new 2011 model has plans for major engine updates, it still uses technology base on the 2003 model which is 20 years old. The 2002 BMW Series 7 was more forward thinking. These cars came equipped with a beautifully integrated

Windows Mobile system. It was new and it was hot, but the software was already out of date before the car hit the market. These scenarios show that unforgiving intersection where fast-moving technology crashes into slow-moving car design and development.

Ford and Microsoft have taken a very different approach. In 2007 Ford partnered with Microsoft when faced with stiff competition from other auto manufacturers, including GM's OnStar navigation system and DaimlerChrysler's MyGIG. Urban legend has it that Microsoft was caught completely off guard by the meteoric rise of the iPod, and that was the push to enter the technology free-for-all.

Microsoft had been working with Fiat to develop Bluetooth capabilities in the auto market. At the time, Microsoft had decided to focus its limited automotive development resources not on the high-end solution with a company like Daimler but on the broader market that Fiat offered. The collaboration combined Fiat Auto's experience and research with Microsoft's expertise in providing standard platforms, services, and applications.

First Fiat and then Ford tapped into the possibilities that this new approach to autos that technology offered. Both companies felt that the best way to keep on the leading edge of quickly changing technology was to key into a standard platform and tools that their engineers could customize and update as swiftly as the auto market was beginning to move. By looking outside of their typical design and development road map, they could buy into an open platform—Windows Automotive—that allowed their engineers to quickly create powerful in-car computing solutions that would go beyond the initial introduction in 2007. As other automakers have seen, dressing up old technology and calling it new won't cut it in today's market.

The dedication to new solutions has paid off for Ford. Its SYNC technology makes them agile today and continues to let the company lead in the innovation race. *Fast Company* recently put Ford on the top 10 "Most Innovative Companies" in mobile technology.[5] They are not at the top but share the upper levels with Google, Apple, Amazon, and HTC—one of the world's "most creative electronics firms." This is the first time an automaker made the Top 10 Mobile list. Innovative, agile, and successful are the new modifiers for Ford. And you know that this is going to continue to win the company a big piece of that billion-dollar automotive market pie.

It Takes a Village to Build a Better Car, Faster

Technology in the car isn't the only smart way that companies are using technology to remain Agile and innovative. Technology within the company can mean shorter design and production cycles. As Henry Ford once said "Coming together is a beginning. Keeping together is progress. Working together is success."

In 2008 BMW committed to connecting its 100,000-member village to ensure that everyone was working together to keep the company successful. Even in the tough global market, BMW continues to report strong earnings and sales. It attributes its success to its highly efficient operations and the value that it places on employees. No matter where employees work, they are dedicated to maintaining BMWs reputation for high-quality engineering, luxury, innovative design, and first-class performance.

The challenge is that there are 100,000 employees are spread across 24 production sites in 13 countries. To optimize the strength of this work force, BMW needed to go from a Basic technology infrastructure to a more Dynamic one. Microsoft uses an optimization model that helps companies assess and improve their information technology capabilities. One of the key areas to assess is a company's communications and collaboration resources. These two areas directly impact business productivity. Done well, companies can reduce communications and IT management costs while speeding up decision-making and project completion times. With poorly done communications, a company risks being left in the dust.

To move from Basic functionality to a Dynamic model, BMW looked at its hardware devices, communication options, employee locations, and vendors. Like most basic infrastructures, its hardware used multiple platforms, communications were not easy, and the multitude of vendors supporting communications could not easily plug into BMW's systems. A Dynamic model—one of the key indicators of company agility—needs to be fully automated, customizable, manageable, and easy for everyone to access and use.

In about 2005, BMW deployed a communications and collaboration solution from a large networking hardware company. The up-front cost was small, which made it easy to sell to decision makers. However, it took a lot of expensive engineering to make it work in a way that was acceptable. After it was set up, the system was still hard for employees to use and did not integrate well with BMW's Microsoft Office tools. The village was certainly not working together.

In round two of going from a Basic to a Dynamic infrastructure, BMW switched to Office Communications Server 2007 and Office Live Communications Server 2005. This combination provided a unified approach to communications and collaboration. Now the village had instant messaging, presence monitoring, voice communications, as well as audio, video, and Web conferencing that plugged into current development tools. Engineers were particularly happy with some of the new security levels that let them share designs without the risk of losing confidential or proprietary information.

The results have been reduced conferencing and communications costs, faster project completion times, reduced IT issues, and reduced IT management costs. Designers, engineers, and manufacturing sites are in constant communication regardless of their location across the globe. Innovations don't sit on a drafting table in Munich when they need to be in South Carolina, South Africa, or Kuala Lumpur. This move from a Basic infrastructure to a Dynamic one gets better BMWs to market faster.

I Want It and I Want It Now

Innovative car designs and Agile production teams are only part of the technology evolution picture. We have looked at cars and we have looked at automotive productions cycles, but what about the customer? Can a company use technology to secure and retain valuable customers? What does it mean to be Agile and innovative in the customer care segment of the auto industry? Volvo knows the answer—not only to the "I want it and want it now" demands but to the "How much is this going to cost me?" questions.

Volvo is known around the world for the quality of its trucks. Product quality is essential to success, but it's not enough. It's also important for a company to make doing business with it as easy as possible. Volvo Truck North America has over 300 truck dealers in North America and a wide web of fleet customers. They know that making it easy for customers to do business is great for the bottom line. They also knew that their financial transaction process was slow, inaccurate, and as painful as possible to navigate for fleet customers and dealers alike. Remember BMW's challenge to go from Basic infrastructure to Dynamic? Volvo Truck North America wasn't even on the technology map.

The sales transaction processing system worked something like this. When a customer came to a dealer for a repair, the dealer had to obtain a credit authorization over the phone. Then a paper copy of the invoice would be forwarded to a third-party processing center, which would check that the customer had been charged the right amount, according to its contract with Volvo. The processing center would then send an adjusted invoice to the customer, collect payment, and forward it to the dealer. When the customer finally got an invoice, the prices on initial invoices often didn't match the amounts billed by the processing center. Frequent errors on invoices—such as the wrong purchase order number or vehicle identification number—made it tougher for customers to process invoices. The good news was there was plenty of room for improvement.

Volvo looked to its sister company—North American Transaction Services (NATS), a division of Volvo Financial Services—to design and implement a solution. NATS first identified criteria for a new transaction processing system. It had to provide consistent pricing across their more than 300 dealer locations. It had to provide real-time pricing information that integrated with the dealers' own point-of-sale and business systems to ensure that the price on an invoice was correct before a customer left a dealership. And it had to provide real-time confirmation of purchase orders, vehicle identification numbers, and related data to ensure that customers had all the information they needed to process invoices properly.

The new financial management solution has helped to increase parts sales more than projections and to cut development costs. It has also helped Volvo serve its customers with faster and more accurate parts support. Sales are up. Development costs are down. Customers are happy. The results are definitely not as sexy as Web-based browsing from your car or proprietary engine designs going from Munich to China in the blink of an eye. But the technology solution makes Volvo Truck North America more Agile and able to retain happy customers. The company went from nowhere on the technology infrastructure map to a Dynamic leader in customer support.

Getting Left in the Dust

We've looked at how agility gives companies a competitive edge. Let's look at what happens to the companies that missed the IT infrastructure boat. General Motors Corporation and Toyota Motor Corporation formed New United Motor Manufacturing Inc. (NUMMI) in 1984 as an experiment. For Toyota, the joint venture was an opportunity to test its ability to use its production methods in a U.S. setting. For GM, it provided a way to learn how to build cars more efficiently using Toyota's "lean" production system. Since GM also wanted to manufacture a small, high-quality car, Toyota seemed like the perfect partner.

Toyota achieved its goal from NUMMI. A year after joining, it began opening plants in the United States. And GM? What did it do? The NUMMI plant continued to crank out approximately 250,000 cars (Toyota Corolla, Pontiac Vibe) and 170,000 trucks (Toyota Tacoma) per year. The cars were high quality and cost less to build. NUMMI was a stellar success for U.S. car production. But the lessons learned and infrastructure necessary to support the new way of building cars was never transferred to other GM plants.

It is a classic story of gross lack of change management and a definite lack of company agility. Granted, many of the problems GM experienced taking the learning to other plants were rooted in the GM culture. Workers hated the new system—they were paid to get cars off the line and out the door. Toyota instead focused on high quality. GM workers and management were combatively at odds. Toyota formed collaborative teams, and anyone could stop the line at anytime to fix a problem. GM plants were run by the plant manager who was king. Toyota, again, relied on teamwork and quality. GM just didn't get it.

GM's market share slid from 45 percent in 1975 to 35 percent in 1985. The company blamed external factors. It refused to look internally at the processes and infrastructure throughout the company that doomed it to failure. It missed the big picture and how the system worked.

What GM didn't understand was that the system required an infrastructure that guaranteed quality at every level—from the parts suppliers, to management, to the line workers, to the designers. As one employee puts it, "We had the throw-it-over-the-wall approach." One team would work on something and then throw it over the wall to the next team. Once it left your desk, it was someone else's problem.

NUMMI was opened in 1984. It wasn't until 1992 when Jack Smith, who had negotiated the deal between Toyota and GM, took over as CEO. Facing a $2.7 billion loss, he implemented the Japanese system rapidly—by GM standards—but not rapidly enough and not completely by any means. GM finally pulled together its findings and implemented its "global manufacturing system," improving its quality and cost structure. However, by then all its competitors had done the same thing.

GM went bankrupt in 2009—the largest corporate bankruptcy in U.S. history. Ironically, at the time the company was probably in its best shape ever. But it was too little too late. It was too slow and lacked any agility to innovate in the quickly changing global market. GM basically got run over.

If only that was the end of the story. In 2008 Toyota earned the distinction of being the world's largest automaker. However, Toyota got there making many of the same mistakes that GM made before GM learned the value of productivity and quality—lessons that Toyota had taught at NUMMI. The current global recall has tarnished a brand built on quality. The head of Toyota is Akio Toyoda, grandson of Kiichiro Toyoda (the founder of modern-day Toyota). At a congressional hearing, he summed up the issue: "I fear the pace at which we have grown may have been too quick. . . . Priorities became confused and we were not able to stop, think and make improvements as much as we were able to before." Akio Toyoda got his start in the business at NUMMI.

If you look back at Figure 4.3 outlining Core IT Infrastructure and business productivity maturity, you have to wonder where Toyota would fall, and whether it could have avoided some of its problems by improving BI, collaboration, content management, communications, and enterprise search. Basic infrastructure just isn't enough these days to stay Agile and innovative.

Are willingness and determination to improve business processes that important to some of these companies? Are they ready to leave the ineffectual legacy systems behind? In spring 2010, GM and Toyota went on the offensive with massive investments into public relations and image management. Both companies ran multimillion-dollar television commercials across the networks with a key message: "We didn't have the right processes in place, we didn't listen to our customers enough, and our communication and processes were not working well enough. Our key priority is fixing these process issues." Is this just marketing, or is it real change? Based on what we have learned so far, we will have a good indicator soon by their improvements in the IO capability models.

Technology in the Finance Sector

Smart people + access to knowledge + smart technology = smart and fast decisions. We discussed earlier that people *and* knowledge *and* insights are the key success factors for innovation and organizational wins. Nowhere has this been as evident as it has been in the financial sector over the past few years. Because of the speed of decisions and ability to lose or gain huge amounts, even small advantages can be leveraged and small mistakes can be devastating. Smart people and proven recipes—most people would say this is how you get ahead in business. The financial market meltdown proved that sometimes this just isn't so. Complex financial bundles layered with lightning-fast transaction times and then multiplied by an insane number of financial transactions in a single day can be the perfect recipe for disaster. "Good enough" technology and infrastructure often is simply not good enough to succeed or even to survive.

Today's financial landscape is vastly different from that of 2007. Many of the big players are gone, and others are struggling. Those that have remained face an ever-changing landscape where costs of business, compliance, security, risk tolerance, and operational efficiency are just a few of the challenges that stand in the way of recovery and growth.

Those that have survived and flourished continue to look at ways to improve their Core IT Infrastructure and BI as well as how they manage, review, and protect valuable data. The truly Agile companies not only recruit the best minds in the industry, they give them versatile and innovative tools to access information as well as expertise and derived knowledge for decisions.

He Who Hesitates Is Lost

Goldman Sachs is one of the companies that has consistently put the smartest people in the room with the best tools. I often tell a cautionary tale about working with several major players in the financial markets in the summer of 2008. I had the opportunity to host a customer roundtable discussion with IT executives from various financial institutions from the U.S. East Coast. The discussion focused on how to efficiently tackle typical software version migration challenges. While the chance to ask questions of Microsoft employees was a key draw for participants, the opportunity to discuss with their peers and to learn from each others' experience was at least as important.

The temperature in the streets of Manhattan was relatively cool for the season, but the discussion inside was definitely heated. The group quickly self-selected into two distinct subgroups. One group discussed specific technical issues of the migration: interoperability challenges between different components and how to get resolutions more quickly via the support or the product development teams. The other group—let's call them the hesitators—had very different questions and concerns. Their discussion was more along the lines of "Is it really worth the hassle of retraining and redeveloping solutions?" There were no benefits in their minds, just the cost in time and money and hassle. All the people in the room were very knowledgeable in their subject matter. But I could not help wondering if this is how they view all IT projects and how this would affect them in the long run.

The following 18 months gave me my answer. The financial crisis hit hard. And one of the first to go was Lehman Brothers, one of the most vocal of the hesitators. Right after the roundtable discussions, the Lehman Brothers logo was nearly everywhere in Times Square. A few weeks later, the company was gone—the first domino in what would become the largest financial crisis since the Great Depression. The other hesitators didn't do much better. Merrill Lynch got taken over by Bank of America, and other major institutions failed, were acquired under duress, or were subject to government takeover.

What happened to the organizations where "getting the new stuff to work" was the leading topic? They suffered too, like most of us. But after only 18 months, they came back and are doing better than ever before. These companies are dominating the new market. As we have learned, profits can be made in up- and downward moves of an economy; and knowledge and timing often decide where a company lands. And Goldman Sachs has truly demonstrated over the last years how to leverage timely knowledge into staggering bottom line results and influence. I clearly wouldn't call the whole thing cause and effect, but attitudes toward change *can* make a difference. And leveraging technologies and knowledge has been proven clearly to have a bottom-line impact.

Like all organizations, financial institutions deal with device and server management and applications delivery. However, some of their biggest IT challenges revolve around security and compliance issues, data management and analysis, and with communications internal to the organization and externally with customers.

Managing Growth

Growth for a regional organization supporting 70,000 customers looks very different from growth for a global company with over 35 million customers in 40 countries. But companies at both ends of the spectrum need tools that help them manage ever-increasing numbers of customers, transactions, and data streams. A small hedge fund has different scale and compliance challenges than an organization like Fidelity. However, knowledge access and speed of transactions and decisions are absolutely business critical. And companies based on Wall Street or in the Petronas Towers in Kuala Lumpur act and compete in a global market, have access to similar information, and face not-too-different challenges.

EFG-Hermes, launched in 1984, is one of the largest investment banks in the Middle East and the second largest in global emerging markets. It serves corporations, institutional and individual investors, as well as regional governments. It has gone from adding fewer than 9,500 clients a year to adding over 12,000 per year over a two-year period. Its fragmented information systems were at capacity just as growth was gaining momentum.

Kareem Azzouny, head of software development at EFG-Hermes, wanted absolute confidence in the availability and security of any IT solution. "We have clients who depend on our service every minute of every day—from Egypt to the U.S. As the number of clients grows, we need to make sure that they retain complete trust on our organization and infrastructure." Nesma Mounie, a database architect for the organization, was more specific in his analysis: "We were starting to experience bottlenecks which threatened to diminish the quality of our services."[6]

At the other end of the growth spectrum is the *UniCreditGroup* based in Germany, with over 142,000 employees and over 35 million customers in 40 countries. Its Markets & Investment Banking Division (MIB) has taken off. The primary objective of UniCredit MIB is to establish itself as one of the leading and most profitable European investment banks. Offering structured derivatives for retail, corporate, and institutional clients is key to its growth. Andreas Kokott, manager for the Structured Derivatives Platform Strategy, explains: "The structured derivatives business segment is characterized by investors constantly on the hunt for better yield-enhanced or tailored risk-reward structures, which creates high pressure on financial engineers and traders to supply increasingly sophisticated and complex products. A traders' burning concern is time to market, because being first means reaping the most profit. Speed is king." These computationally intense problems need powerful computing resources that span multiple data sources.

These are two very different growth issues that must be managed carefully or the companies lose the advantage over competing institutions. Both companies looked to technology to keep in front of their growth issues instead of being run over by them.

EFG-Hermes wanted absolute confidence in the availability and security of any new database technology. It also wanted to work with a single supplier for the majority of its technology rather than with a mix of organizations or resellers—IT complexity was *not* a goal. The company migrated to SQL Server since it could handle the company's growth capacity and reliability needs. It also provides improved BI features, allowing EFG-Hermes to be more competitive in its region. From a business capabilities view, the company created a scalable system optimized for data integration, reporting, and analysis.

UniCredit Group needed raw computing power to handle complex computational problems. It built a second-generation high-performance computing cluster on the 64-bit Windows Compute Cluster Server. Much like EFG-Hermes, UniCredit wanted to standardize its IT environment as much as possible. To UniCredit, the algorithms could be complex but the IT management could not be.

Complex IT infrastructures are expensive to support. The theme of cost control runs throughout this book and for good reason: A basic IT infrastructure is very expensive to support. To truly understand the impact these numbers have on your overall IT spending, let's look at

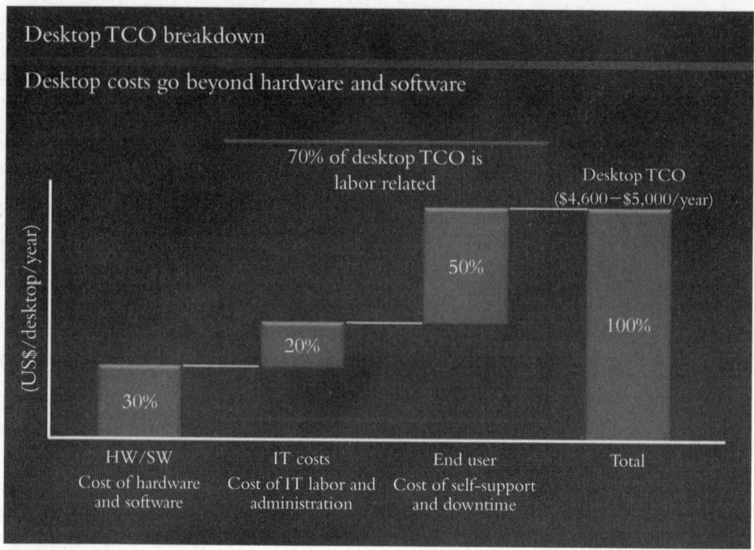

Figure 4.4 Desktop Total Cost of Ownership

the total cost of ownership (TCO) shown in Figure 4.4. Hardware and software typically make up about 30 percent of the overall IT budget. However, when you look at the labor cost in a budget, you quickly see it sucks up 70 percent of the budget.[7] Reducing labor costs has a huge impact on the overall budget, regardless of the size of the business or the size of the problem.

Data Management

Companies with a Basic infrastructure to support BI leave their data sitting in data silos and rely on very basic analysis tools. Companies with a Dynamic infrastructure have well-integrated data warehousing, reporting, and analysis capabilities that provide real-time access to relevant data. Organizations with Basic data management capabilities are not allowed in the financial sector. It's an evolutionary thing—they went the way of the dinosaurs. And truth be told, those organizations sitting in the Standardized level with their data management are not going to be far behind the dinosaurs.

Producing monthly reports and quarterly financial statements is Basic. Aggregating, compressing, and storing high-quality, real-time data in a scalable, integrated system that allows employees to identify hidden trends, problems, or relationships; develop insights extracted from patterns, clusters, and trends; and perform ad hoc queries and analysis of large amounts of complex data across all aspects of your business—*now* we are talking Dynamic. The end goal is that employees spend less time searching for the right data and more time on higher-value work and better decision making.

Lloyds TSB is a prime example of how organizations use high-quality accessible data to gain a business advantage. Remember, in the financial sector where every organization has a fairly mature IT infrastructure, it takes some innovative solutions to really make a difference. Lloyds TSB is one of the largest financial groups in the United Kingdom. The group serves more than 16 million customers across three divisions—U.K. Retail Banking, Insurance and Investments, and Wholesale and International Banking. It has more than 2,100 branches throughout England, Scotland, and Wales.

Lloyds TSB relied on a single data warehouse supplied by Teradata systems. Although the data was stored in a "single" warehouse, anyone who needed to access information needed advanced SQL training and database knowledge. All reports for decision makers had to come from Lloyds TSB's Customer Value Management (CVM) team—the only group with the skills to mine the data. Decision makers in the various business units could not gather the exact information quickly enough to make effective assessments of business opportunities. Basically, a group of about 60 analysts held the keys to the information for the entire organization.

The CVM group didn't want to be the information bottleneck. It wanted to offload the day-to-day analysis so its members could spend more time on detailed analytics that were more strategic and time critical. Teradata let Lloyds know that it was partnering with Microsoft to improve the interoperability between Microsoft's BI tools and the Teradata Warehouse.

What was particularly interesting was the partners' push to help users with minimal training quickly access, analyze, and report on critical data. From a business productivity standpoint, this would put relevant data into the hands of business decision makers faster. Business units are able to understand their customers in more detail—they had access to much more targeted and focused intelligence when they needed it. The Teradata Warehouse provides the data from one underlying data source so there is a single version of data. A BI portal also provides a central place where any of the analysts can upload work that they've done, making it available to others in the organization. Again, everyone has fast access to answers.

Managing Security and Compliance

Information is currency anywhere in the world, and financial service providers must take all available precautions to safeguard mission-critical information. Hostile Internet activity, malicious employees, and just the day-to-day security breaches all corporations face are further compounded by changing compliance and disclosure rules. Mergers and buy-outs mean legacy systems, disparate platforms, and communication obstacles.

In the United States, we have a bowl of alphabet soup financial regulatory bodies. For banks, there is the Federal Reserve and the Federal Treasury followed by the Office of the Comptroller of the Currency (OCC), Federal Deposit Insurance Corporation (FDIC), Office of Thrift Supervision (OTS), National Credit Union Administration (NCUA), and the Federal Financial Institutions Examination Council (FFIEC). I am sure I've missed a few. All countries have their own local laws and requirements, with Basel II adding the global perspective to regulatory policy. Money moves around the world at the speed of light—24/7. Financial service IT infrastructures handle immense amounts of data, communications, loan systems, general ledger systems, customer relationship management systems, trading systems, collections systems, and originations systems. It is easy to see why these infrastructures require a Dynamic level of maturity in this industry. And like all industries, IT teams must strike a balance between cost savings and innovation.

Piraeus Bank Group, another dynamic financial organization that went through the task, also is a best practices for the organizational management of change. This bank has a particular expertise in retail banking, capital markets and investment banking, and financing for the shipping sector and was one of the first in their home country to offer a comprehensive electronic banking service. Business and IT teams continually worked to increase efficiency in all areas, including its technology infrastructure. While the infrastructure worked well, the bank wanted to improve secure access to corporate resources, protect its critical data, and continually meet regulatory requirements.[8]

Throughout this book, I continually talk about building the business case to garner leadership support and organizational adoption. How to do this right? Here is how this financial organization made it happen. After assessing the business case and IT needs, the bank's IT department first prepared a detailed deployment plan to gain support from business stakeholders and build momentum among the ranks. The IT staff identified 200 computers that would comprise the pilot deployment group. It took a cross-organizational approach and targeted computers used by employees in the treasury, Internet banking, and IT departments.

Demonstrating the strategic advantage of a unified platform, the bank did not have to replace any of the three types of desktop hardware and deployed the new solution—Windows 7—using a single, hardware-independent image. The team achieved one of its goals—reduce IT costs through easier desktop management—but the business goal of improving security was the strategic victory. The advanced features of the new Windows 7 platform put multilayer processes into the system that hardened the infrastructure against malicious software and other attacks. "Hardening" means infrastructure capabilities reduce the number of points to defend in the system while putting in a layered security system that forces attacks to break through multiple layers of security.

Protecting assets from external attacks is one thing; what about internal attacks? Identity and access management control who has access to data, especially customer information and account data. Mature IT infrastructures automate policy-based identity and credential management by reducing the number of manual "touches." *Banque de Luxembourg* is a private bank that offers its clients wealth management services. Employee access rights management capabilities were at the bottom range of the Basic IT infrastructure. Spreadsheets were passed to as many as 30 people via email each time the bank hired a new employee, each time employee access rights changed, or each time an employee terminated employment.[9] You can see where this system could include lengthy delays, data inaccuracies, and innumerable ways to get around security systems.

I talk more about the actual technology behind the improved security capabilities at Banque de Luxembourg in Chapter 5. What is important for you to know here is that by improving the overall technology infrastructure, the bank was able to completely automate identity management and at the same time simplify IT management and take advantage of additional capabilities to improve compliance reporting. Time and time again, companies spend money to implement one solution but gain additional critical capabilities for pennies more.

U.K.-based accounting firm *Mulligan Williams* provides critical tax, bookkeeping, and accounting support and services. Mulligan Williams has continually invested in IT solutions. However, no matter how good the solution, technology continues to evolve, as do security concerns. And like all of our IT examples, keeping costs continues to be an IT goal.

Mulligan Williams did face security and productivity issues caused by legacy systems. Booting up and waiting for computers to respond at the beginning of the workday could take 15 minutes or more, cutting into valuable work time. Employees would joke they could turn the PCs on and put on the kettle for a cup of coffee—the coffee was usually ready first. Employees also dealt with multiple sets of data and applications, but their data silos and lack of robust data warehousing capabilities further reduced productivity. The legacy systems were sometimes unstable, so system crashes and data loss were not uncommon.[10]

While some of these issues related to productivity, the Core Infrastructure is was where the issues could be resolved. The organization implemented Windows 7 Professional, which improved hardware performance—boot and resume times were immediately improved. And like the Piraeus Bank Group, Mulligan Williams could use security capabilities to harden its network infrastructure against intruders and malicious software.

I've talked about security, but it often goes hand in hand with regulatory compliance. One colleague likes to joke that in the banking industry, it's good business to know who your customers are—it is also a regulatory requirement. It takes the warm fuzzies out of customer relations when organizations now need not only verify to their customers' identities but also to check names against multiple "watch lists" maintained by U.S. and international entities. The lists—like many compliance laws—are updated constantly. An automated solution is the only way to remain competitive and compliant in this highly competitive industry.

Instead of looking at another financial services organization, I'd like to look at a company that supports more than 6,500 financial institutions by offering a range of financial software and services. *Harland Financial Solutions* is based in Lake Mary, Florida, and employs about 1,400 people throughout the United States. Its Intrieve Core System offers a range of integrated back-office financial services for small community banks and savings and loan institutions.[11] Offering compliance solutions is not a huge competitive advantage anymore. However, making it easier and faster for compliance officers and bank operations managers to streamline compliance responsibilities is.

In late 2006, Harland Financial Solutions began to offer WatchDOG Pro version 6.0 as part of the new release of the Intrieve Core System called IntrieveAdvantage. WatchDOG Pro is a Web-based compliance application from ATTUS Technologies. It provides the automated compliancy capabilities but also has greater control over risk tolerance levels, reduces the time spent on routine compliance tasks, and provides additional data protections in areas such as reporting and disaster recovery.

Harland Financial Solutions houses the WatchDOG Pro application in its Enterprise Services Center, making its functionality available to clients via a protected Web connection. All clients have to do is a Web sign-in, and they have immediate access to their reports. The Harland application processes the clients' account records against the watch lists behind the scenes so the reports are ready for the clients immediately. Advanced name-matching algorithms and disqualification schemes limit false positives, and risk tolerance levels can be set to match the needs of financial intuitions.

A robust compliance solution as an integrated Web service that saves clients' time and increases data security gives Harland Financial Solutions a differentiating and competitive advantage in the market. More important from an internal IT perspective, the move to an integrated, Web-based system delivered lower costs and better maintenance capabilities. The solution eliminated issues arising from different or out-of-date software versions being used by Harland clients. And because Harland fine-tuned the application's work flows and user interface using the Microsoft .NET Framework, programmers can code more quickly and use capabilities like .NET tools that allow for the reuse of programming objects and include system-wide use of style sheets.

Technology in Healthcare

In this section we look into the healthcare sector and how technology is making a huge impact on people's care and providers' bottom lines. However, we see this agility impact at very few organizations.

In the United States, we currently spend over $2 trillion on healthcare annually. Some analysts predict that number will double to $4 trillion by 2015. Today, the United States has the highest per capita healthcare cost in the world but ranks low in global ratings of birth complications, medical mistakes, and illness survival rates.

With those numbers in mind, we can look into the healthcare sector and see how technology is making—or, unfortunately, not making in many cases—a huge impact on people's care and the providers' bottom line. I say "or not" because, until recently, we haven't seen the kind of mature IT infrastructure innovations that we see in other industries. Simply put, the company supplying your child's gaming device has better IT infrastructures than her pediatrician.

The most conservative estimates report that implementing Agile process and patient management systems would save the United States hundreds of millions of dollars and save tens of thousands of lives every year. If we follow the argument that technology and process improvement are a key lever to cost containment, improved data handling, more efficient processes, and more secure transactions, then the opportunities are tremendous on multiple levels.

Peter Neupert is Corporate Vice President of the Microsoft Health Solutions Group and is an authority on the intersection of technology, health, and business. He is also the former president and board chairman of drugstore.com. In a recent posting on the *Harvard Business Review* blog The Conversation,[12] he writes, "For too long we've held healthcare to a different standard than other businesses—a lesser one. Patients complain they are paying too much while doctors complain they are being paid too little. They're both right—it's time to shift the value chain in health care, fundamentally changing the business of health care."

This book is not long enough to go into all the areas across the healthcare sector that could be improved by IT infrastructure maturity. I am also not going to get involved in the ongoing battles about the best way to deliver and pay for healthcare services. Instead, I'd like to pique your interest in the possibilities that IT infrastructure brings to the sector. I'm going to focus on data management and how it impacts everything from patient safety, to improved drug development, to radical reductions in the cost of doing business.

Managing Data, Patients, and Costs

Throughout this book, we look at how businesses use data and analytics to create a competitive advantage in the market place. This applies to healthcare industries as well. However, we are talking about more than product revenue costs, profits and losses, or transportation logistics or marketing numbers. The data we are talking about relates to health and safety—our health and safety—data that affects our quality of life, cost of living, and life expectancy. I, for one, do not want to hear that my insurance provider and healthcare team are still manually pushing my data around on paper.

The patient data scenarios are endless, so let's just look at a typical patient who is ready to leave the hospital. Remember, the healthcare system—with all the associated cost in time for people and equipment, facilities, medications, and so forth—just worked very hard to get our patient well again. Before the patient leaves, he is given specific follow-up instructions: what to do and not to do, which medication to take at what time, if there should be follow-up with a primary care physician, and on and on. While doctors and nurses do their best to explain the details and the patient listens carefully, after several days or weeks, the instructions are lost or forgotten (or ignored). Unfortunately, our patient's health regresses and, more often than not, eventually he ends up back in the hospital.

Hospitals measure these far-too-common cases in their patient readmission rates (people who need to be readmitted to the hospital, often because they forgot to take their medication). Readmissions are expensive and often avoidable. The U.S. government agrees with this and is changing how it pays hospitals that have high readmissions rates on common health issues. Starting in 2013, the government will enforce payment reductions if 30-day readmission rates for heart attack, heart failure, and pneumonia exceed "risk-adjusted expected rates."[13] If hospitals can't reduce readmission rates, Medicare pays them less.

How can technology help solve the issue? Creating a personalized reminder for the patient could prevent many of these instances. But not many hospitals can take the time to work with individuals to create such a plan and to deliver the reminders. However, a software solution that automates creating a customized treatment handbook for the patient to take home doesn't sound like rocket science. Making it accurate and engaging might be a little harder, but there are out-of-the-box solutions available today that use the already existing patient treatment data and patient characteristics and create an "individual patient user manual." Progressive hospitals that are using this technology already have seen their readmission rates drop by an average of 30 percent.

Two hospitals piloting this technology are *Washington Hospital Center* and *Union Memorial* in Baltimore, Maryland. Both have nationally recognized cardiovascular programs. The technology allows patients to access their discharge summary online and lets them share it with their primary care doctors and healthcare providers. For example, say a patient outside the Washington, DC, area receives treatment at Washington Hospital. The hospital discharge clinic sends an online discharge report to the patient with care instructions. Our patient can't remember specifics once she is home so she goes online and checks directions. Washington Hospital Center wants a local doctor to monitor the patient's progress, so she shares the report with her doctor, who then monitors medications and blood pressure results. If there are any questions, the primary doctor connects with Washington Hospital Center and immediately troubleshoots any issues.

It's not surprising that Washington Hospital Center is part of the pilot program; they are dedicated to IT solutions. The hospital's technology solutions have been putting patient data on PCs next to patient beds in the cardiology care units for several years.[14] Doctors don't wait for someone to go gather X rays or lab results down the hall. The information is bedside when the doctor needs it. The system reduces any delays in treatment and improves patient monitoring while people are in the hospital. The system lets physicians view multiple types of data onscreen—lab work, reports, images, and pharmacy data. It means less time waiting for data and more time consulting with patients. An application in the system makes a virtual private network connection into the hospital system available to a core group of public health clinics that partner with the Washington Hospital Center to provide follow-up treatment and evaluation for cardiology patients who do not have their own private physician.

Another healthcare service provider handles discharged patients in another way, but the solution still is based on a solid IT infrastructure. Operating as Premera Blue Cross in the State of Washington and as Premera Blue Cross Blue Shield of Alaska in Alaska, *Premera* serves more than a million members through a large, diverse network of providers—nearly 18,000 healthcare professionals and 100 hospitals in Washington and 840 professionals and 23 hospitals in Alaska.[15] Premera has case managers coordinate treatment for seriously ill or injured patients after they leave the hospital. Each case manager handles about 30 member cases at a time; altogether, the team managed more than 8,000 cases a year. In complex cases, each patient might be working with five different physicians or therapists. In addition to working with those direct care providers, case managers had to track lab tests, medical equipment, and pharmacy orders, and conduct postrelease planning that factored in family support or lack of it. It is complex work.

Premera uses the case management model to help control costs and cut down on potentially life-threatening mistakes. Originally the case management was paper based with a great potential for disasters on many fronts. The organization brought in a case management collaboration tool that has about 20 tasks to help nurses follow care guidelines and standards. Because Premera has also replaced its old claims administration systems with a more flexible and efficient standardized platform, case managers interact directly with billing, further reducing costs and mistakes. By pulling together much of the information that case managers need and providing links to other resources, the collaboration tool provides a quick, easy-to-understand view into a complex workload. Better results with fewer mistakes and lower costs—it sounds like a fairly mature IT infrastructure to me.

Why don't all hospitals, healthcare, and health infrastructure providers use such tools and processes today? Ask your hospital or insurance company the next time you are shopping for treatment for yourself or your family and you want to reduce your chances of returning for additional care.

What about the treatment process itself? Is it possible to optimize in and around the operating room? Surgery scheduling and use of hospital assets are an area the University of Washington in Seattle and a local hospital looked into for improvement potential. They moved from the traditional and common approach in scheduling resources—the whiteboard—to the technology of 2010 with impressive results.

Most of us know hospital processes only from watching *House* or *ER* on TV. The scramble in the operating room is always dramatic. Ensuring that the actual room is available and prepared for the scheduled surgery is a significant task. Nurses and anesthesiologists need to be present, as does the right equipment, supplies, and the surgeon, of course. Sometime there are special requirements, such as a translator if a non-English-speaking patient is having brain surgery and will be awake during the operation.

All in all, it is a complex project management task. Most hospitals tackle the task with a whiteboard that has columns for the resources and rows for the different operating rooms. Any change requires a complete row to be wiped out and rewritten after telephone confirmation with the head of the respective resource, such as the nursing or surgery department lead. At a time when Excel spreadsheets are being used by fifth graders, there should be a more efficient way, shouldn't there?

In the Seattle hospital, the challenge was identified and tackled with standard IT components. Whiteboards were replaced with touch screens and resource management was automated in the back end.

The hospital staff felt more in control and less in "emergency mode." More important, the real impact was seen on how the very expensive hospital resource, the operating room, was utilized. In this particular hospital, and based on its estimates, the use of facilities increased by 15 percent. At a cost of such a room of $2,000 to $3,000 per hour across a total of 28 operating rooms, the investment in technology paid off rapidly to the tune of a multimillion-dollar bottom-line impact per year.

If you are a hospital administrator, how long can you afford to underutilize 15 percent of you resources year after year? If you are a medical professional, don't you want your patients to get the best possible care with reduced stress for you and your team? If you are a patient, wouldn't you feel more comfortable knowing that there is a system in place for keeping you alive and well during a surgery that doesn't depend on a whiteboard and markers?

It is good to recognize in the examples what is possible to achieve through optimized processes and technologies. Considering how far the healthcare industry in general is behind other sectors in leveraging an Agile infrastructure and otherwise common capabilities, it becomes clear how far we still have to go in optimizing it. I want to be super clear: Most of the people working as doctors, nurses, administrators, and researchers in our healthcare system are doing an admirable job every day of the week. I would like us to give them the tools to make their jobs easier. By doing so, we will all benefit.

Technology in the Public Sector

I struggled quite a while on how to include the next experience in this book without violating confidentiality or suggesting that the public sector is less interested, capable, or motivated to improve cost structure, efficiency, and agility. To put it up front, the largest and one of the best-executed desktop upgrades I have witnessed was driven by the U.S. Army. And the U.S. Air Force is using technology and business improvement processes in truly impactful ways. To really appreciate their improvements, you would require security clearance. The key insight of the next true anecdote is simply to outline the importance between the "blockers and naysayers" and the people who are driven forward strongly by the external pressure they feel.

So I will start this section with a story about one particular, government-run organization. Whether the reader generalizes across other government organizations or not, I leave up to you. The insight gained here is more general and a question of attitude and environmental pressure to change. I have told this story to a worldwide audience, hurting some feelings and receiving harsh feedback from representatives of the government sector. I am starting this section at the bottom of the sector but close with stellar examples of agility in the government and nonprofit sector that most commercial organizations could benchmark against.

After this disclaimer and introduction, let's go back only a few years. During one of my trips to Europe, I had the opportunity to converse with the CIO of their state correction—prison—system. This gentleman, with a grandfatherly appearance, had a long history as a government official. His passion for technology and deep insights were extraordinarily valuable for me and the other participants during a technology event. One of the agenda sessions was a participant discussion on the challenges and the value of desktop migration and upgrades.

The discussion, like so many others I have seen, split the participants into two camps. One of the groups was arguing how to best utilize technology and how to overcome the unavoidable challenges. The other argued that just following along would be truly sufficient; its members didn't see any reason to rush into anything. The second group felt that the correct course was to study, in great detail, all potential obstacles first and then create a mediation plan with the value of the change clearly proven before considering any kind of technology change.

Eventually our CIO, one of the quiet types, stood up and started to explain his situation. He said that he fundamentally has two user groups to serve and the camps in the room reminded him of the conflict he sees every day. One of his user groups consists of nonprofit organizations that are focusing on inmate resocialization. They help establish and maintain contacts between inmates and their families on the outside, providing services like case and parole reviews. He explained that these people were usually highly motivated by what they were doing but were totally overworked and underfunded. Time was a limiting factor for them, and they saw efficiency as a key to improving their work situation. These were the people who were pushing him and his team to get the latest technologies, such as instant messaging, Voice over Internet Protocol (VoIP), and standardized, easy-to-exchange data formats like Extensible Markup Language (XML).

And then he talked about his second user group—the employees of the correction system. "You must understand," he explained, "for a typical employee, a good day looks like this. They schedule one meeting out of the office, at a location within a comfortable driving distance. Then they drive to the meeting in their private cars, being reimbursed for the mileage as well as claiming expenses for lunch and an afternoon snack. For these employees, the telephone is far too much technical advancement. They could have four or five discussions in a day, but they would not be able to get the expense reimbursements. And for any potential productivity improvement technology could bring here, the pushback from their representatives is enormous, and there is surely no demand for capability improvement coming from them." Talking to the "slow movers" in the room, he added, "You remind me of these employee groups. You and your organizations simply don't have the economic pressure to be effective yet." With that said, he sat down.

Like healthcare, discussions around public sector spending can be divisive. We cannot agree if we spend too much or too little, but we can agree that, as a society, doing more with less is a good concept—and that applies to governments too.

Traditionally, government agencies do not have a reputation for being at the forefront of technological innovation. But this is actually beginning to change. Increased demand on the services and tighter budgets, combined with a limited talent pool for recruiting, have forced many public sector organizations to proactively optimize their technologies. Optimization usually brings better service for the customers (us) at lower costs. All levels of government are beginning to see how technology allows organizations to better leverage dwindling resources and create synergies—and opportunities—between agencies.

Leaders joining our government bodies now bring with them the expectations that they will use technology to be as effective in office as they were in the outside world. We have seen how Michael Bloomberg changed the city government based on his experience. When Barak Obama entered the White House, there was no question that mobile devices—particularly his BlackBerry—and other social media were going to be part of his work style as president. Nicolas Sarkozy felt the same about his email. When he discovered that the messaging platform in the Elysée Palace was outdated, he insisted on improvements to ensure his and his incoming team's productivity.

You don't have to look at the heads of state to see how technology capabilities change the face and agility of government. We are seeing examples on a state or district level of ad hoc collaboration when disaster strikes. Technology fundamentally enables and supports change regardless of political ideology.

Based in Scotland's capital city, the *City of Edinburgh Council* provides a range of services from more than 70 principal locations to 480,000 citizens, businesses, and organizations in Edinburgh and Lothian. In 2005 the City of Edinburgh Council embarked on a service-led IT transformation program with its outsourcing partner, BT.[16] Managing the IT infrastructure was a challenge for the council government, as it is in so many other communities. The council did not know how many computers were in its offices, let alone how to manage them. When a PC broke, it could take up to five days to be fixed. It was a complex, disparate environment with dozens of desktop operating systems, old mainframe systems, and significant obsolescence challenges.

The goals, while seemingly impossible to reach at first, represented a push to mature the council's IT into a standardized and scalable, Zero-Touch infrastructure. The end results would be improved front-line services to citizens, a restored internal customer and employee confidence in the IT systems, and increased business agility to assure business continuity. By 2015 the council wants to make Edinburgh the most successful and sustainable city in northern Europe. In short, it appears very ambitious and hardly possible.

But the results do not lie. Using its matured IT infrastructure, the council now operates with 24 percent fewer employees per 1,000 citizens than any other comparable local government organization. By modernizing its IT infrastructure, the council has raised £40 million in capital receipts because it was able to sell more than 18 separate sites and bring together 2,500 employees in one building in December 2006. The payback period for the changes was just 14 months. The number of line-of-business applications went from 4,500 to around 400. The improvements provided an internal rate of return of 200 percent. The council is also on target to reach £25 million in IT department savings by 2011 from its operational budget. And the council is now 25 percent more efficient in meeting quality of service targets. The list goes on and on.

I wanted to use the City of Edinburgh Council as an example because it shows the power of transforming technologies within an organization. It shows that even the most basic infrastructures can be optimized to provide serious costs savings and improved productivity in a short amount of time with the correct planning. "Correct planning" is the key concept. I am not going to go into all the technical hardware and software specs that went into transforming the technology used by the council. I also do not want to cover the IT services redesign and the improved migration strategy that keeps the infrastructure current. Instead, I want to look at how the council and BT analyzed the infrastructure and used the IO model we have talked about in this book to create a road map to help it meet its aggressive goals.

Let's first look at the infrastructure pre-transformation, as they call it in Figure 4.5. This is an older version of the IO model so it may look a bit abbreviated compared to the one shown in Chapter 3. They did a fair assessment of the IT capabilities—although the two standardized ratings seem a bit optimistic when you look at the original picture.

Edinburgh — Pre-Transformation

	Basic	Standardized	Rationalized	Dynamic
Desktop Infrastructure				
Server Infrastructure				
Change Management				
Operations Management				
Asset Administration				
Customer Service				
Technology Planning and Process Management				
Overall Rating				

(a)

Edinburgh — Post-Transformation

	Basic	Standardized	Rationalized	Dynamic
Desktop Infrastructure				
Server Infrastructure				
Change Management				
Operations Management				
Asset Administration				
Customer Service				
Technology Planning and Process Management				
Overall Rating				

(b)

Figure 4.5 Edinburgh (a) Pre- and (b) Post-Transformation

When we look at the post-transformation results, it is clear that the roadmap focused heavily on improving the Core Infrastructure. Using this strategy, the IT department put in the foundation for a system that was easier to manage immediately and one that would take advantage of newer technologies as they came on the market. In later chapters, I'll talk about how this type of foundation supports continual improvements and innovations in capabilities—no matter how fast technology evolves and employee and customer wants and needs change.

Chapter 8 provides an overview of another government agency—the local authority in the state of Hessen, Germany—that highlights how governments are making inroads into technology innovations at all levels. When we look at government innovation, it is also important to look at nonprofit agencies that work with them. Nonprofits face the same budget and resource restrictions as their government counterparts. Many of these organizations have been around for decades and face aging infrastructure challenges and have their fare share of blockers and naysayers. However, they also have a strong desire to attract and retain new talent while proving to their supporters that they are efficient and successful in program delivery.

One of these organizations is the *American Red Cross*. In addition to responding to catastrophes, such as apartment fires and weather-related events, the organization serves local communities with education, training, and products that enable people to prepare for and respond to disasters and other life-threatening emergencies. The American Red Cross of Greater Cleveland has served the community in and surrounding Cleveland, Ohio, area for more than 100 years. The chapter employs approximately 55 people who provide disaster relief and help 1.7 million residents in Ohio prevent, prepare for, and respond to emergencies.[17]

The need to reduce overhead costs while maintaining core services prompted the Cleveland chapter to take a hard look at its IT infrastructure. Its accounting system needed better integration with donor management software, which needed to operate in the same environment at its volunteer management, training management, and sales and marketing systems.

The Greater Cleveland Chapter worked with CBIZ Technologies to upgrade the infrastructure to support the business needs. The upgraded system lets sales, customer service, finance, and fundraising work together. Data is available anytime employees need it, as long as they have the correct permissions. Work flow controls streamline business processes. IT can set up approval processes so that the system routes purchase orders through the appropriate channels, with review messages automatically appearing in managers' in boxes. By making important business functions available online, the chapter simplifies purchasing processes and helps employees avoid unnecessary tasks. Employees involved in the sales and shipping processes have cut lead times on orders by 40 percent since deploying the solution. Monthly reports are not only easier to review, department heads can collaborate to create a budget faster or investigate discrepancies or issues immediately.

Since 2001, the organization has reduced its paid staff by more than 50 percent—from 115 employees to just 55 full-time staff. Over this period, the chapter's ability to fulfill its mission has remained unaffected, and its annual budget has increased from approximately $7.5 million to $9 million. Imagine what your local government might look like with this type of focus on maturing its IT infrastructure.

The Red Cross is not the only relief organization that mobilizes resources to help in disaster situations. A full-scale disaster—like Hurricane Katrina or the 2010 earthquake in Haiti—are catastrophes that are fortunately addressed with a global response. In the worst of times, sometimes we can see the best of humankind.

Multiple agencies and government responders converge on a scene of chaos and destruction. Split-second decisions mean the difference between life and death. Organizations from the United Nations, to the International Red Cross to Doctors without Borders to local, on-the-ground relief groups join government agencies and military forces to deliver food, shelter, clean water, and emergency health services. The complexity and challenge of coordinating the activities of multiple agencies is immense. Large-scale collaboration is needed to address these large-scale natural disasters.

In my years at Microsoft, I saw innovative and transformational uses of technology every day. However, a visit to the Disaster and Humanitarian Response team left me speechless. Its use of technology and ability to leverage it across global borders and politics was truly amazing. Claire Bonilla and her team provide the tools and expertise that supports large-scale collaboration. The team puts processes and technology in place to streamline information sharing, coordinate aid activities, and connect donors and volunteers with those in need before, during, and after a disaster. Cloud computing is playing a more and more pivotal role here too, as the availability of IT capabilities as a utility "on tap" makes it faster to turn on or scale up capabilities as they are needed for area, an organization, or a specific challenge.

What agencies have learned over the last decade is that in a catastrophe, the first priority is to secure fresh water, the second an Internet connection. Why is connectivity so critically important? Having the right data, with the right person, at the right time can mean the difference between life and death.

Figure 4.6 is a snapshot of the complex interplay of people, processes, and technology during relief efforts.

I want to focus on only a small part of the Disaster and Humanitarian Response team: its Information and Communications Technology

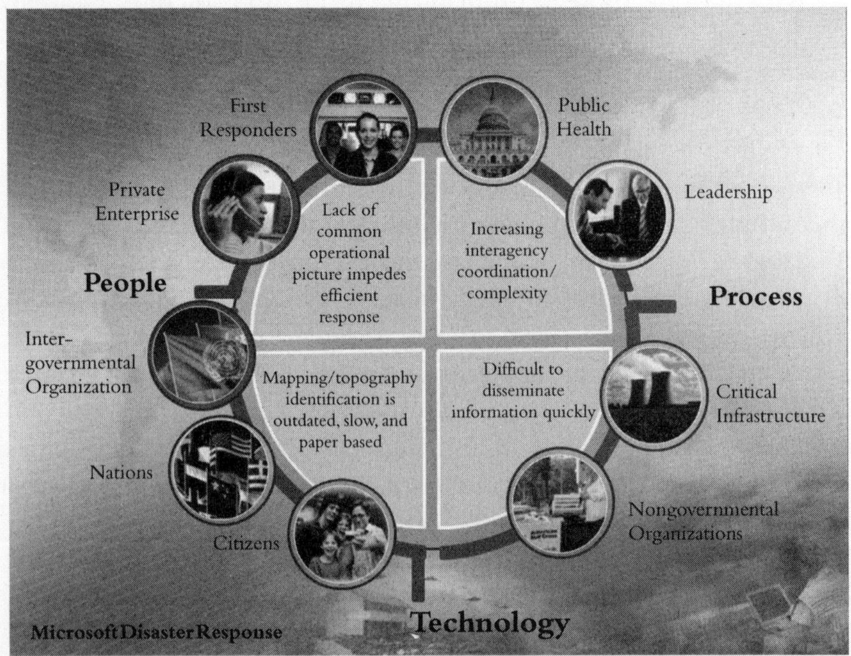

Figure 4.6 Coordination Challenges in Disaster Relief

(ICT) Solutions and Expertise. This is where we see the power of standardized platforms, services, and solutions.

- At least 138,000 people died and millions more lost their homes when a cyclone and extensive flooding devastated much of Myanmar in May 2008. Within days, Microsoft and 19 of its technology partners rallied to help the UN Office for the Coordination of Humanitarian Affairs create a Web-based collaboration portal for aid workers in the region. Built on Microsoft SharePoint Server 2007 and Microsoft Virtual Earth technologies, the Myanmar humanitarian portal offered organizations a single source of reliable data and a standard collaboration tool to coordinate their response.
- During the 2007 California wildfires, Microsoft worked with Infusion Development to provide the local government Emergency Operations Center with Joint Emergency Planning and Response System (JEPRS), a crisis and consequences management portal that provides real-time communication and collaboration on data, mapping, incident reporting, and other critical information for enhanced situational awareness and disaster response. JEPRS was used in the recovery phase of the incident to aggregate and report damage assessment information.
- Microsoft facilitated the exchange of information between civilian and military actors working together in Haiti earthquake relief efforts, through the provision of a SharePoint-based portal called the Civil-Military Overview. The Civil-Military Fusion Centre manages the SharePoint portal as an Allied Command Transformation initiative and monitors events and facilitates communication among the international community on specific crises.
- Bing Maps worked with satellite imagery provider DigitalGlobe to rapidly publish up-to-date imagery after Haiti's earthquake captured by the company's Quickbird and WordView II satellite sensors. Relief groups could better understand the location and extent of the catastrophe and deploy appropriate teams and resources.
- Following Hurricane Katrina, the Red Cross and Microsoft launched a consolidated Web site on missing persons and evacuees

to help families locate displaced relatives. Katrinasafe.org was used by governments in the states of Louisiana, Alabama, Texas, and Mississippi, and an estimated 340,000 inquiries were made to the site. The site has evolved to the current Red Cross Safe and Well site. Microsoft also provided servers, laptops, Tablet PCs, and software to first responders, such as the Red Cross, Navy and the Army Corps of Engineers, to integrate communications. The hardware used Groove technology to establish communication links and portals in areas with little or no electricity or infrastructure.

- Microsoft arranged to have three-dimensional oblique aerial photography performed in a few days after Katrina hit and hosted the images on the live.local.com Web site in conjunction with National Oceanic and Atmospheric Administration imagery to allow New Orleans residents to remotely inspect their properties to determine flooding or damage.

Having such an incredible positive impact in very hard circumstances is by itself a huge accomplishment.

What it also demonstrates is what is possible when motivation and technology meet. Often I hear from IT departments or their people in charge that implementing a specific capability is too hard or takes too long. Projects are planned for many years out. Does it have to be this hard or slow? No! When the earthquake hit Haiti, the response team was able to build on an existing SharePoint environment of the North Atlantic Treaty Organization and had a working collaboration and communications platform for relief organizations from all nations up and running in 15 minutes! Building a complete such infrastructure from scratch takes up to 72 hours. Leveraging cloud computing opportunities is shortening this time to a fraction again. And the capability of donations sites to receive an increase in donations when help is pouring in can also be scaled up in under 20 minutes.

Your organization might not be hit by a physical earthquake but by competition. And giving you the capabilities you need should not be a project of years. Yes, your team might not have experience in managing international disasters, but your environment is likely less complicated than hundreds of organizations with independent processes and IT systems across all geographies and many languages. IT, it is time to get moving!

NOTES

1. www.ENR.com sourcebooks.
2. Stephanie Overby, "Bechtel's New Benchmarks," *CIO* magazine, October 24, 2008.
3. Microsoft maintains a Web site that provides access to Infrastructure Optimization (IO) online maturity model assessments and comparisons at http://www.microsoft.com/optimization/tools/overview.mspx.
4. *Automotive News*, "2008 Global Market Data Book."
5. *Fast Company*, Issue 143 (March 2010), "The World's Most Innovative Companies."
6. Microsoft, "Leading Middle East Financial Group Sustains Rapid Growth with Database Deployment," 2010.
7. Data comes from a leading analyst firm, December 2005. Note: It excludes server and network costs for centrally managed services.
8. Microsoft, "Bank Boosts Security and Control of Desktop Computers with New Operating System," 2009.
9. Microsoft, "Financial Institution Gains Efficiency with Automated Identity and Access Management," 2010.
10. Microsoft, "UK Accounting Firm Boost Productivity, Strengthens Security with Windows 7," 2009.
11. Microsoft, "Financial Service Provider Helps Ease Banks' Compliance Burden with Web Service Solution," 2009.
12. Peter Neupert, "Stop Demanding Too Little of the Health Care Industry," *Harvard Business Review* blog The Conversation, April 8, 2010.
13. From the Patient Protection and Affordable Health Care Act (HR 3590) and Reconciliation Legislation (HR 4872).
14. Microsoft, "Cardiology Service Sees Gains in Efficiency, Core Measures with Data Aggregation," 2008.
15. Microsoft, "Leading Healthcare Insurer Avoids $9.6 Million in Costs with Case Management Tool," 2006.
16. Microsoft, "City of Edinburgh Council Works Towards Delivering Smart City Vision with Infrastructure Optimisation Model," 2007.
17. Microsoft, "Efficient Operations Help the American Red Cross Succeed in Its Mission," 2009.

CHAPTER 5

BUSINESS IMPACT: TECHNOLOGY SOLUTIONS FROM THE SHOP FLOOR TO THE TOP FLOOR

Does your business view IT as a cost or as a creator of value? If IT expenditure is viewed as a necessary cost but not a critical business or production factor, is that approach a conscious strategy or simply a default? Driving down IT costs will deliver some tangible value to an organization. But what happens when there are no more costs to remove and/or your competition goes to the next level with technology to improve business competitiveness? When do we start to be penny wise and pound foolish?

In February 2009, the *Harvard Business Review* reported: "The power of IT reaches far beyond the technology itself. IT averages only about 5 percent of the total cost in a business. Shrinking IT cost by

50 percent will generate fewer savings than cutting business operations costs by 3 percent."[1]

We have seen that the right investments into IT infrastructure help the core business. It also reduces the short- and long-term cost necessary to maintain the IT environment on which the rest of the organization depends. Let's look more at the upsides for the business. Increasing numbers of organizations and managers want to and expect to further leverage IT as a potential asset to create business value. This is especially true in an economic environment in which agility and lower costs are a key asset. But what are the appropriate IT capabilities and priorities? How do you align IT capabilities to improvements in business performance? How do your investments and IT capabilities compare with your industry? Even if your organization is in a market leadership position, you still need to ask: Where do we invest to sustain sector leadership? Where are our competitors gaining ground? And in which segments can we grow share and profits?

IT AS BUSINESS ENABLER INSTEAD OF COST CENTER

As companies grow, their IT infrastructures grow along with them. But the pace of that growth typically is uneven. It rarely follows a comprehensive long-term strategy; as a result, organizations are left with a heterogeneous environment that is difficult to manage and integrate. You add an application here. You add functionality there. You add people across the board. Valid business reasons drive the growth, but the more variables you add to your infrastructure, the harder it can be to manage and, more important, to keep secure. And, of course, there's more pressure than ever on IT to keep costs down and functionality high. Even as the costs for hardware and software decrease, the costs of managing and supporting your infrastructure increase. Today the bulk of the IT budget is spent just treading water rather than adding new business value. With typically an 80 percent allocation of the IT budget on maintenance, the chief information officer (CIO) can't redeploy budget and resources to shift IT to drive strategic business asset investments.

In 2007, *CIO* magazine published its "State of the CIO Survey," which reflected three years of survey data (see Figure 5.1.). The top priorities at the time (on the business side) were controlling operating costs; attracting, retaining, and growing customer relationships; and improving workforce effectiveness. With regard to technology, CIOs were focused on business intelligence applications, security technologies, and service-oriented architectures. The biggest shift over the time period was that change in how CIOs see their role in an organization's overall business picture: Their role switched from enabler to an active driver of the business with technology solutions. But how can you invest in new capabilities if your hands are tied to maintaining the status quo?

Fast forward to the 2008 survey, and you find that only a year later, CIOs had blown past the "should" be proactive in envisioning business possibilities. It's not even a question now: The demand on

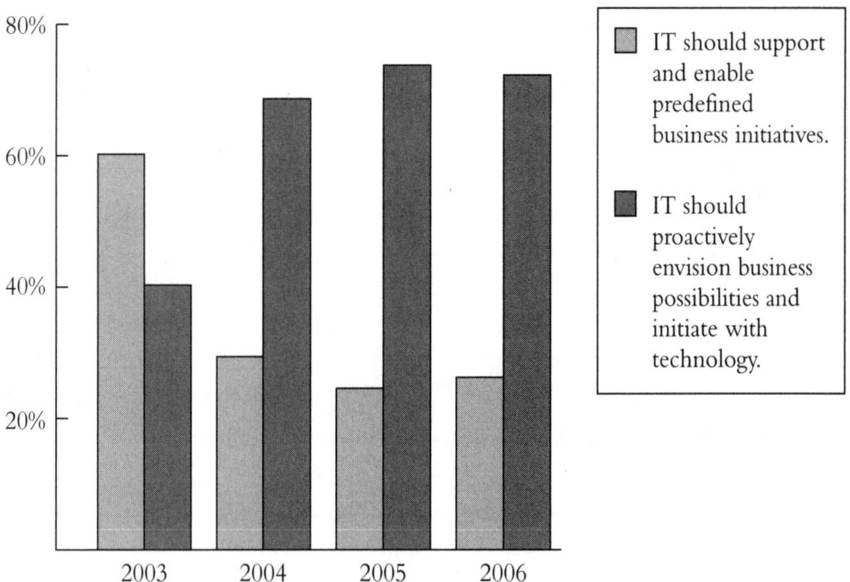

Figure 5.1 Changing Role of the CIO

Source: "State of the CIO," *CIO* magazine, data from 2003 to 2006.

the role is a fact. But so is the limitation in discretionary budget. The latest survey does not pull punches:

> We can't imagine a CIO who doesn't know that technology must support the business's processes and goals. If you don't understand that, nothing in this survey will help you. In our 2008 "State of the CIO" survey, 82 percent of respondents said that aligning IT and business was their number-one activity. Of course it was. Does a therapist listen? Does a general command?
>
> A strong, balanced, successful CIO doesn't heed pundits and he doesn't pay attention to buzzwords. Strong CIOs don't align technology and business. They work with their peers. They guide them, educate them, persuade them, debate them, hear them, help them, decide with them and execute the enterprise's strategy with them.
>
> Strong CIOs don't innovate. They figure out ways to make money for the business. They cut waste and plow those savings into projects that create value. Sometimes they create whole businesses where none before existed.[2]

CIOs and chief technology officers must take the lead in explaining how IT infrastructure creates business value—especially in challenging economic times. This mandate comes at a time when almost 70 percent of executives rank information- and technology-based capabilities among the top three corporate levers for creating competitive advantage. Executives also say they would like to dedicate almost 40 percent of their technology spending (up from 20 percent today) to the development of business capabilities that match or surpass the competition.

Before you can spend that 40 percent, you need to get IT costs down. The current service level is the baseline of expectations, and delivering against it must be possible with reduced resources. The examples I use over the next pages focus heavily on business practices since these are the capabilities most visible to the business—the Business Productivity Infrastructure Optimization portion of the Maturity Model. However, the underlying IT infrastructure and IT management—the Core Infrastructure Optimization (IO) capabilities in the model, is the part that is least understood and appreciated by the company at large. The Core is where pitfalls trip up many IT deployments and capability improvements and where many maintenance and security challenges present themselves.

If your organization has a poor understanding of the required infrastructure or if your business needs are not well defined, you may not be able actually to deploy solutions, or project costs may climb the farther into deployment you get. The comprehensive optimization models make sure you understand the dependencies and synergies before you begin. It gives you the tools you need to guide, educate, persuade, debate, hear, and help decide your enterprise's business strategy based on how IT can contribute and leverage investments in one area or across many functions. You don't just buy technology for point solutions; you use the technologies broadly and synergistically. You own the technologies and their advantages for your business and organization.

CREATING BUSINESS INTELLIGENCE FROM DATA OVERLOAD

Bloomberg is delivering and managing information, and information drives knowledge that directs the business. But it isn't just any kind of information. Bloomberg gathers, synthesizes, and distributes the most up-to-date and relevant information to hundreds of thousands of analysts and decision makers worldwide. Business intelligence is a critical asset, and Bloomberg delivers it like no other organization in the world. The world is not going to become less connected, so understanding and managing these increasingly complex and interconnected systems will make the difference in how effectively and agilely we can maneuver in our environment.

The Infrastructure Optimization (IO) Model documents the maturity of information technology capabilities that streamline the management and control of content, data, and processes across all areas of a business—business intelligence and content management. As we saw in our drill down into the automotive and financial sectors, companies with a Basic infrastructure to support business intelligence leave their data sitting in data silos and rely on very basic analysis tools. Companies with a Dynamic infrastructure have well-integrated data warehousing, reporting, and analysis capabilities combined with sophisticated search and broad information sources that provide real-time access to relevant data.

Organizations can either build these capabilities or leverage third-party solution providers. For example, Bloomberg created its competitive advantage in the business of "information management" and provided customers with information essential for their business intelligence to stay competitive in their markets. In the highly competitive, visible, and sensitive energy and commodities market, predicting supply and demand as well as the impact of environmental factors is essential to be effective. Gaining the edge in accuracy and speed in reacting to market movements often determines the difference in huge profits or losses. For these traders, having access to real-time information and forecast is more than business critical.

Bloomberg has been providing the data for many years, but it developed a new tool for customers that changed how they derived insights to a new level. Think about a military leader who is trying to oversee and manage the battlefield with list of resources versus his opponent who sees the terrain and all the relevant information on a map. Who do you think has the better overview and can make better Agile decisions? Bloomberg's "Interactive Maps for Energy and Commodities" (BMAP) is such a next-generation tool, providing critical business intelligence in the energy and commodities world. BMAP is a strategic decision-support tool that represents data and analytics in a visual manner. It combines vast amounts of data—100,000+ so-called energy assets (drilling platforms, refineries, pipelines, etc.), real-time weather feeds, damage/impact forecasting tools, breaking news, global shipping vessel loads and movement, fuel and commodities pricing by area—with an interactive map that lets analysts really "see" what is happening on a global scale. With this knowledge, companies can predict regional impacts that influence oil or natural gas process while or even before they happen. As we mentioned, access to information is critical, but being able to combine and analyze the data sources effectively is what makes the difference in quality and usefulness. By providing big-picture understanding of activities and events in both predictive and real time, while simultaneously providing granularity of information, this tool enables users to build complex impact and response models based on current data. It is about getting potential answers to questions before and as something is happening instead of after the fact—when it is much too late to make a decision. On the trading floor, those with the fastest and most informative information can act quickly to benefit from shifts in market prices.

For example, say a cold snap in Europe hits and a natural gas trader wants to understand supply, likely rising demand, and potential impact on pricing. Utilizing BMAP, the data shows that only 2 liquefied natural gas tankers with supplies are on their way to the area but that 10 liquefied natural gas tankers full of product would be necessary to meet the demand increase. The trader can see the shortage before it happens and know that natural gas prices are very likely to be going up as soon as the demand increase surpasses the existing inventory and temporary shortage. A supplier, however, might use the data to redirect ships heading for a different destination with predicted lower prices to Europe instead and optimizing their return.

Or our commodity trader might follow the latest hurricane coming into the Gulf of Mexico and can access potential damage/impact forecasts on the oil, gas, and power infrastructure before it comes ashore, anticipating and leveraging changes in demand and supply for profit optimization and resource redirection. A much broader audience now can generate high-quality data insights and predict outcomes, allowing their organizations and the system of supply and demand to be more efficient, faster, and Agile.

It is easy to understand the business need for BMAP for this market. The innovation in the available tools creates a competitive advantage for users and quickly (because of the speed of the market) becomes a "must have" for every participant to stay competitive. How did Bloomberg come up with and realize the solution idea? Building on its experience for its fixed income and equity analytics, the goal was to provide a tool that brings data to customers in a Dynamic and easy-to-use interface. Bloomberg utilized cutting-edge technology and data sources with an interface people have used for thousands of years: the map. With the readily available global mapping through Google and Bing, the canvas did not need to be reinvented. Building on standard technologies, the key then became integrating mapping technologies with relevant data sources to maximize the business impact. An interesting side note is that the quality of the maps was not the factor in deciding which competitive technology Bloomberg used. The development tools and integration into research and development and information infrastructure led Bloomberg to choose the Bing mapping technology for BMAP.

For most business decision makers, the story would end here, but if we go a little deeper, the key point of combining and leveraging standard technologies with the stuff that truly makes Bloomberg's offering different becomes clearer. And for the technology decision makers and the other geeks (like me), it is simply cool to look at how Bloomberg actually built the solution utilizing standard technologies and interfaces with its own proprietary information management tools.

Bloomberg uses a proprietary computational environment and distributed application model: the BLOOMBERG PROFESSIONAL service, commonly known as the Bloomberg terminal. Enhancing the service with the new desired capabilities required some "nonnegotiable" cornerstones:

- A very mature and Dynamic infrastructure that was fast and adaptable as the foundation was required.
- The platform needed to be architected, designed, implemented, and deployed as a new addition to the existing computational environment
- Scalability of and interoperability with data sources and presentation layer infrastructure were critical.

BMAP had to be both a niche-specific application supporting all energy and commodity business requirements while simultaneously being generic enough to be the mapping foundation for other groups within Bloomberg. The technology had to be extremely scalable; the number of servers required to support the numbers of requests users put across was massive. And since coming late to the party is rarely a benefit, time to market also was an issue.

And one size does not fit all. Customers wanted to commingle their own data with data supplied by Bloomberg. They wanted to use the platform as their own infrastructure tool, as if it were a proprietary, in-house tool—while still getting updates and upgrades from the Bloomberg service. Obviously, these were not simple business needs and were impossible and cost prohibitive to achieve with only Basic or Standardized IT capabilities.

What happened next was also a cultural change within Bloomberg. Historically, Bloomberg relied on in-house proprietary solutions unless someone could prove an existing, off-the-shelf tool or technology could save time and money and provide an end product it couldn't get on its own. When Bloomberg business lead Andre Parris and Research and Development (R&D) Senior Executive Steve Ross looked at developing and maintaining their own mapping technology, the cost and level of engineering effort would be the absolute opposite of developer or organizational agility or fiscal responsibility.

One of their senior architects, Mitchell Brody, put together a simple proof of concept using Microsoft's Bing, which is not only a search engine but a fast and interactive mapping platform with—here is the key—standardized application programming interfaces (APIs) and development tools.

Best-of-breed or integrated solution? Here is where the synergies of a platform come in. Bing utilizes Microsoft Silverlight—a Web application framework that integrates multimedia, graphics, animations, and interactivity into a single runtime environment—as a container, with standard APIs and development integration. Leveraging this platform lets Bloomberg control how its data is managed but gives it the required visual mapping technologies. Everything is inside the map, running in a Silverlight application, which can be imported into any Bloomberg application that uses its standard Graphical User Interface package.

The flexible architecture is important for customers, who need to have true real-time access to insight and information that gives them a competitive advantage. They can use the data to understand factors influencing the markets, capture market share, and make money. The technology infrastructure allows customers to analyze both the data within the Bloomberg programs or use it easily to plug in their own data. The services model provides the users with constant updates and upgrades. Both Bloomberg and their customers are using and leveraging the benefits of a platform infrastructure to advance their own business intelligence capabilities without having to re-create the underlying plumbing or even create an electronic map of the world by themselves.

The Rationalized infrastructure allows Bloomberg not only to provide a one-of-a-kind tool but to stay ahead of competitors going forward by expanding without the need to completely rebuild. The company chose an infrastructure that allows it to easily add additional capabilities as new data sources come online.

So why not use a tool that works for the analysis of natural gas transportation to other fields? BMAP was developed (and funded) originally in Bloomberg's Energy and Commodities business. But both Bloomberg and its customers could leverage the standard components and interfaces for additional business opportunities, especially as it became clear that the combination of maps and information could make a real business difference. And because the original implementation was homogenous and well integrated by utilizing the platform and standard API approach, adapting it to new business scenarios was mostly a question of business creativity and identifying the most appropriate data sources. It did not require a complete reinvention, which would have been necessary if the original commodity solution had been built with proprietary best-of-breed components.

Bloomberg's Research and Development department helped build the solution and leveraged the new platform for optimizing its analytic and prediction capabilities for its Network Services. Naturally the other commodity management areas, such as agriculture and shipping, imported their specific needs and data into the mapping solution. But use went quickly beyond commodities to other areas where knowledge advantage means business advantage. The tools are now available for the analysis and modeling of diverse things such as commodities, municipal bonds by county, and foreclosure rates by city.

IMPROVING CUSTOMER CONTACT THROUGH WEB SITE DESIGN AND DATABASE MAGIC

It is not a secret that consumers today want easy access to product and service information. For the IT services organization, this means they not only need to deliver the consumers' access to the information and product they look for, they need to have the flexibility to support in-house sales and inventory management that can change as the whims of the customer change. How investments into better customer insights, improvement of business intelligence capability, and leveraging of data and content management can improve the customer experience and competitive advantage is covered in the next, literally explosive, story on how capability improvement—supported by robust IT infrastructures—can drive ecommerce and boosts sales and customer satisfaction.

Established in the 1800s and located in Alton, Illinois, *Winchester Ammunition* has seen every technology change from the introduction of the light bulb to the rise of the Internet.[3] Keeping such a venerable brand relevant and fresh and in touch with the next generation of customers can be a challenge. Reaching new, younger consumers means extending its reach via new technologies.

To leverage this "Internet thing," the company has launched several Web site redesigns over 13 years to ensure that customers experience a contemporary and relevant site. The latest redesign prompted Winchester and its Web design and hosting partner, Quilogy, to find out if the goals were actually being reached. Together, they conducted site surveys and focus groups to identify whether Winchester.com met the needs of the company's customers.

The Web visitors were a mixture of experienced, occasional, and novice hunters and shooters. A new insight was that the third most popular reason for going to the site was for ballistics information—how bullets and specific loads will perform in a variety of guns and under variables such as wind speed, altitude, range, and scope site height. When the company looked at its core customers—the experienced hunters, who also constitute the largest segment of site visitors—ballistics information jumped to the number-one reason for visiting the site. Focus groups confirmed that fact.

The company realized the insight could create a competitive advantage. None of the ammunitions manufacturers provided this information to their customers, and Winchester spotted a way to put itself ahead of its competitors. The data was available in different forms. However, the company that could provide an online tool that would allow customers to generate ballistics information on several products under different variables would own the proverbial silver bullet in delivering customer value.

As Winchester and Quilogy personnel began to think about producing a ballistics calculator, they realized the need extended beyond Winchester.com. Such a calculator could be a marketing asset at highly trafficked trade shows. It could be the basis for in-store kiosks at gun shops. It might even be the basis for a mobile application. Any solution that they developed would have to take flexibility into account. By putting the right infrastructure in place for one business need, the company was more than halfway to also implementing solutions in other areas—without adding new infrastructures at a greater cost.

Leveraging standard components and external expertise were the way to go. Brett Flaugher, the Vice President of Sales and Marketing at Winchester Ammunition, was part of the evaluation and strategy development with the IT organization. He summarized the decision reasons: "We looked at a lot of approaches but decided that software plus services would provide customers with the best experience, regardless of how they were accessing the calculator. They wouldn't have to download and install an application, and we could provide a highly visual experience tailored to the way that customers were accessing the calculator."

With the architectural direction established, the team considered the technology options for their development road map. Under traditional circumstances, an application with the highly visual, animated interface that Winchester wanted would have been designed in Adobe Flash. But these circumstances weren't traditional. Winchester envisioned its ballistics calculator powering several applications and running on several hardware platforms. Flash technology would have required the development team to create a separate Flash front end for each version—and then to maintain all those versions and keep them synchronized. Winchester had worked extensively with Flash in the past, but now it wanted one solution that would work across multiple versions of the ballistics calculator. Because Internet access is uncertain at trade shows, this version of the calculator had to be able to run when a device is not connected to the Internet. While Flash technology was the dominant media technology on the Internet for many years, when Apple's CEO and founder Steve Jobs publicly declared in 2010 that Flash is not good enough for mobile platforms, it became time to move on for many.

Better is the enemy of the good. Cross-platform and standardization won out here too, and the project at Winchester was implemented on a Microsoft Silverlight browser plug-in and Presentation Foundation that was already in use in other groups in the company. Knowing the calculator would be a hit at trade shows, Winchester took it a step further and used Microsoft Surface software and touch computing platform for its trade show displays. Using standard interface and development tools allowed this presentation of the actual ballistic calculator tool.

Utilizing the standard platform of a Rationalized collaboration platform allowed the integration and addition of features like a Web version of the calculator running on Microsoft Office SharePoint Server. System integration and content and data updates were a breeze, using out-of-the-box work flows. Portability is key, and, yes, there is "an app for that" on Apple's iPhone too.

"One of the biggest benefits of the ballistics calculator is that it provides a phenomenal tool to educate customers on the value of our products in a way we couldn't easily educate them before," says Flaugher. "It defines our leadership position in the industry."

From the traditional manufacturing company on the banks of the Mississippi River, we are now traveling to an e-commerce provider in the desert to look at a much younger organization that is using infrastructure improvements and adding capabilities to extend its leadership into a new business sector. *MeMega* is an online and retail technology provider based in the Kingdom of Saudi Arabia.[4] The company was one of the first technology specialists in the region and has introduced a number of unique products there, including next-generation interactive gaming technologies. Consumers in Saudi Arabia are using European and U.S. Web sites, such as Amazon, to order product, and MeMega saw an opportunity to develop a sophisticated, locally based, online retail experience for the customers there.

The pioneering company knows that first impressions count, so it wanted to create a highly competitive offering from the get-go, including fulfillment. The site had to get new products into consumer hands quickly and reliably. In early 2007, the company asked several vendors to submit proposals for a solution that could provide a unique shopping service while also being easy to support, use, and deploy. MeMega considered a number of options, including a solution based on Storefront. The organization chose to work with BTAT—one of the kingdom's most experienced international e-commerce providers. The BTAT solution for MeMega is based on Commerce Server, which provides a set of tools for developers, IT professionals, and business users to develop, deploy, and manage end-to-end e-commerce applications. It incorporates a range of technologies, including Microsoft Dynamics customer relationship management and enterprise resource planning (ERP) software, with Microsoft SQL Server as the database. The combination allowed it to get its Web site up and running quickly, beating out local competitors by having a Web presence fully integrated into its business application and processes. By choosing a standard platform, not only was the rollout fast, but the company is also able to react quickly to changes in the market and consumer tastes. Analyzing, learning, and improving are critical in the online space.

The business results were impressive, exceeding the original expectations. In a short time, online sales already exceeded targets by 50 percent. Reliability and system integration played a key role in capitalizing on the additional business potential. The underlying infrastructure handles customer orders immediately—most orders ship the next day.

MeMega is a perfect example of a major player in a market that chose an IT infrastructure to support and extend its business leadership position into a new market opportunity by leveraging existing strengths. Having a Standardized and Rationalized IT infrastructure built on standard components and interfaces allowed the extension of the core business platform quickly and ahead of the competition. It had a competitive edge going into the development and came out even farther ahead at the end.

Other companies use their infrastructure to go into entirely new markets. Expedia, Inc. began offering online travel services toward the end of 1996. It was one of the first commercial Web sites dedicated to the travel industry. Since then, sites devoted to travel take you anywhere in the world. They let you compare prices and book rental cars, hotels, insurances, event tickets, and many, many more things you might (or not) need when getting to your destination. A complete industry was reshaped in just a decade.

What's true for the travel infrastructure also holds up for the travel destinations. Standing out in the travel industry crowd is tough, but *VisitBrighton* has used mapping technology to get people to come to its little corner of the world. Brighton & Hove, a city created from the merger of two towns, is a popular seaside destination on the south coast of England. VisitBrighton is the tourist board for Brighton and Hove city council; its purpose is to attract visitors to the towns and support local businesses.[5] The area hosts more than 8 million visitors each year, but the city council wanted to rebrand the city as a cool and exciting place to be. The business need that started the infrastructure update was the push to increase bookings by getting people more involved with vacation planning. Their target audience is younger and hipper so their Web presence was their biggest marketing opportunity. However, the site was too static, with data presented in lists and only a few truly interactive elements – think "the Web in 1995." Someone looking at the site could find only basic geographical information and a few business listings. It did not scream "cool place to visit."

VisitBrighton chose to work with Web tourism specialist New Mind. Together, they created a site—leveraging the same technology as Bloomberg does—Bing's Maps for Enterprise, to help potential tourists visually plan their trips. Site visitors can create itineraries of local attractions and businesses and view their plans on a map, travelling between locations virtually. They can also use unique features, such as bird's-eye view, which shows detailed aerial photography taken from a 45-degree angle, giving a more accurate sense of scale and distance than top-down images or maps alone could provide. It is way better than a customized guidebook.

On the business side, local businesses around Brighton & Hove can integrate their details directly with the maps on the Web site, uploading images, text, and links. In 2009, VisitBrighton and New Mind added the latest technology to their site experience. Again, having decided to build on a platform, plugging in another component, such as walking virtual tours of some of the city's most famous attractions—the Brighton Pier and the museum or the Royal Pavilion—with Photosynth was easy and added tremendous value. What is Photosynth? It is an advanced imaging technology originally developed by the University of Washington that stitches together images into three-dimensional models. The VisitBrighton team used it to give its online visitors an experience otherwise available only for places like the Great Pyramids, the Vatican, or Singapore's marina.

The results of the investments? For the Internet marketers: Since the redesign, users spend an average of eight minutes using the site on each visit. For the business folks: Bookings for Brighton businesses, such as hotels and attractions, have jumped 120 percent month on month since the relaunch of the VisitBrighton Web site. And using the latest technology helps VisitBrighton engage with its Internet-savvy target audience and highlights the city as one of the most creative in the United Kingdom. The changes VisitBrighton made have other tourism sites scrambling to catch up now.

STREAMLINING THE PRODUCT DEVELOPMENT CYCLE

Winning in the market often means being first or second in the market. As customer preferences change or new technologies or material become available, product updates or new developments become possible or necessary. This is especially important in product development, where creativity, teamwork, and IT infrastructure unlock the potential of engineers and researchers by providing better access to collaboration and knowledge tools.

Tyson Foods is one of the world's largest processors and marketers of chicken, beef, and pork. The company has approximately 104,000 employees at more than 300 facilities around the world. Tyson has roughly 15,000 information workers who need to share development and marketing information, respond to customers, keep production lines moving, and handle all the operational details that keep the enterprise running. Original Web-based IT solutions at the company had powerful creation and management tools. But only a handful of employees—and really it was just a handful—had the skills to use it, which resulted in information bottlenecks, out-of-date site content, and a lack of effective collaboration among employees.[6]

Upgrades and changes to the system broadened the number of content managers from 50 to 150 people by simplifying how content was managed via an intranet. Information remained fresh, and people took greater advantage of the tools. Again, as technology innovated, Tyson upgraded its intranet offerings. Changes were incremental, but each one improved information sharing and reduced IT support requirements.

With customer and product data growing exponentially and cycles accelerating for everything from new-product development to customer response, Tyson needed to look across the enterprise to find ways to mature its IT infrastructure to support the growing needs. Large mergers created all sorts of organizational headaches. Data and people were hard to find. When you could find data, making sense of it was challenging.

In July 2007, Tyson's IT staff invested more in its collaboration infrastructure for two reasons: to save money and to gain more capabilities. A more complete Web collaboration solution included content management, business intelligence, enterprise search, work flow, line-of-business (LOB) integration, and sophisticated rights management capabilities.

Tyson employees discovered the power of powerful business intelligence capabilities immediately. Dashboards, Web parts, key performance indicators, business connectivity technologies, and reporting tools were easily accessible. The employees could use these capabilities to self-service their information needs and to create, publish, and distribute information more securely, with little training.

The IT staff could use the new platform as a useful general-purpose development tool. Because it had more time to support business needs as opposed to user support needs, IT could address requests from small groups needing specific capabilities that would boost productivity. The cost to these incremental changes was minimal both in dollars and time. For example, the IT staff created an application that pulled data from LOB systems to help a small group of employees speed contract revisions. Quarterly reporting for customer account managers went from two-week headaches to a Dynamic contract tool that pulls live, up-to-date information from LOB applications into a template, automatically updating contract variables. Built-in work flow determines next steps and routes the contract to the appropriate Tyson personnel. Capabilities like this across the company continually reduced the amount of time spent on connecting people with data. The results are a modern content management system that improves collaboration via project data sharing, blogs, wikis, announcements, employee contact information, competitive intelligence, and more. Business intelligence is not for just a few analysts. Product development, sales, and executive teams have easy access to useful data that is current across the enterprise.

IT spends less time on employee support and can spend the time looking at business problems differently than it did using a more traditional development effort. The IT staff can deliver solutions to users sooner and less expensively. The integrated system provides overall company efficiencies but specifically has helped managers rethink how they deliver information to the business and to customer. With better business intelligence tools, groups can be more proactive instead of reactive. This case study shows how when a mature IT infrastructure—specifically in this case one that supports a unified communications (UC) plan—can solve issues across multiple areas of an organization that reduce the amount of time it takes to connect the right people with the right organizational knowledge.

Food production is a highly regulated sector, and companies test their products thoroughly before they go into broad production and distribution. But this oversight pales in comparison to that of new pharmaceutical products. A mandatory testing and government approval process controls every aspect of the development process. These companies invest heavily in R&D. When a new compound is found that might turn into a medication down the road, the invention is quickly patented to ensure exclusivity for the inventor. The patent protection doesn't last forever. The timing between filing for the patent and its expiration determines if the company will recover some development costs as well as generate profits. As the government-regulated medical testing and approval process falls into this protected time, a company has to do everything it can to streamline processes to get a product to market as quickly as possible.

Clinical drug trials generate thousands of documents. Keeping track of all of those documents is the responsibility of the contract research organizations (CROs) that conduct or oversee trials on behalf of the pharmaceutical companies. CROs adhere to strict regulations set by the U.S. Food and Drug Administration (FDA). A system that manages those documents must be validated to be in compliance with Part 11 of Title 21 of the United States Code of Federal Regulations, which determines the rules for electronic records. These rules cover system access authorization, document audit trials, electronic signatures, and validation requirements for computer systems.[7]

Clinilabs is a CRO that provides early phase and specialty clinical drug development services to the pharmaceuticals industry. Since 2001, Clinilabs has conducted more than 170 trials and contributed to 9 successful new drug applications. As part of its clinical trials, Clinilabs must ensure that the flow of documentation is smooth, prompt, and accurate. Many of the documents are created by clinical investigators located all over the world, typically on paper. Data from these documents is rekeyed into Web applications known as electronic case report forms (eCRF), a time-consuming and laborious process. The pharmaceutical companies then have to send monitors to the research sites to conduct reconciliations and confirm that the eCRF data matches the original paper source data. This is time and money eating away at the window of development opportunities. But it is also a safety issue since paper forms introduce all types of errors into a process. Audits are a nightmare.

Paper documents aren't the only area for error; electronic documents can introduce inaccuracies into the system. Documents saved to hard drives or file share computers are distributed through email systems, creating multiple copies of files and potential version-control problems. Security is a concern when documents can be sent freely internally and externally.

Clinilabs saw an opportunity in the challenge of document management. It decided to address the problem by digitizing and centralizing documentation to reduce the time and cost of reconciliations and audits. It also wanted to look at ways to cut travel time and cost for monitors and auditors, reducing expenses for pharmaceutical customers. It considered a range of options. Commercial hosted document management services for the pharmaceuticals industry, because of the massive numbers of documents generally stored and managed, are prohibitively expensive for a smaller company seeking an edge over larger competitors. Products such as EMC Documentum were also too expensive and didn't fit the Clinilabs business model. The company felt that one way to remain competitive was not to force clinical investigators to change the way they worked in the fields. Instead, the company wanted its solution to flow into the clinicians' work.

Clinilabs created a solution based on Microsoft Office SharePoint Server. It worked with Perimeterwatch to develop and deploy "Clinical InSite" in the course of about six months. Validation by an outside company returned a report of full compliance with the FDA regulations regarding clinical document management systems. Clinilabs has cut trial costs by 35 percent, saved customers up to $465,000 per trial, boosted the quality of its service, and made its customers happier—all with a solution that sped to market in just six months. While the reduced cost is a bonus, for drug companies, the true value lies in reducing the amount of time and removing the possibility for human error. Bringing a new drug to market sooner—even by just a few weeks—adds significant opportunities to both the pharmaceutical company and patients.

Agility in the product research and development process makes the key difference. Technology can remove hurdles and streamline processes. The researchers at the Institute for Global Work at Boston University outlined this in their analysis of the ability of teams to solve problems that need an innovative approach. Their work concludes that if the solutions and related behaviors are novel, then the value potential of improved collaboration processes and technologies can increase dramatically. In sync with their referenced research findings, the argument that when faced with novel problems, groups that develop effective knowledge-sharing mechanisms will outperform those that do not is supported. The right capabilities can unlock knowledge and drive the team synergies.

Not many organizations are disclosing their development processes in much detail to the broader public. What we can see is that the companies recognized for their innovation and ability to bring products to market are also the ones that are leveraging technology and have mature business productivity capabilities. Collaboration and content management capabilities seem to be a key asset for those innovation leaders in their industries.

RETAINING CONFIDENTIALITY WHILE OPERATING "IN THE CLOUD"

The IT professional's role is changing—from making sure that servers are up and running, to advising management on how IT capabilities can help the business, to strategizing how to procure, build, and integrate new capabilities into existing infrastructure and processes. Using and managing technology capabilities effectively differentiates businesses and often leads to market success. The agility of an organization improves with its ability to meet business requirements rapidly and inexpensively through the reallocation of technical infrastructure resources and the provisioning of new or enhanced capabilities.

In the past, building capabilities in-house or outsourcing the building and management to an outsourcing partner were the best options. Now organizations consider purchasing an IT capability just as they would purchase electricity or water supply—as a utility. Cloud-based offerings play a major role in today's economy. Companies are driven to expand and to grow customers, revenue, and profit while reducing costs. The evolution of cloud computing, along with the convergence between applications and LOB process, has facilitated this expansion. There are still a few different definitions of cloud computing out there, based on specific products a manufacturer has to sell. For our purposes, "IT capabilities provided like utilities" will do.

Leveraging cloud computing has become another standard way to procure IT capabilities. For companies like Amazon, Salesforce.com, Microsoft, Kelly Blue Book, or Coca-Cola, offering and utilizing cloud computing is part of their daily businesses. Having the alternative to "switch on" an IT capability is fundamentally new. But it works seamlessly only if the other components of your infrastructure support the "standard way" this particular capability is provided. If your organization has a mature IT infrastructure, then integration of additional capabilities—either on-premises or through a services provider—is relatively easy and fast. And it allows your business to take advantage of the scale of the service provider's operation.

From the development standpoint, cloud computing provides great business opportunities. My main experience is with Microsoft Windows Azure. While my examples are Azure based, they still give you an idea of the breadth of opportunities for companies using the cloud. On the highest level, Azure is a platform for running applications and storing their data in the cloud. Companies use the platform to develop new ways to extend their businesses. For example, *3M*—a recognized world leader in technology research and development—wanted to make its decades of expertise in the workings of the human visual system available as a service to customers. 3M created a Web-based application that gives designers the ability to invoke complex algorithms to analyze the effectiveness of a design, based on how the human eye will respond. The innovative service reaches a global audience with minimum investment in hardware infrastructure and ongoing administration for 3M.

Another example is the Royal National Lifeboat Institution. Responding to high numbers of deaths at sea in the fishing industry, the organization contracted *Active Web Solutions* (AWS) to create an automated sea-safety application. AWS developed a location-based service infrastructure, code-named GeoPoint, which transmits position data to a centralized tracking and alerting system. AWS used GeoPoint to build a search-and-rescue application for fishing vessels. To extend GeoPoint to more scenarios, AWS migrated it to the Windows Azure platform. By hosting GeoPoint in the cloud, AWS attained massive scalability, richer functionality, and lower infrastructure costs. AWS was able to quickly convert its application to a hosted service and avoid the expense of building and managing a data center. In addition, AWS has the flexibility and scalability to take GeoPoint into more markets.

This ability to scale is a hallmark of the cloud. *Lokad* is a software development company that delivers sales, demand, and call volume forecasts for more than 300 customers—from one-person e-commerce companies to multinational retailers. To improve its forecasting capabilities, the company developed advanced forecasting tools and models. However, the more powerful forecasting models required significantly more computing resources than the company had available. Lokad decided to implement its software-plus-services forecasting application in the cloud—a quick, efficient process. As a result, Lokad reduced IT maintenance costs compared to traditional approaches, delivered more powerful and accurate forecasts to its customers, and improved its ability to expand into new markets.

Of course, social networking is another development hot spot. For example, *sharpcloud* enhances strategy development efforts by using the interactive and collaborative tools familiar to people who use social networking sites. But turning that idea into a real service for corporate users required a global series of data centers—far beyond sharpcloud's reach. The company developed and now hosts a cloud solution that it estimates to be 200 to 300 percent more productive than it would have been on a competitive platform, saving up to $500,000 annually. Sharpcloud has gained the confidence of major corporations such as Fujitsu, which finds that the sharpcloud service reduces its strategy planning time by 75 percent.

While some companies use the cloud to pull customers to data, some use it to push data out to customers. The *Associated Press* (AP) is the world's largest news organization, with bureaus in 97 countries. AP wanted to broaden its reach by encouraging developers to incorporate AP content into their applications. AP created a highly scalable solution that simplifies capacity planning and creates new business opportunities using the cloud platform. TradeFacilitate helps importers and exporters in the European Union to exchange trade data using a paper-free online system. To meet new regulation requirements for preshipment data exchange in the United States, TradeFacilitate sought a solution that would permit the company to scale its applications to a significantly larger market without proportionately adding more personnel and technology resources. The company quickly migrated the code base from its primary application to a cloud services model—hosting and managing its Web application and services on the Internet through data centers. With Windows Azure, TradeFacilitate quickly developed a scalable and reliable solution that helped the company improve its ability to focus on delivering new services to customers.

It is safe to say that cloud computing has also changed competitive relationships and provided new synergistic opportunities. At a high level, Windows Azure is simple to understand: It's a platform for running Windows applications and storing their data in the cloud. *Intuit*, the maker of QuickBooks and TurboTax, and Microsoft have not been the best of friends in the past. Actually, Microsoft has competed directly with Intuit. However, the cloud has provided a win-win opportunity for both companies in the area of small business customers. They integrated the capabilities of their cloud services platforms—the Intuit Partner Platform and Microsoft Windows Azure platform—to enable developers and channel partners to deliver solutions to businesses that use QuickBooks financial software. In fact, this will allow developers to jump-start development and distribution of new Web-based applications.

Alex Chriss from Intuit and Liz Ngo from Microsoft were in charge of making this collaboration a reality. Chriss is clear on Intuit's customer needs: "With the changing economic landscape, millions of small business customers will need—more than ever—new services and a greater support infrastructure." By combining the vast ecosystem of more than 750,000 development firms and channel partners, both companies are reaching the market more quickly and provide a greater diversity of offerings and services on one common platform to over 27 million small business customers.

Cloud computing is still in its infancy but is explosive in its growth. It provides opportunity for fast movers to extend reach into services, capabilities, news sets of partners, and new routes to markets. Opportunities for new services and for net-new models and revenue stream are emerging now. We will see Agile companies taking advantage of the broader platform adoption beyond Azure and staking the claims before 2015.

IT maturity will rely heavily on this new platform if organizations want to extend offerings into new markets.

As you have seen here, cloud computing is not an alternative to our capability models, It is a very powerful addition for organizations of all sizes to gain access to the latest IT capabilities.

MANAGING SUPPLIERS AND INVENTORY

Managing suppliers and inventory can be a competitive advantage. Mismanaging these areas can be a disaster. A mature IT infrastructure allows complete control over production, inventory, and distribution as well as leveraging optimization potential and ensures compliance. It can also improve supplier management and allow companies to comply more easily with government standards and regulations for their industry or region.

Leading pharmaceuticals manufacturer *Riva Pharma* provides high-quality, cost-effective products to healthcare markets across Africa and the Middle East.[8] Riva relied on a locally designed, custom-built system. The homegrown IT infrastructure played a business-critical role in manufacturing and supply chain management. However, it was more often in the way than leading the way. Data was inconsistent across business units, and there was no system in place for handling complex purchasing needs and sales orders. Sameh Mohsen, System Administrator at Riva Pharma, was facing the business challenge that, on some occasions, the sales order process took hours and at other times it took days. Why? Because information needed in the process was simply inaccessible. Out-of-date information led to stock shortages. Occasionally it would get to the point where Riva was unable to fulfill customer orders on time, resulting in lost revenue and unhappy customers pushed to the competition.

Management of the supply chain also suffered. Employees struggled to calculate stock needs in relation to supplier lead times, plan for purchases, and access important administrative information such as supplier quotations, trade agreements, and previous purchase orders.

Working with *BayaNet*, a Middle Eastern consultant that focuses on enterprise-level business solutions, Riva assessed the key issues in its basic IT infrastructure. It realized the need for capability improvements not only on the business application side but also in the underlying IT Core Infrastructure. The team prioritized the standardization of its server infrastructure, consolidated the information management with Microsoft SQL Server, provided employees standardized access to information and processes through the latest version of Microsoft Office Professional, and implemented Process Industries for Microsoft Dynamics AX to manage the business infrastructure.

The resulting solution today manages the entire production process, from purchase planning to finance. Purchasing agents, for example, can easily compare the delivery times and prices of different vendors. They can process purchase orders and create receipt lists that are then seamlessly passed to the inventory department. Inventory can view the items arriving at the warehouses, complete with information such as where items are from and trade agreement details, with the push of a button.

Results were immediate and impressive. Greater control over warehousing and stock levels helps the business to increase revenue by reducing the costs associated with wasted stock. Procurement power increased, while employees can compare supplier quotations and delivery details to keep supply costs down. Meanwhile, the production team can compare actual and estimated production costs to keep budgets on track and make optimizations where necessary and most effective. When necessary, employees can quickly generate supplier performance reports that meet industry regulations as well as ensure that product information meets export requirements. A clear view of real-time data helps managers review production rates and sales across the business, monitor performance in departments, and predict market fluctuations. By ensuring that the Core IT Infrastructure was standardized and the implementation of business intelligence and supply change management were working hand in hand, Riva Pharma turned a difficult competitive situation completely around.

Another highly regulated manufacturing sector is military equipment. Much like Riva, *BMI Defense Systems* struggled with a basic IT infrastructure that was completely unable to handle key business needs when growing rapidly from a small- to a medium-size organization. BMI Defense Systems began the year 2009 with fewer than 10 employees and QuickBooks accounting software.[9] Good news: BMI won a multimillion-dollar U.S. Department of Defense contract to supply energy-absorbing protective equipment to U.S. military stationed in Iraq and Afghanistan. Bad news: It had fewer than 10 employees and no system in place to ramp up quickly.

After BMI Defense won the contract, the company not only had to hire many more employees but also needed to upgrade its business systems to handle the increased warehouse, manufacturing, and financial accounting activity. It went from a handful of employees to about 80 people in less than a year and ran the company by using QuickBooks and Excel spreadsheets. Those tools and processes were not able to handle the rapid growth. BMI needed a system that would tighten up processes, help eliminate opportunities for error, and make tasks more efficient.

To solve these problems quickly, BMI Defense performed an expedited survey of different ERP systems. Understanding that it is often far more efficient to adjust processes to the software than the software to a company structure, BMI optimized for affordability, excellent government contract accounting capabilities, ease of installation, and extensibility. Ensuring that it had a Rationalized IT infrastructure in place on which to build its solution, the resulting Microsoft Dynamics handled the government contracting requirements and light manufacturing needs of BMI. Having selected SIS—an IT system integrator specialized in business management solutions—BMI developed and deployed the new infrastructure in just four weeks. And that included the financial, manufacturing, and warehouse capabilities as well as the integration with an existing timekeeping system.

What works for organizations of all sizes? It is being clear on the priorities, deciding to implement capabilities relevant for the core business, and building on integrated standardized solutions allows quick turnaround. IT simply doesn't have to take years. BMI continues to grow and recently used the system to win a contract to provide ballistic blankets to the U.S. Marine Corps for direct deployment in light armored vehicles in the field.

We have looked at two smaller companies and their IT issues. What happens when the inventory is energy and the customer is the general public with millions of customers? *Invensys Operations Management* is out to make it easier and less expensive for small electric utilities in the United States to participate in smart grid technology.[10] "Smart grid" includes smart energy metering and distribution; Dynamic optimization of grid operations; and standards for communication and interoperability of appliances, equipment, and electrical infrastructure. Utilities need a high-performance, low-cost way to distribute real-time pricing data to customers so that they can make smarter consumption decisions. The company has approximately 9,000 employees and is a division of London-based Invensys, which makes industrial and railway control systems.

There are multiple technical challenges in bringing smart grid to fruition. Utilities need to upgrade and expand the nation's electrical infrastructure to reliably and securely deliver power from a variety of energy sources, including not only coal, water, and oil, but also wind and solar power. They also need to figure out how to deliver constantly changing pricing data in near real time to huge numbers of customers over a broad geographic area using a wide variety of existing network infrastructures. The U.S. government is creating and mandating standard formats for electricity pricing data as the energy moves through a lengthy supply chain from regional transmission operators, to aggregators for retail markets, to local utilities, and finally to residential, commercial, and industrial customers. However, there has been no common, scalable, and affordable communications infrastructure for communicating this data up and down the supply chain.

Invensys saw and realized a business opportunity by creating a smart grid communications platform leveraging newly existing technology and services offerings in the cloud. Why build it yourself, if you can build on a growing and innovating platform? Invensys leveraged standardized services, such as service bus and access control service—both part of the Windows Azure platform. Azure is the cloud services platform hosted in data centers that provides development, computing, storage, and communications services for creating scalable, pay-as-you-go Internet services. Invensys solutions live right on top of the platform and allow utilities to quickly launch smart grid services at a very affordable price, as neither the utility corporation nor Invensys needed to invest into the data center infrastructure. Leveraging the platform and standardized development tools approach, Invensys developed its pilot solution in just three months, delivering key customer scenarios for smart grid–compliant products and services.

In one solution, an electric utility sends real-time electrical pricing data to customers in different geographic areas and pricing zones every five minutes. A client application running in a home or business receives the pricing information through the Service Bus. The consumer can respond to the pricing data by turning off certain appliances during expensive, high-demand periods. Local utilities could create business intelligence applications and reports on the pricing and usage information flowing to them in real time and better plan for reallocation of power supply, new energy sources, or new facilities.

In another scenario, a consumer on vacation could log on to a home energy portal, powered by Silverlight and hosted on the Windows Azure platform, and notice that he left his air conditioner on. He can remotely turn off the unit over the Web. Once the instruction is delivered over the Service Bus, the consumer immediately sees his cost savings calculated from forecasted electricity prices. In an industrial scenario, factory operators could save a great deal of money by shifting equipment usage times to lower-priced power times. For example, an automaker could decide to swap its sheet-metal stamping shift for a sheet-metal assembly shift to save electricity.

Using the Service Bus as their communications highway, utilities using the Invensys solution can easily scale their smart grid infrastructure to keep pace with need without spending a fortune on IT. Invensys has calculated that using the Service Bus to serve 1 million customers should cost utility companies roughly $189,300 a year. Compare this to building a data center to serve the same customers. A small data center costs from $500,000 to several million dollars, with annual maintenance adding another 50 percent.

Being on the edge and leveraging new technologies and trends creates the business opportunities of today and tomorrow. Invensys is clear that new infrastructure not only lowered its development costs but made the project possible in the first place.

While all three of these companies began their infrastructure improvements at various levels of maturity, they assessed their starting point and holistically improved the capabilities necessary for the desired solutions. Like many other organizations we have seen and have the privilege to work with every day, they ended with a more mature infrastructure, smoother supply and inventory processes, and—most important—new ways to use the technology to increase revenues, reduce costs, and be better prepared to compete.

SECURITY, SECURITY, AND MORE SECURITY

Security and the protection of intellectual property and trade secrets are top concerns for many organizations today, especially if they work internationally. While managing IT in a secure way is an absolute requirement today, many breaches are actually happening through social engineering. A spy simply calls an employee, pretends to be from the help desk, and asks for the person's credentials. Or the spy simply walks through an office facility and collects information in plain sight—usually from an unsecured computer. Why do many people leave their PCs unlocked when taking their lunch break or getting some coffee? Because they are tired and cannot remember the myriad of different passwords necessary to log into the different systems they need to use.

It is a well-known secret that employees who are expected to remember five or more different passwords just write them down. Employees use a handy Post-it note that they tape to the underside of a keyboard. Office 2010 implements a tiered approach to security that we call layered defense. The aim is to reduce the number of points to defend. Microsoft calls it "hardening the attack surface." It means attacks must automatically pass through multiple layers to crack into a system. There is a "protected viewer" that allows files to be opened without allowing harm to the system, and a gatekeeper provides file validation. Data can be isolated in a secure area, preventing harmful actions, and users have a chance to make informed decisions on document trust. For an employee, it means tighter security without all the password hassles. If you are still not convinced that there are holes in your security system, take a walk around some offices and lift the keyboards.

This is easier if you have a small number of offices to canvass; however, if you need to secure an organization with thousands of employees, you may need a different approach. Headquartered in Bangalore, India, *MphasiS* is present in 23 geographical locations across the world.[11] With over 34,000 employees, the company provides infrastructure, applications, and business process outsourcing services to global clients. Identity management and the ability to move employees from one project to another is a very important and costly affair. A simpler, cheaper, and automated process was required to stay competitive.

While the company has a robust IT infrastructure to manage employees and resources, at the same time, it found it extremely cumbersome to keep users, computers, and other directory objects in sync among various databases. MphasiS has seen unprecedented growth of employee count in the past few years. This growth, coupled with the usual challenge of attrition in the India technology market, requires the IT team to manage a large number of identities. The company wanted password synchronization, password reset, and user self-service functionality across the enterprise to enhance users' productivity and company security. Employees who had multiple digital identities and the company found it challenging to manage access rights to business information and safeguard applications and data from unauthorized access and security threats.

MphasiS was looking for a standard solution to resolve all these issues at a reasonable cost. Because the company was already using Microsoft Server products, it consolidated on Active Directory and chose Microsoft Identity Life Cycle Manager. The deployment took three months, and the new application automates identity management based on business roles. It automatically maintains consistent identity information across a wide range of directories, databases, and other system across the enterprise. Help-desk costs were reduced by over $1 million, and the company resolved security issues that had drained its intellectual property assets and kept executives up at night.

While no organization should have its security processes sitting in the Basic basement, this type of immature IT infrastructure is completely unacceptable in the financial world, as *Banque de Luxembourg* discovered. This private bank offers its clients wealth management services.[12] The IT department maintains an IT infrastructure that provides tools to facilitate key banking tasks, including processing thousands of transactions on a daily basis. With this comes the task of managing the identities of 780 employees and the access they are granted to more than 50 LOB applications and to several heterogeneous databases. Identity and access management control are critical, as several other European financial institutions and their customers discovered publicly and painfully over the last years.

For each business application, the IT security department relied on time-consuming manual processes for managing employees' identities and access. Using multiple spreadsheets, the access management department maintained access-rights information. Spreadsheets were passed to as many as 30 people via email each time the bank hired a new employee, each time employee access rights changed, or each time an employee terminated employment. Not only did this method create lengthy delays and potential for inaccuracies, it increased—if not guaranteed—security breaches. Describing this capability assessment as Basic in the IO Model is still an overstatement but daily reality for many organizations across the globe.

Banque de Luxembourg sought a centralized solution for identity and access management. It had to eliminate manual processes for provisioning user accounts in an effort to improve IT efficiency and internal compliance. Even more important, the bank wanted a solution that would give the access management department granular control over employees' identity and access, enabling it to protect sensitive and confidential information that, if breached, could put operations at risk. This doesn't sound like an unreasonable request, does it? Shouldn't every organization control the access to its most precious information in the same way?

The bank's IT team, working with Telindus, implemented an Active directory based Identity Manager. Granular and role specific access? Check! The access management department identified more than 300 roles at the organization and defined policies for each of the roles, which determine every employees' level of access and which applications and data they can access. The bank now provides appropriate access to systems and data when new employees join the company. At the same time, when employees leave the company, the IT department can centrally and automatically deprovision user accounts to ensure that they no longer have access to sensitive banking and customer data, which helps to ensure compliance with internal (and highly appreciated by customers) security policies.

Improving security was the key driver for this project, but the move from a Basic IT infrastructure to a more mature one increased employee productivity, simplified the IT management, and improved regulatory compliance. In the process, the role of the IT department changed: Its focus switched from manual upkeep of information to more strategic IT-security tasks that support critical bank operations and future business growing priorities.

WORKING ANYWHERE, ANYTIME

Working anywhere, anytime can be as simple as using a smart phone or a more technical hardware, software, cloudware solution at the back end. The goal is to keep employees securely connected and informed regardless of their location.

Senior System Engineer Rainer Gold managed a global IT team at *Voith IT Solutions*, which is based in Heidenheim, Germany.[13] Voith AG, the parent company, is a global leader in paper production, power transmission, hydro power, and industrial services with 43,000 employees at 300 locations worldwide. To help ensure that the group's supporting IT infrastructure is operating efficiently, Gold must travel frequently to work with the local teams. "If I'm in South America and need to consult with someone back in Germany about a problem, I can't wait hours for a response," he says. "I have a critical need for both voice communications and easy, mobile access to my email and instant messaging."

There are many good and cool point solutions out there. But in the business environment, the platform approach unlocks the capabilities while allowing manageable and future prove integration. The Voith Group uses a variety of mobile phones and adopted the Windows Mobile operating system as its standard several years ago. For email, the group relies on server computers using Microsoft Exchange Server. Voith also uses Microsoft Office Communications Server and the Microsoft Office Communicator Mobile client, which provide presence awareness for mobile users, so they can see at a glance when contacts are available to communicate. Everyone, from the IT team, to salespeople, to executives, to service workers who construct machines for paper production, need and now have mobile computing capabilities.

Gold and his IT colleagues piloted several phone models in April 2009. The IT team tested phones with specific users in mind. If you think back to our scenario discussions in Chapter 3, you'll remember how mature IT infrastructures look at different job scenarios when considering new technologies. Some Voith Group workers needed to use email or create Office documents from the field. Others, such as managers and salespeople, needed to conduct meetings using whatever mobile device was available. The phones that the IT team eventually introduced take advantage of Direct Push Technology, which uses Microsoft ActiveSync technology to send email messages directly from the mail server to the phones, without the need to initiate a connection. The ease of use, lower costs, and efficient operation with Microsoft infrastructure made the deployment easy on the team and easy on the budget.

But anywhere, anytime scenarios usually have to go beyond an employee and a phone and require more organizational and IT capabilities. Companies like design firm *Wimberly Allison Tong & Goo* (WATG) design everything from boutique hotels and destination resorts to spas and conference centers around the globe. Many of WATG's sites are in remote locations that lack high-speed Internet connections. "Our designers could be working from the middle of a jungle or the middle of the desert, which, among other challenges, makes it difficult for them to exchange files and work with their teammates who are in offices half a world away," says Lawrence Rocha, Vice President and Chief Information Officer. Together with its system integrator DynTek, WATG established 65 department portals for sharing information about such specialties as sustainable architecture or spa design based on a SharePoint integrated peer-to-peer technology called Groove, which is included in the Microsoft Office suite. The firm and its partner also built project sites where geographically dispersed teams can find and exchange relevant documents and drawings. The system supports ongoing ad hoc collaboration, including sharing compound AutoCAD files and delivering feedback in an unstructured way—a valuable capability in the design process. In addition to replacing unsecure and limited email attachments or sending CDs via mail or courier, WATG now has file transfer capabilities with external partners and customers. Transfers are secure, across firewalls, and use the Internet. WATG has also automated paper-based processes to enhance management of documents and information in a mobile environment, moving its content management capability to the next level. As seen earlier, while capability improvements often are driven by a specific and initially quantifiable business need, the resulting capability improvement can have additional fringe benefits. Improving WATG's content management and collaboration infrastructure enabled switching on additional capabilities included in the platform. One of the more surprising outcomes for the company was how employees embraced the new wiki and blogs to capture and reuse project knowledge and information. Information no longer sits in project silos, and the employees (and the company) feel more productive and empowered. The $2 million U.S. WATG saved in automating manual processes was a nice outcome too.

One final example of how workforce mobility impacts how Agile an organization can be comes from *Ecole de Management de Lyon* (EM Lyon Business School).[14] As part of its mission to "educate entrepreneurs for the world," EM Lyon recognizes the importance of technology in business education.

Just as today's business workplace has become increasingly decentralized, with employees using technology to stay connected while working remotely, EM Lyon students need to remain in contact with peers and complete group projects while working at off-campus internships and other assignments. Students found this difficult using traditional desktop software and experimented with purely Internet-based but functionality- and security-limited alternatives. The school explored and implemented options for building a robust collaborative platform that would facilitate communication while also teaching students about real-world information-sharing strategies.

Before the new tools came on line, students were frustrated by the difficulties inherent in a distributed work environment. In these types of situations, it's always the weak link that creates problems. New capabilities based on an integrated collaboration platform allowed students to access tools from any location; they no longer need to be in the classroom or in the same location as colleagues to complete projects and assignments. Remote synchronization kept collaborations moving forward without losing or overwriting data. A variety of features enable virtual workgroups to function as cohesively as those who work face to face in traditional settings.

Not only these French students, but most people joining and leaving the academic world come to school digitally wired and expect the institutions and companies they work with and for to support their use of technology. Students often make the most of email, chat, and desktop applications but also need to process the expanding data formats that newer technologies leverage.

MAKING SUSTAINABILITY PART OF THE BOTTOM LINE

Throughout, we have looked closely at the impact technology management has on the economic bottom line. But maturing your IT infrastructure pays off in more ways than just in reduced cost or more effective businesses. Across different studies and consulting approaches, it becomes clear that organizations that are more resourceful with their traditional assets often have a positive impact on the environment as well.

More organizations are establishing their own tools to measure their ecological impact and reporting details openly to the public and their shareholders. Not only is awareness on the rise but so is the ability actually to analyze the impact of process and technology decisions. The key business drivers and needs we have seen when it comes to sustainability are:

- Reduce the carbon footprint by minimizing the environmental impact of technology.
- Measure and track internal resources and environmental impact goals.
- Support creation, management, and monitoring of compliance frameworks.
- Normalize corporate compliance with external environmental regulations.
- Respond to consumer expectations that industries take a holistic approach to sustaining the environment.
- Participate in business opportunities that sustain the environment.

Where Can Information Technology Help?

We have seen many examples of improvements in an organization's performance throughout this book. We can also consider the ecological impact on those organizations through the lens of infrastructure maturity. When the topic of sustainability hits the boardroom, these are the most frequent conversations:

- How can we better understand the business's carbon position, footprint, and liability?

- What are alternatives to in-person meetings to reduce cost and carbon footprint?
- How do we measure the performance and productivity of remote workers?
- How do we comply with environmental sustainability regulations? And what are they?
- What do others do? How can we learn about, share, and reevaluate opportunities to sustain the environment?
- How do we analyze and optimize not only our carbon footprint but that of the supply chain?

In its 2009 "Green IT" study, the analysts of Forrester documented that the conversations are in full swing.[15] Twenty-five percent of IT executives stated that their organizations were actively implementing green IT practices and an additional 61 percent were creating or currently considering green IT strategies. And there is investment behind it, with an estimated growth of 60 percent year over year for "Green IT Services."

Companies are realizing that "green means green." More sustainable computing operations are also more efficient and less costly. It is a very encouraging data point for all of us in the IT industry who have been promoting the energy savings and reduced total cost of ownership of more efficient hardware and software for several years. It's also a strong signal that cost reduction must stay at the center of any green-IT-related value proposition from supplier to customer.

The positive environmental impact of a mature IT infrastructure goes far beyond energy savings in the data center and across PCs and devices. However, it also raises new business challenges. For example, remote working scenarios reduce facility cost and emissions as well as commuting emissions and traffic. But performance management and collaboration styles are impacted, and companies need to adjust policies and possible team structures.

In our work with customers, we saw a direct correlation between IT maturity and environmental impact in these areas:

- Reduction in energy costs for PCs and data centers
- Reduced CO^2 footprint through reduction of travel
- Reduced CO^2 footprint through reduced space and space management requirements

- Increased efficiency in time and timing
- Reduced paper consumption
- Increased awareness and accountability through insight generation and reporting capabilities
- Increased diversity and inclusion of different work and lifestyles into the organization through more flexible work processes and environments

For organizations that look at these factors for their overall organization, estimating the projected impact of an IT and business capability improvement is actually relatively easy. Getting the people in charge of sustainability on board projects in the early phases ensures that both return on investment and environmental impact are part of the project analysis.

Companies are looking at a variety of ways to reduce their carbon footprint. Some focus on changing the way they manage their business, such as putting the infrastructure in place to enable a total migration to a paperless forms system to reduce paper waste and increase workflow efficiency. Others look at technologies that let them better manage their IT device environment. Newer technologies allow IT teams to switch on computers remotely overnight for a brief time in order to apply patches, eliminating disruptions to users during the day and saving on electricity each year. Other technologies enforce the shutdown of PCs and laptops when not in use. Virtualization technology reduces the need for computer hardware, power and cooling, and office space, for a more cost-effective, environmentally sound operation. A UC environment reduces communications and travel costs. The innovations and ideas are endless, and the companies with a mature IT infrastructure have a built-in lead in the race to become more environmentally sound.

NOTES

1. Cyrus Gibson et al., "Don't Waste a Crisis: Use the Economic Downturn to Lift IT's Business Value," *Harvard Business Review* (February 2009).
2. Kim S. Nash, "The State of the CIO 2008: The CIO's Time to Shine," *CIO* magazine, December 10, 2007.
3. Microsoft, "Ammunition Maker Uses Software-plus-Services to Boost Web Traffic and Sales," 2010.

4. Microsoft, "Pioneer Retailer Beats Online Sales Target by 50 Per Cent with E-Commerce Solution," 2009.
5. Microsoft, "Tourist Board Boosts Local Bookings by 120 Per Cent Using Mapping Technology," 2009.
6. Microsoft, "Tyson Foods Improves Collaboration and Business Insight, Creates Process Efficiencies," 2009.
7. Microsoft, "Contract Researcher Cuts Costs by 35 Percent with FDA-Compliant System," 2009.
8. Microsoft, "Pharmaceuticals Firm Cuts Costs and Streamlines Processes with Business Software," 2010.
9. Microsoft, "Defense Contractor Helps Save Lives and Sees 100 Percent ROI with ERP Solution," 2009.
10. Microsoft, "Firm Uses Internet Service Bus to Enable Smart Grid for Dynamic Energy Savings," 2009.
11. Microsoft, "Services Company Reduces Helpdesk Costs by U.S. $1 Million," 2010.
12. Microsoft, "Financial Institution Gains Efficiency with Automated Identity and Access Management," 2010.
13. Microsoft, "IT Group Gains Mobile Solution Estimated to Save up to 20 Percent in Operating Costs," 2010.
14. Microsoft, "Business School Enhances Student Learning with Collaboration Software," 2009.
15. Doug Washburn and Onica King, "Inquiry Spotlight: Green IT, Q1 2009," February 10, 2009, www.forrester.com/Research/Document/Excerpt/0,7211,48132,00.html; and Christopher Mines, "Market Overview: Green IT Services," April 24, 2009, www.forrester.com/Research/Document/Excerpt/0,7211,46824,00.html.

CHAPTER 6

ASSESSING YOUR SITUATION

My favorite ice-breaker in a business meeting came from a chief information officer (CIO) at a German media company. On our first meeting, I had barely introduced myself and my colleagues when he growled, "I don't know why I bought your software." Shareholders don't like to hear that company executives don't know why funds are spent. The *Financial Times* once stated that there would be two types of CIOs in the future—the ones who reduce costs and others who go a step further to innovate in their company's businesses. After this meeting, I thought they should have added a third type—the one who has no imagination, no vision, and soon no job.

Is this the CIO you want in charge of assessing your business strengths and weaknesses and making recommendations on how IT infrastructure supports innovation in your organization? Most think not. As a business owner, employee, or shareholder, you want the forward-thinking CIO who views IT infrastructure as your stealth bomber and road warrior rolled into one. You want a team of dedicated professionals who think a Basic and outdated IT infrastructure is for wimps and fiscally irresponsible. The goal is Rationalized or Dynamic—anything else doesn't make business sense and is unacceptable.

Not all IT projects need to focus on total change at once. Sometimes identifying a few capabilities to start with might be the right choices. An IT road map can engineer a one-time technology boost that allows a firm to catch up with capabilities a competitor has already mastered.

Recent technology changes also provide more flexibility and choice for the best path for an individual organization and its unique conditions. For example, virtualization technologies allow a company to consolidate physical resources like computer servers or deploy virtual machines on employee desktops. The control of the resources remains centralized with IT. Virtualization simplifies deployment and administration because fewer physical computers need to be managed, so an upgrade or fix to one affects many users but only limited hardware. Through virtualization in the data center, power use can be reduced and security and backup can be simplified. Many organizations are on the path to evaluate or are already leveraging virtualization technologies today. Not surprisingly, the topic is on many decision makers' minds these days. Understanding that their competitors were on the road to IT simplification, the CIO from a 2,500 employee manufacturing company wanted to meet with us to talk about virtualization technologies.

The CIO started the conversation by noting that most of his colleagues from other companies already had virtualization projects. What could Microsoft offer? He felt his team was behind the times and the competitors were moving ahead. How fast could his team catch up? What were their options? The customer here was ahead of the game because the company already was leveraging a platform strategy. After discussing the pros and cons of how Microsoft's virtualization technologies would roll right into the existing Microsoft infrastructure, a fast and effective way to meet the company's intentions was found. The solution would not only meet its immediate, competitive needs but also be a stepping-stone for future capability improvements in its customized road map.

Another IT road map for capability improvement came from the chief technology officer (CTO) of a car manufacturer. Managing the heterogeneous environment was consuming more and more of the scarce resources. The CTO wanted a long-term solution for the various platforms used within his organization. After an ability-based assessment of the current and desired capabilities, his team created a road map that took into consideration different aspects of infrastructure, such as employee desktop requirements and what type of desktop infrastructure would fit his users. It also covered server management, identity issues, integration efforts, application dependencies, migration cost, as well as business cases and cost savings. In this case, the result was a plan in sync with the business priorities that would increase infrastructure capabilities year after year. Utilizing the Microsoft Infrastructure Optimization (IO) methodology helped the final plan ensure clear project ownership, progress milestones, and results measurements.

So, let's go back to the CIO of the media company who did in fact keep his job. Fortunately, we had experience and content to bring to the table to help him and his team. We have seen people under similar pressures to justify their investments, strategies, and successes far too often. After this awkward and bumpy start to the conversation, we discussed the basic merits of his cost savings plan but also probed deeper to uncover actual business needs—not only for the IT team but for the media business itself. We mapped the insights against the IO model's capabilities. Upon seeing how IT capabilities actually could innovate business processes, the CIO agreed that his IT needs went beyond cost savings. The company's journalists were away from corporate headquarters for a month at a time but needed to access and send in information 24/7. Also, a small army of freelancers had to be integrated in the company's business processes somehow. Looming deadlines always added a frantic nature to a story, and the logistics complicated things even more. After using the IO model, it became clear in a structured (and less overwhelming) way that the company's current IT infrastructure simply didn't have the capabilities to support all the new requirements. As a next step, we agreed to help the team analyze the IT capabilities necessary to support the new business challenges. Based on the IO model and mentoring by our and other specialized consultants, the CIO's team created a multiyear infrastructure road map that showed the role the company's IT team and its leadership would play within the broader organization.

In thousands of these engagements over the years, we have seen that infrastructure road maps come in all sorts of forms. To be fully impactful, they need first to be based on a sound analysis of the business. Assessing where your business and your IT infrastructure are today informs where the business can go in the future. And as you have seen here and likely have experienced yourself, the people making that assessment can be moving you forward or holding you back.

Change is nearly always hard. Changes in business can be discomfiting, expensive, annoying, or just plain difficult to accomplish. So why would any manager make changes? Maintaining the status quo is, in most instances, the path of least resistance. But leaders take on change either to gain something for the company, such as new market share or a simpler balance sheet, or to avoid the pain they'll face if they continue in their current direction, such as product or organizational obsolescence. Tough economic times have the highest potential for change because the pain is greater, but the gain may be greater too. And while many businesses change things that are uncomfortable, the smartest ones go beyond removing discomfort to lay a foundation that fosters their capabilities to master future challenges and create opportunities for execution and growth.

WHERE IS YOUR STARTING POSITION?

Before hiring a consultant for a more in-depth analysis, it can be helpful to do a very informal back-of-the-envelope calculation and leverage available tools for an initial gut check. This way you can at least have the right numbers in place before you begin to work with a consultant. You can also schedule time with the other organization leaders for the initial assessment and to get them at least philosophically on board.

Very few companies have this data readily available in detail but often they have a pretty good idea of the ballpark numbers. Here are a few of the questions you should be asking before you plunge into real planning.

Productivity

- Does my company calculate productivity of knowledge workers?
- If so, how? And what is the amount per year and employees?
- If not, can I use an industry-comparable number for productivity?

- What is the age range of my workforce? As older workers retire, many companies see an increase in productivity as younger workers are more willing and able to embrace new productivity tools.
- If neither is available, what are my fully burdened cost per knowledge worker and my saving potential? In the United States, we often use $150,000 per year. To be clear, this is not about calculating a potential reduction in force. Assuming that all (or most) employees are generating value for the company today, this identified potential would actually grow the business.
- Apply a 10 to 40 percent productivity increase against this initial number for the likely bottom-line impact.

Sick Leave Cost

- Calculate it per employee, per year, or total for the organization. Sick leave reflects the corporate culture. Bad morale and bad management lead to high sick leave percentages. Companies that support a work-anywhere-anytime ethos typically see lower sick leave rates.
- Apply 2 to 20 percent of those costs as savings.

Attraction and Attrition

- Attraction: Here assess recruiting costs, including headhunters, relocation, sign-on grants, and so forth.
- Rate of attrition: Bad company morale definitely impacts attrition rates.
- Apply 5 to 30 percent of those costs as savings.

Office Space

- Real estate is a big cost-savings driver. However, lease contracts determine when and if you will be able to reduce costs.
- Apply 15 to 50 percent of those costs as savings.

Travel and Work Time

- Apply 5 to 30 percent of these costs as savings. Costs and potential savings depend on the nature of the organization. The structure of the sales force, global presence, and type of products all influence the numbers. The more mobile your workforce is, the greater the number of tools you will need to support them, but you can also realize greater savings.

Total Cost of Ownership of Workplace

- This is the total of direct capital investment in hardware and software plus indirect costs of installation, training, repairs, downtime, technical support, and upgrading. The single largest factor affecting total cost of ownership is staffing cost—60 percent, according to the IDC.[1] Recent IDC[2] research has shown that such technology initiatives coupled with organization-wide improvements in IT management processes can reduce IT labor costs by as much as 50 percent.
- Overall, factor a 25 to 30 percent savings through the capability upgrade.

Cost of Communication and Collaboration

- Where do your employees work—from a desk, in the hall, in meeting rooms, on-site with clients, from the airport, from home? What technology does your organization provide?
- How much do you spend on messaging costs: storage, third-party mobility, archiving, and backup solutions?
- If employees are spread across geographic areas, how do they communicate and conference: in person, over the phone, or not at all? Are they using the Web, video, and audio conferencing capabilities?
- Cost savings here are a worst-case scenario versus a best-case scenario. For the worst-case scenario, you have a legacy system that needs to be replaced. You will spend more initially as a necessary improvement. However, the investment pays off, and those companies can expect the best-case scenario cost savings of up to 25 or 30 percent.

IT and business optimization is a journey. The first step in moving forward is determining where you are today. It is always helpful to see examples of companies that have done in-depth studies into success factors in their sector. *Mastering Automotive Challenges* by Bernd Bottschalk and Ralf Kalmbach examines the German car market to better understand and show why German cars continually rank higher than other global brands.[3] The authors, two leading experts in the German automotive industry, describe the strategies that have led to the German industry's great success. They also discuss how German auto manufacturers are meeting challenges from emerging worldwide competitors. Their book outlines and explains the results and impact that can be achieved with first-class management, marketing, branding, and innovation and clear strategic aims.

Figure 6.1 shows what Bottschalk and Kalmbach list as High-Success and Low-Success indicators.

The pillars in this comparison are easy to understand. Many of us are car owners, and we expect the bullet points in the High column from a car manufacturer when we look to buy a new car. Getting into that category is sometimes a learning process. For example, customer knowledge can become outdated quickly, especially for companies entering a new market. Have you ever wondered why the cup holders in older German cars are so flimsy and feel like

High	Low
In-depth customer knowledge	Failure to identify fundamental trends
A clear vision and clear goals	Failure to redesign systems (too little or too late)
A long-term perspective	No long-term corporate strategy
A strong focus on customer loyalty	A lack of vision
Consistent delivery on the promise of value for money	No distinct profile
Consistently high quality	Failure to deliver value for money
A global presence but a regional orientation	Inconsistent brand management
An entrepreneurial spirit	A lack of entrepreneurial courage
Early warning system	No early warning systems

Figure 6.1 High- and Low-Success Factors

Source: Bernd Gottschalk and Ralf Kalmbach, *Mastering Automotive Challenges* (London: Kogan Page, 2007), p. 42.

an afterthought? Well, they were just that. The concepts of a cup holder and cruise control in a car were completely foreign to the experience of German vehicle engineers but necessary for cars going into the U.S. market. Both features make perfect sense for the long-distance highway driving common in the United States and are expected by U.S. consumers but are virtually unused and unknown to the German driving and traffic patterns. The engineers from Swabia and Bavaria had to expand their horizon and understanding of what U.S. customers need to close this knowledge gap. Thriving organizations understand the importance of success indicators—cup holders and cruise control—and are self-critical about improving against them.

But even organizations with a self-critical culture rarely look systematically for challenges or optimization potential in the Low column. When utilizing a capability-based assessment and planning approach, both highs and lows are often identified, as they map well to the IO matrix discussed in Chapter 3.

This matrix gives companies a baseline of where they are today. An organization doesn't rate itself as good, bad, or ugly. It simply measures IT infrastructure and capabilities across a common set of questions. This measurement enables you to classify your IT capabilities across a common set of question. It's interesting to look at how some automakers companies rank on the Basic to Dynamic maturity continuum. As you look at Figure 6.2, keep in mind the highs and lows from Figure 6.1 and consider how companies avoid the lows and reach the highs by using their IT infrastructure. For privacy reasons, we have not listed the company names, but these are true assessments done by IT departments and experts.

While the assessment looks at IT capabilities, it is interesting to notice that the maturity on a capability level often correlates with the company's business focus on supply chain management, just-in-time production, or product offering expansion strategy. For example, Company A has definitely invested resources into developing its IT infrastructure to support business processes. It has also put a particular focus on developing sound business intelligence capabilities, leveraging the data existing in the organization and its processes. Company B is working to move away from Basic to Standardized maturity overall and has put some resources into improving its data management.

Core Infrastructure – Automotive					
Capability	**Sub Capability**	**Basic**	**Standardized**	**Rationalized**	**Dynamic**
Identity and Access Management	Identity and access management	● ◆ ○	■		
Desktop, Devices, and Server Management	Desktop management	●	■ ◆ ○		
	Mobile device management	■ ● ◆ ○			
	Server management	● ◆	■ ○		
	Virtualization	◆ ○	■ ●		
Security and Networking	Security and networking	■ ● ◆ ○			
Data Protection and Recovery	Data protection and recovery		■ ● ◆ ○		
Security Process	Security process	◆	● ○	■	
ITIL/COBIT-based Management Process	ITIL/COBIT-based management process		■ ◆ ○	●	
Business Productivity – Automotive					
Collaboration	Collaborative workspace and portals	◆	■ ● ○		
	Social computing	■ ● ◆ ○			
Enterprise Content Management	Documents and records management	◆ ○	■ ●		
	Forms	■ ○	● ◆		
	Web content management		■ ◆	●	○
Business Intelligence	Performance measurement	■ ○	●	◆	
	Reporting and analysis		● ○	◆	■
	Data warehousing		◆	● ○	■
Unified Communications	Messaging	■ ● ◆	○		
	Instant messaging/presence	◆ ○	●	■	
	Conferencing	○	■ ◆	■ ●	
	Voice	●	■ ◆ ○		
Enterprise Search	Enterprise search	● ○	■	◆	

Company A ■ Company B ● Company C ◆ Company D ○

Figure 6.2 Automotive Infrastructure Maturity Comparisons

Companies C and D, however, are just plain behind in their use of technology versus their competitors.

ANALYZING WHERE YOU WANT TO GO

Once you determine where you are today, you can begin the process of mapping out where you want to go. In December 2009 I was invited by an IT organization to give a speech about IT technical trends and cost reduction. I was told that I shouldn't talk about products and technologies; the audience was management and business decision makers.

In searching for the right introduction for the presentation, the movie *Christopher Columbus: The Discovery* came to mind. Columbus was the perfect match for today's manager in IT. There are many new topics, ideas, and technologies arriving on the horizon. Like Columbus, IT managers have to define and find the New World. Columbus never built ships, and his primary skill wasn't as a good sailor. He was a visionary commander and his foundation was navigation.

Navigation is one of the most important skill sets of today's IT managers. You know where you are and you know where you want to be. And you have the skills and knowledge to create a map that gets you to your goals.

Part of the navigation process is doing a complete business analysis, focusing on change requests from business; identifying, collecting, and understanding the requirements expressed by business; and ensuring change is in line with the IT capability road map. As Gartner has put it:

> The process enablement team's primary relationship will be with the users and super-users of the business community. This team will play a critical role in the development, measurement and performance of service-level agreements, and will assume the primary responsibility for developing and prioritizing the [business] requirements for other teams.[4]

The discipline, therefore, will contribute to continuous improvement along the company's value chain. Many IT decision makers today understand the demand and arm themselves with tools and knowledge traditionally used by the MBAs.

Key responsibilities of the business analysis discipline in IT impact on a business are:

- Understand strategic goals and objectives of the business.
- Work with the business to identify, collect, and understand its requirements.
- Outline the business scenarios for resolving business pain points and driving new ways of working.
- Define success measures.

As a recent study by the *CIO* Executive Board[5] shows, engaging with the business is the most important IT governance capability; it is also the least developed.

DEFINE WHERE YOU WANT TO BE

After understanding your starting point and your business priorities well, the project can move into the next phase: defining the desired or needed project end state and prioritizing capability improvements.

When writing this book, I sometimes felt like the writers in *Car & Driver* or *Road & Track* magazine, who often have to defend themselves against accusations of having a positive bias toward BMW. The cars from Munich are often category winners and used as benchmarks for their segments. But a key reason why I can refer to BMW in this book on business and IT agility so frequently is simply that its teams have, over the years, done an outstanding job in continuously assessing optimization potential and leveraging technology to do so. On a beautiful Bavarian summer day in 2005, we had an interesting meeting with one of the strategic architects at BMW in Munich. One of his team's key responsibilities is to identify business trends in the automotive sector, assess the business units of BMW in terms of obstacles and challenges, talk to IT analysts and leading IT companies to learn about the area of automotive challenges, and be aware of IT trends that could help to address these challenges. In BMW, once the team is ready to get a project going, it secures support and sponsorship from the business. Then a build department is set up and runs prototypes to evaluate if there are any obstacles that might lead to changes in the IT infrastructure.

The build department not only runs prototypes but also performs cost calculations and creates operation guidelines with the operation department. Their intention is to reduce costs as much as possible and speed up the time it takes to deploy the technology or solution. For BMW, defining where it wants to be starts with the business case and proceeds in a highly directed path, focused on delivering the planned result in a meaningful, timely manner. For many readers, this isn't exciting news. But you might be surprised how many of your peers in other IT departments are not organizing their projects around a structured and repeatable process to first test, then build, and finally implement and run.

I've talked to hundreds of IT managers who told me that of course they have an IT planning department doing work like the one just mentioned. Unfortunately, in some companies, the planning process can take years to complete. Meanwhile, the technology has changed, or the competition has already deployed a solution; or worse, both of these things have happened and your plans still sit in committee.

Planning IT is a crucial part of the IT departments work, but the real business value comes when those plans become actual projects in the business units. In other words, the value of your new world arises when you've reached it, not when you talk about it.

Of course, every development scenario has natural forcing and blocking forces. Moving you toward your goal would be cost savings, technology capabilities, competitor actions, and market trends. Blockers would be a desire to save money in the short term by not spending it on new software, equipment, and training.

IMPACT Planning

Is there a way to learn from successful organizations, standardizing the process from assessment to solution, and empowering as many people as possible to leverage the insights and methodologies? A growing ecosystem of service organizations out there sure think so.

People—employees, partners, customers—are a top focus area for an organization to realize its business strategy. Technology is the number-one enabler for organizations to mobilize their people. We have also seen that amazing results are possible when people and technology are successfully combined. The Microsoft marketing machine calls this People Readiness and The-People Ready Business. A proven model of assessment and planning that helps get companies people ready is called IMPACT: How to Build a People-Ready Business.

IMPACT's co-creator Ilco van der Bie describes the approach as "a structured methodology to create synergy between people and technology." IMPACT leverages multiple assessment and insight tools and enables organizations to make technology the accelerator of organizational change. It is really about three things:

1. **Change has multiple formats and drivers**, but it is people who will make or break a successful change program.
2. **Every organization is different**, but the activities that people perform are more or less the same.
3. **Change is about big things**, but these big things are in fact many small steps that are correlated.

To drive change, we need to focus on the behavior and changing capabilities of people. If people change their behavior, the organization will change. We know that people tend to change their everyday way of doing things very slowly. So unless a dramatic event forces people to change, technology changes must align to their everyday activities. And changes are made methodically and step by step. To make sure these changes are adopted and internalized, a change must bring instant or short-term benefits.

IMPACT focuses on people's everyday activities and changes that can support these activities. Change also is designed to bring immediate and measurable effects. Everyday activities have three basic elements:

1. **People** who perform the activities
2. **Place** where the activities are performed
3. **Technology** that is used to perform the activities

IMPACT balances and maximizes the synergy among these three. *Technology* is the accelerator of change and determines the dependencies toward *People* and *Place*.

How to Use IMPACT

While most of us think or feel that our organization is fundamentally different from others, as an organization we first must acknowledge the 80 percent similarities between organizations and the people who form them. Of course, the content of organizations is totally different, but the activities that the people perform are the same. For example, an oil company does something completely different from a financial institution. However, the people within these organizations go to meetings, read their email, search for information and expertise, design products, and so on. These are the everyday activities.

If we agree that people are the focus and activities are comparable across organizations, then driving change by changing everyday behaviors is done in the same manner, regardless of industry. There is only about a 20 percent difference in activities between organizations in different industries. Keeping the 80/20 rule in mind, making quantum leaps in the 80 percent are likely to pay off handsomely.

Once organizations acknowledge the possibility to leverage what is working somewhere else, they need to get to get the right stakeholders and decision makers at the same table. The catalyst for change can vary—a move to a new building, new technology, a big crisis, an aging workforce, and so on. These are all major factors, so any organizational change program will involve multiple senior stakeholders. These stakeholders all have different views, opinions, and starting points. The big challenge is to acknowledge these differences and, at the same time, make them work toward the same future. The one constant in all of this is "people."

People perform activities related to their *work style*. For example, one work style is "supportive with high predictability of job." In a production-driven environment, this could be a machine operator or a painter. In a knowledge-driven environment, this would be a call-center agent or executive assistant. Another work style is "technical role." This is pretty self-explanatory and would cover engineers, product installers, or developers. An engineer's activities are different from a painter's and so on. We call these work styles *persona*.

The activities take place within a *scenario*. It could be an individual scenario, such as email or project management, or a collaborative scenario, such as a conference call or project meeting. Within each scenario, our personas use specific *tools*, such as email or project management software. Personas and scenarios are fundamental to making change understandable and tangible. And it is important to remember that people look at change through the lens of their jobs or scenarios.

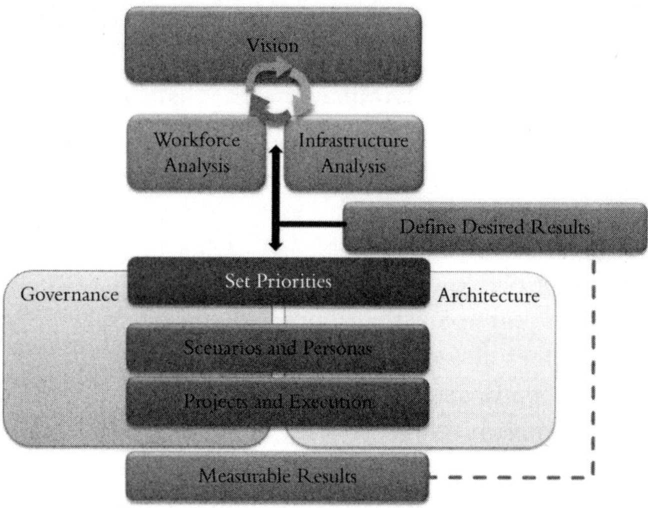

Figure 6.3 IMPACT Model

For example, a CIO asks how an investment in a new platform can deliver real value, beyond cost cutting. A Human Resources director wants to know if the change supports people working from home, an office, or the airport. A facility manager needs the change to support the idea of open space to help reduce the amount of office space required. A business manager demands that the change helps her salespeople be more productive by reducing common internal tasks. A CFO wants to know how the change is going to affect the bottom line. These are all different reasons why an organization wants to change—all different opinions and interests.

Change can happen in *any kind of sequence.* Why any kind of sequence? The rationale behind the change can be completely different for each stakeholder. Having all the building blocks in place is much more important than the sequence. Vision, IO, and Workforce Analysis are the key building blocks of the IMPACT model (see Figure 6.3).

- The **Vision** visualizes and clarifies the way the organization should operate in the future. How will people work, what will the customers experience, what is the partner, and business ecosystem, and so forth. Technology will never drive a vision, but will enable and probably slightly adjust the vision.

- The **Workforce Analysis** shows what the workforce is actually doing and what the possible accelerators and blockers of change.
- The **Infrastructure Analysis** shows what the current status of the technology.
- The **Business Case** shows the financial value of the whole change.

Once building blocks are in place, stakeholders can create a comprehensive, multiyear road map. Figure 6.4 provides a detailed look into the actual steps and components of each block. Remember, the three blocks can be developed on separate paths but consolidate and influence each other in the process.

Once these three major tasks are completed, the organization can move forward on the real nuts and bolts of its plan. Figure 6.5

Building blocks	Deliverable	How	Benefits
Vision	Vision document that describes how your organization's world of work will change between now and five years—and what to do, based on available technologies and best practices	Interviews with stakeholders in business and IT	Vision and road map to realize this vision where people, processes, and technology are directed toward company goals
Infrastructure Analysis	Assessment of the current infrastructure and how that relates to the ambition level defined in the vision document	Infrastructure optimization profile Gap analysis	Clear insight in the current status of technology and processes Recommendations on next steps (immediate and longer term) to realize benefits and cost savings and align IT with business goals
Workforce Analysis	Assessment of the current readiness and skills sets of people and people-driven processes and how they relate to the ambition level defined in the vision document	Workforce assessment based on skills, readiness, and ambition level by Factor 4 Index or Productivity Impact Measurement Interviews or survey from workforce Gap analysis	Clear insight in the current status of people readiness Recommendations on next steps (immediate and longer term) to align IT to enable and empower people to realize personal and company goals

Figure 6.4 Components of IMPACT Building Blocks

Building Blocks	Deliverable	How	Benefits	Duration
Define Desired Results	Business case—how will recommended changes affect strategic metrics like cost, productivity, time to market, etc.?	Rapid economic justification Business case with recommendations related to infrastructure, solutions, people Hard, quantifiable metrics based on customer specific, strategic objectives Soft, people- and process-defined results	Cost savings Improved people achievements Alignment of people, processes and technology Measurement tooling	1–2 months
Set Priorities	Definition of priorities based on the Impact Analysis Tool (balance impact on people, business, short-versus long-term results and cost involved)	Impact analysis Balanced scorecard Quick wins list	Tool to take well-balanced decisions about IT and workforce-related issues Recommendations based on quantifiable metrics	1–4 weeks
Scenarios and Personas	Description of the way of work (tasks and activities) of people (roles) in the organization. These are archetypical situations, not directly related to the current organizational structure or existing job descriptions.	Scenario and persona descriptions High-level solution overview	Picture of the future of work within the company Recommendations on measures to be taken and solutions to be built	2 weeks per scenario
Projects and Execution	Execution: realization of the scenarios—People, Processes, and Technology	Developed and implemented solutions End user adoption training	People-ready IT environment Skilled employees to get maximum value out of IT investments	On request
Governance	Guidance during the implementation process	Road map planning Program management Resource to monitor process Center of excellence	Making sure projects are executed on time and on budget	Continuously
Architecture	Definition of the necessary IT infrastructure	Example environment Quick plans Reference architecture Risk management Best practices	Making sure solutions are built supporting the infrastructure of the future	Continuously
Measurable Results	Through all phases and measurement, monitoring and assessment of metrics set	Progression report with metrics Recommendations and guidance	Demonstration of success	Continuously

Figure 6.5 Sample IMPACT Project Overview

outlines the level of projects that will help the customer organization to become more Agile. The indicated project durations are based on typical length within a large organization.

Let's look more closely at workforce analysis. This is an assessment of the current readiness and skills set of people and people-driven processes within your organization and how that relates to the ambition level defined in your vision document. Understanding your workforce is more than just knowing people's names, ages, and titles. To do a truly in-depth analysis of your employees, you need to look at a multitude of factors: where they work, what their job-related challenges are, how predictable their work is, what tools they use, and even with whom they really work. Figure 6.6 gives you a good idea of the scope of your analysis.

As part of a complete IMPACT study, we are using the Factor 4 workplace study. The Factor 4 Index is a tool that lets a company understand the barriers that keep employees from being successful in their jobs.[6] Many people in organizations have their own ideas about how they can work more efficiently and how to make the best of their abilities. Studies show that people would gladly increase their productivity, but they encounter a number of barriers in the process. These barriers can be found in the four spheres:

1. **Inspiration**. The degree to which people are inspired to make the most of their abilities
2. **Organization**. The manner in which the organization is structured
3. **Culture**. The manner in which people within an organization treat one another
4. **Technology**. The degree to which technology is supportive

The Factor 4 Index has been developed to measure the ambitions of companies and their employees with regard to these four dimensions. The index is based on a series of 64 statements, categorized according to the four spheres. Each sphere has four categories. Each category consists of four statements. For every statement, participants are asked to indicate their own experience regarding a certain aspect of operational management and what they would like to see happen in that area.

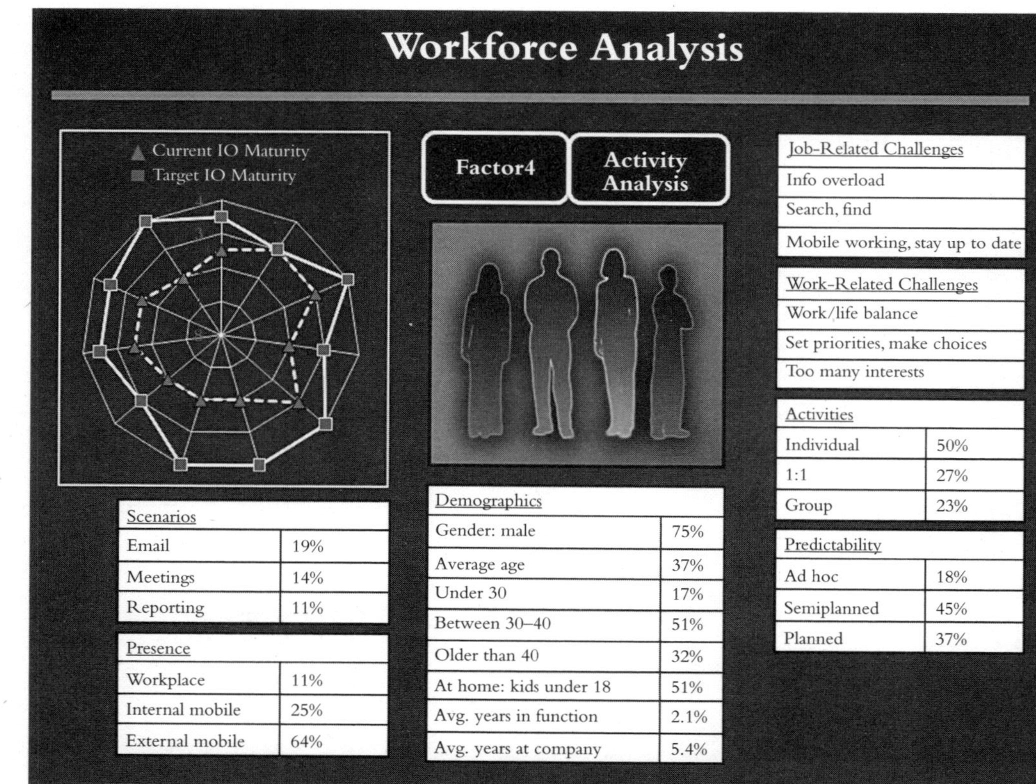

Figure 6.6 In-Depth Workforce Analysis

You now have your vision and a good understanding of your workforce, but without the infrastructure in place to support the vision and people, you won't get far. In Chapter 3, we looked at the IO maturity model. We are coming back to it now. The IO assessment is your starting point to assess what tools you have and what tools you will need.

Company ABC, our fictional example, completed the online IO assessment tool at www.microsoft.com/optimization/tools/overview.mspx. Like many other organizations, much of ABC's core capabilities (shown in Figure 6.7) and business productivity capabilities (shown in Figure 6.8) are at a Basic level. However, its enterprise content management, enterprise search, and reporting, as well some Core IO, are in a Standardized level and for the protection of their information the current level is even Rationalized. In the next step, the capabilities are prioritized, including against competitive threat, risk exposure, and business priorities. For this organization, improvement of collaboration infrastructure and portals are a key priority, as is the ability to manage and access information. In determining those as first-priority capability improvements and leveraging a standard platform for the implementation. Provisioning additional capabilities, such as social computing and dashboard, is nearly free, as the necessary infrastructure in hardware and software and processes is already implemented. So these second-priority capabilities are added to the first phase of the improvement projects.

The team goes through a similar thought process when planning the necessary messaging/mail and instant messaging upgrade. Again, choosing an easily extensible messaging platform that provides these two capabilities will give the organization the infrastructure to add integrated conferencing and voice capability relatively easily. As contracts with existing providers of these technologies are not up for renewal for two years, the customer decides to roll out the integrated functionality in a second phase of the improvement project.

WHERE TO BEGIN?

Where to begin is a tough question regardless of the size of your company or the complexity of the project. Company ABC has set strategic

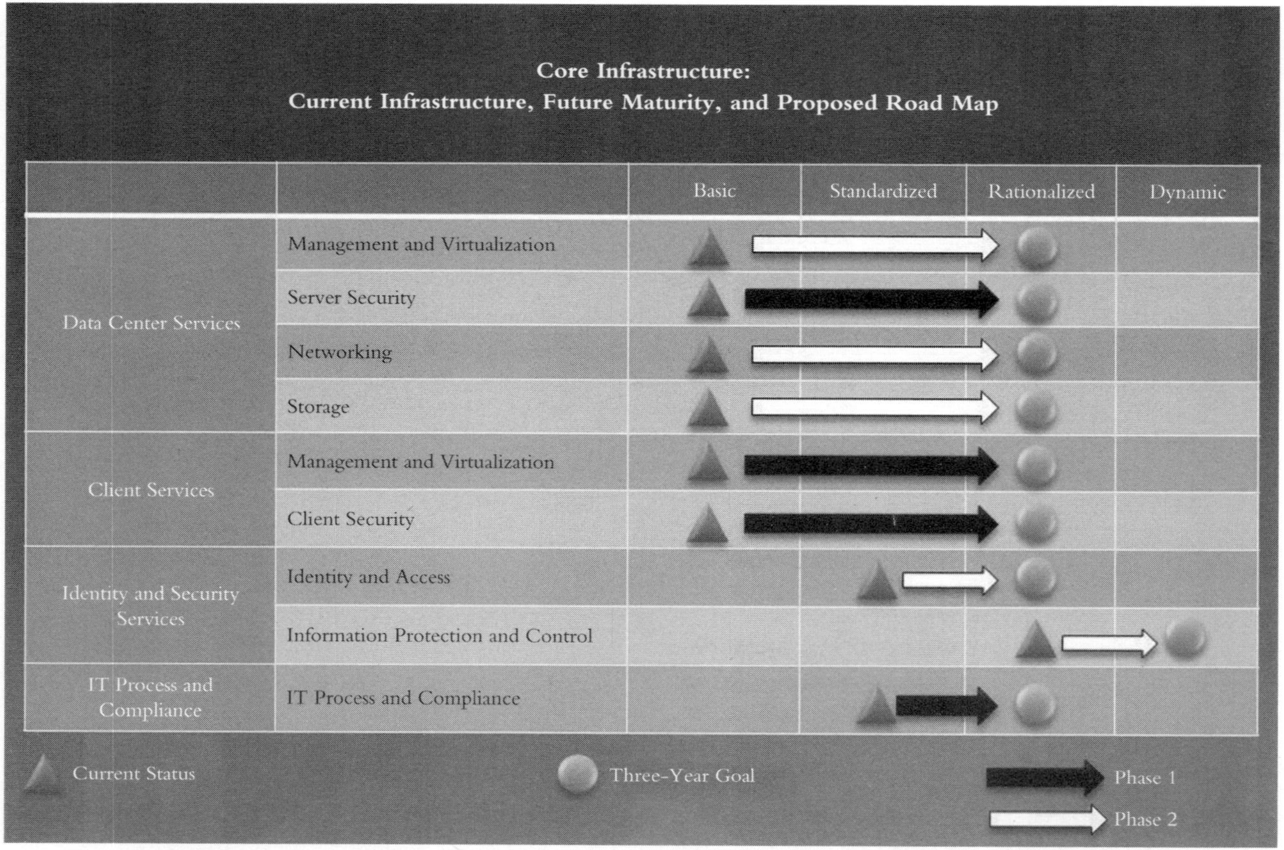

Figure 6.7 Core Infrastructure Assessment and Planning Example

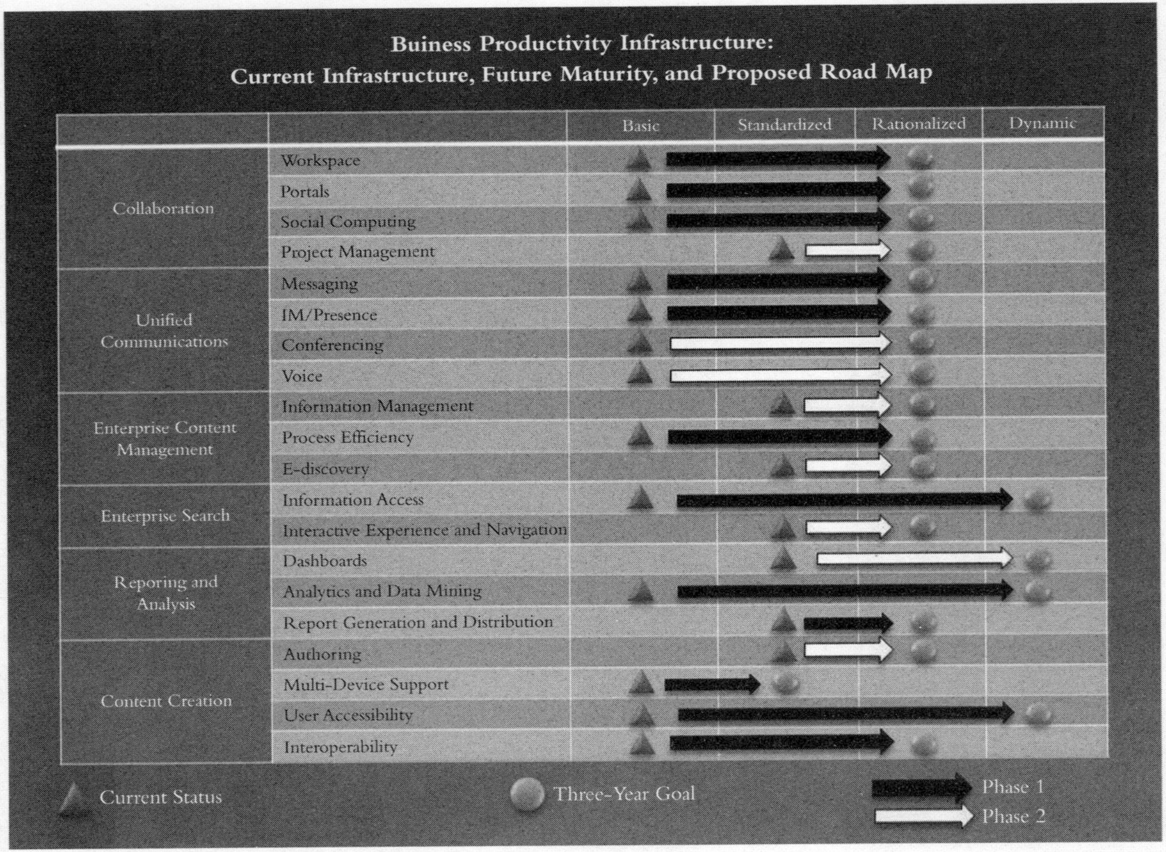

Figure 6.8 Business Productivity Infrastructure Assessment and Planning Example

goals that will color all priority decisions. It needs to boost revenues but cannot do it by adding more costs. It will focus on improving processes surrounding communications and collaboration but also needs to reduce the complexity of how individuals and teams work together. Time to market in its business sector is continually getting shorter, so it needs to boost productivity in a number of areas. ABC has created a list of possible measures and how it will measure success with all projects. IT has also looked at the complexity of IT solutions, the time it will take to adopt the technology, and the time to implement new tools and processes. The IT department wants to find the sweet spot that will give them a few quick wins while it also focuses on longer-term strategic processes. Since cost is a huge issue with this company, getting the most bang for its IT buck is critical.

The gap analysis shows that our fictional company aims to make the greatest advances by having a unified communications and collaboration strategy—and with good reason. Without a unified communications strategy, a company is powerless to stay competitive in today's business climate.

This is especially true in the financial services sector. In Chapter 3 we looked briefly at *Bank of America Bank* (BOA); we will now analyze it further. BOA is one company that set a goal of developing a mature IO infrastructure capable of supporting advanced communication and collaboration processes. To recap, BOA has more than 18,000 ATMs and nearly 3 million active online banking users. It serves one in two households in the United States, and its retail footprint covers 80 percent of the U.S. population. It also serves 59 million consumer and small business clients. These numbers are impressive enough by themselves. But in 2008, with the acquisition of Countrywide and Merrill Lynch, BOA grew to over 300,000 employees. Email is the communication channel, not only within the company but to its customers as well. After the mergers, it was crystal clear that BOA's aging messaging infrastructure could not handle the communication flow, let alone support its need for 99.999% availability. In addition, federal regulations require BOA to archive roughly 100,000 of their 320,000 mailboxes located across five data centers in the United States. Market pressures and budgetary constraints further complicate the communications issue.

Email is a business-critical communication channel. "People in this company frequently communicate with customers through email.

In some cases, it's the only way we communicate with customers. If we don't have functioning email, then people can't respond to customers in a timely manner. The last thing we want is failed interaction," says Allan Tagg, the Senior Vice President Global Messaging Executive at Bank of America.

While other business executives in stormy waters are trying hard not to rock the boat, BOA set a clear course and steamed full speed ahead. It combined the just-released versions of Microsoft Exchange Communications Server and Office to improve its current and now combined and integrated messaging system. Was it worth it? Did the change impact the business negatively? The opposite is true. Across the board, BOA has seen improvements in communications and collaboration capabilities company-wide. It was great for day-to-day business operations, but the IT department is especially pleased with the numerous ways the solution has cut costs. The new system takes fewer resources to manage but still provides a high level of availability and disaster recovery. A Database Availability Group reduces the use of tape backups, cutting backup costs by about 25 percent.

NOTES

1. Randy Perry and Al Gillen, "Demonstrating Business Value: Selling to Your C-Level Executives," IDC, 2007.
2. Al Gillen, Randy Perry, and Seana Dowling, "Optimizing Infrastructure: The Relationship between IT Labor Costs and Best Practices for Managing Windows Servers" (January 2008).
3. Bernd Gottschalk and Ralf Kalmbach, *Mastering Automotive Challenges* (London: Kogan Page, 2007).
4. Gartner 2003.
5. *CIO* Executive Board, "Driving High-Value Business Decisions," 2008.
6. www.factor4index.com.

CHAPTER 7

MAKING IT HAPPEN

Over the years, I have seen many IT leaders, as well as many business decision makers, struggling to make sense of the changes in our industry and how to take advantage of them. It sometimes feels as if a cloud of resignation had surrounded smart people, making them feel more comfortable putting their heads in the sand instead of trying to clear the dense fog of rapid change.

It is not because a lack of will. Many of these businesspeople simply didn't know where to start: how to identify areas of impact and how to prioritize them. The people on the other side—the software, hardware, and services sales folks—know their core competencies but are not as knowledgeable about trends and resources that affect specific businesses or industries. And let's be honest: Most people in the IT industry make their money by selling products and services to you. They need to pay their mortgages and ensure that their kids have food on the table too. Many—but not all—aren't paid to spend time consulting and strategizing with you on how to leverage the technology advances. Most salespeople are coin operated. Their motivation is not working with you on organizational process improvement. Selling their products and services is their goal.

Technology and resources are forcing a change to this model. I truly believe that effective use of limited resources allows organizations, individuals, and society to achieve a higher potential level. It's not about spending more; it's about spending wisely. This is a belief shared by some in the industry and academic world, and I have had the privilege of working with some of them throughout my career. Over the last five years, it was a great experience to witness how much effort people like Paul Lidbetter, Principal Strategy Consultant for Microsoft Strategy and Architecture Consulting, or Samm DiStasio, Senior Director for Microsoft's Infrastructure Business Architecture, and his team invested in improving the Microsoft Infrastructure Model. They have developed great insights into infrastructure maturity and created customer and partner enablement tools, sharing them freely with customers and the ecosystem.

What surprised me quite a bit over the years is how relatively few organizations fully leveraged the tools and guidance available to them. I was always surprised how few participated in educational opportunities or used the resources available beyond the initial assessment that was often driven by salespeople to identify product and services sales opportunities. I've covered the initial situation assessment to identify the best starting points in Chapter 6. Now let's look at the next steps of driving actual organizational capability improvement, looking at the usual challenges and how to mitigate, overcome, or circumvent them. In the next few chapters I'll share with you some powerful tools and best practices to leverage. I'd like to take the fear out of the journey and work with you to identify the steps and milestones on the way to reaching your organization's goals.

You are not alone on this journey. In addition to literature and tools, there are thousands of partners in the industry who are capable and motivated to help you on this journey. They know the methodologies outlined here and how they create agility in an organization. Just remember, though, that independent advice is rarely free; we consultants have mortgages and hungry kids too.

An excellent starting point to learn more about the infrastructure optimization process is the Innovation Value Institute (IVI).[1] The IVI is a consortium of leading industry, consulting, not-for-profit, and academic organizations that has been developing and testing innovative ways to align IT investments with business results. The group's key members include such companies as Microsoft, Chevron, SAP, BP, Ernst & Young, and Boston Consulting Group.

The IVI has published its execution-planning-focused IT Capability Maturity Framework (IT-CMF) to guide an organization in developing a concise road map to optimize business value derived from IT investments. The holistic framework approach of the IT-CMF is shown through four macro processes: Managing the IT Budget, Managing the IT Capability, Managing IT for Business Value, and Managing IT like a Business.

BIG-PICTURE GOALS DURING CHANGE

Bringing maturity to your IT infrastructure and agility to your business processes often can seem complicated and even overwhelming. But as we have seen over the last years, it is a necessary step if your organization plans on maintaining market share or winning in new markets. The Infrastructure Optimization (IO) Model guides your maturity road map, but what happens when you start the actual deployment? How do you keep employees productive during the change? Are your systems going to remain safe and secure as you change infrastructures? Are costs going to spiral out of control before you reach your business goals? As you begin to make it happen, your team needs to keep its eyes on the big picture so business does not stall or grind to a halt. The synergistic effects of capability improvements become clear when we look at actual organizations and their projects. We can look at the challenges they faced and not only see how they overcame those but learn how the process created a far more Agile organization, ready to take advantage of the next big thing as soon as it comes along.

Keeping Employees Productive

Few people know that Microsoft invests between $700 million and $1 billion into the development of productivity software for every new version. Assuming that the money is put to some good use, the resulting products should be far more powerful and empowering for the actual users with every new version. And, fortunately, research confirms that not only does every version increase customer satisfaction and customers' assessment of their own productivity, but they actually are realizing higher improvements than they originally expected when they made the decision to upgrade. However, for many organizations, the upgrade of an Office version or any desktop application is a huge and costly challenge.

Here is where process and IT maturity make the difference again. IDC estimates that desktop upgrades in a Standardized environment cost only 20 to 33 percent of those implemented within a Basic desktop management infrastructure.[2] For IT organizations with a Rationalized infrastructure, those costs can be expected to be reduced by another staggering 66 percent. If we add these numbers up, IT departments moving from the Basic to a Rationalized Desktop Management infrastructure can expect to save 90 percent of their previous desktop upgrade cost when migrating going forward.

Atlanta, Georgia, is home to several large corporations. We are all familiar with Coca-Cola, but you can also find *Cox Communications* there. Cox is a multiservice broadband communications and entertainment company offering digital video, high-speed Internet, and telephony services to 6.2 million customers. The company employs 26,000 people. Employee computers are spread over 20 offices. The central IT group in Atlanta deploys and manages all computers, but each site maintains its own IT and help-desk staffs who are responsible for deploying and supporting the applications and services needed by their office.

"With the current economy, everyone at Cox is being asked to do more with less," says Chip Gandy, Senior Systems Administrator on the Cox Communications Atlanta IT staff. "We are driving standardization and automation wherever possible to reduce desktop support costs."[3] Cox IT refreshes 8,000 of the firm's client computers annually. Deploying operating systems and applications to a new computer took 4 hours, which added up to 32,000 hours of work. The team spent another 500 hours annually performing application compatibility testing.

Cox looked at a software solution that would allow their IT team to use virtualization capabilities to install software more efficiently. Whereas the typical application takes 30 to 60 minutes to deploy manually, streaming applications take minutes. The annual time savings from deploying just two popular applications, Microsoft Office Project and Microsoft Office Visio, to 800 users is more than 300 hours. The IT staff can also upgrade applications and security updates without disrupting user productivity. Marcus Oh, a Lead System Administrator at Cox Communications, remarks, "Employees are no longer sidelined while we update their computers. They can continue doing whatever they're doing and let all that happen in the background."

The IT changes that keep employees productive in the office have also impacted call-center and mobile workers. "Virtual application delivery really benefits our call-center workers, because they're able to move from machine to machine and have the applications they need," Gandy adds. "This saves a lot of time when they're taking customer calls. We're able to make mobile users more productive by making them independent of specific computers."

The changes Cox Communications developed are part of a typical desktop optimization plan. Companies with a mature IT infrastructure often look to desktop optimization as a way to keep employees productive regardless of where they are in a deployment cycle. An organization can use desktop optimization to take its Core Infrastructure Optimization (IO) from a Basic to a Rationalized or Dynamic level and realize tremendous savings and give its employees the better tools they need and want. Because the desktop is the interface of many of the business capabilities we are discussing here, managing it maturely is absolutely essential. With hundreds of millions of people using Windows and Office and the feedback that comes with it, it is fair to assume that Microsoft knows a thing or two about managing those applications. All the experience has been packaged for IT departments and partners to freely use and was a key cornerstone for the first iteration of the IO Model. It still is a key capability that no organization should neglect. Figure 7.1 outlines the best practices for desktop optimization and what each practice looks like along the maturity continuum.[4] Desktop optimization is really about providing an infrastructure that helps organizations control costs, improve systems availability, and enable greater business agility.

Keeping Systems Safe and Secure

The threats for an organization from the Internet are nearly as old as the commercial use of the technology. Mitigating the risks is a key priority, just as it has been for any risk to an organization in the past. However, the risk continually morphs into new threats as hackers and criminals work to stay one step ahead of a company's IT team. The

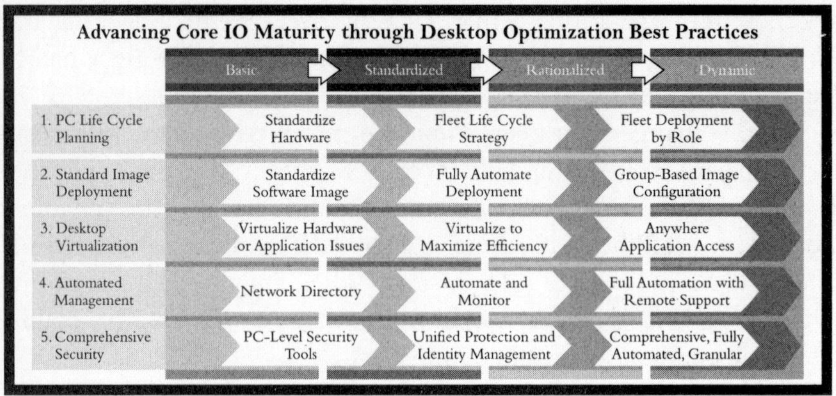

Figure 7.1 Desktop Optimization Best Practices

head of the IT department of the British MI-5 summarized it several years ago pretty well: "The only secure computer is anchored in concrete, in a completely sealed room with no connection to the outside world. Everything else is unsecure, but we have to make informed decisions how much risk is acceptable for a specific environment."

Consider the next data from the most recent *Microsoft Security Intelligence Report*:[5]

- The most significant trend in the first half of 2009 was the large increase in worm infections detected in many countries and regions worldwide.
- In the United States, the United Kingdom, France, and Italy, trojans were the largest single category of threat; in China, several language-specific browser-based threats were prevalent; in Brazil, malware targeting online banking was widespread; and in Spain and Korea, worms dominated, led by threats targeting online gamers.
- Phishing attacks are on the rise due primarily to a large increase in phishing attacks targeting social networking sites. Financial institutions, social networks, and e-commerce sites remain favored targets for phishing attempts. Researchers also observed some diversification into other types of institutions, such as online gaming sites, Web portals, and large software and telecommunications companies.
- Worms rose from fifth place in the second half of 2008 to become the second-most prevalent category in the first half of 2009.

- The prevalence of password stealers and monitoring tools also rose.
- The top category for data loss through a security breach continued to be stolen equipment, such as laptop computers (30 percent of all data-loss incidents reported), accounting for twice as many incidents as intrusion.

Companies cannot afford to have a Basic IT infrastructure when it comes to security. There are tools and processes organizations can choose to gain necessary IT capabilities. They can implement and manage processes themselves, have a service provider take care of it, or even have the capability delivered from a remote data center in the cloud.

Headquartered in Pune, India, *KPIT Cummins* specializes in consulting, solutions, and services in the fields of finance, accounts, and manufacturing. KPIT Cummins used multiple antivirus solutions and antispamming applications to protect its computers, email boxes, and database repositories from viruses, worms, trojan horses, and spam mails. Unfortunately, the results were not very satisfactory, and employees and executives experienced some nasty surprises. The time and resources the company's old multisolution system required was massive and even a single miss could result in an enormous amount of viruses and junk mails and other inappropriate contents.[6]

Enough was enough. KPIT Cummins sought a solution that would effectively filter unwanted email and strengthen protection against security threats while reducing IT overhead and cost for maintaining the system. In the capability model, this meant a move from a Basic messaging system to a Rationalized email system. KPIT Cummins decided to leverage a combination of on-premises and cloud services to build on both the in-house strength as well as quickly leveraging external expertise.

With a cloud solution, there is no overhead of managing the server. The entire infrastructure is managed by a trusted partner, allowing the IT department to focus on developing innovative business solutions instead of fighting the antispam war. Mandar Marulkar, head of Technical Infrastructure Management Services at KPIT Cummins, put it in numbers: "The services have freed up IT staff members and lowered the administrative burden for IT staff by 20 percent. The support calls to the IT administrative team have drastically reduced from 25 calls to not even one call per month." At the same time, the system is flexible, easy to deploy, and does not require any additional capital investment.

This is the hallmark of a well-developed IT infrastructure. Companies cannot afford to have a Basic IT infrastructure when it comes to security. Security threats come in many variations, but all threaten a company's security and core assets.

Keeping Costs under Control

The theme of cost control runs throughout this book and for good reason: A mature IT infrastructure reduces the total cost of ownership for a company. Optimization models provide companies with a methodology for understanding IT optimization for each of the IT capabilities. The models also provide an actionable road map to help an organization transition from one optimization level to the next. Figure 7.2 looks at the cost savings a company can realize as it matures its infrastructure.

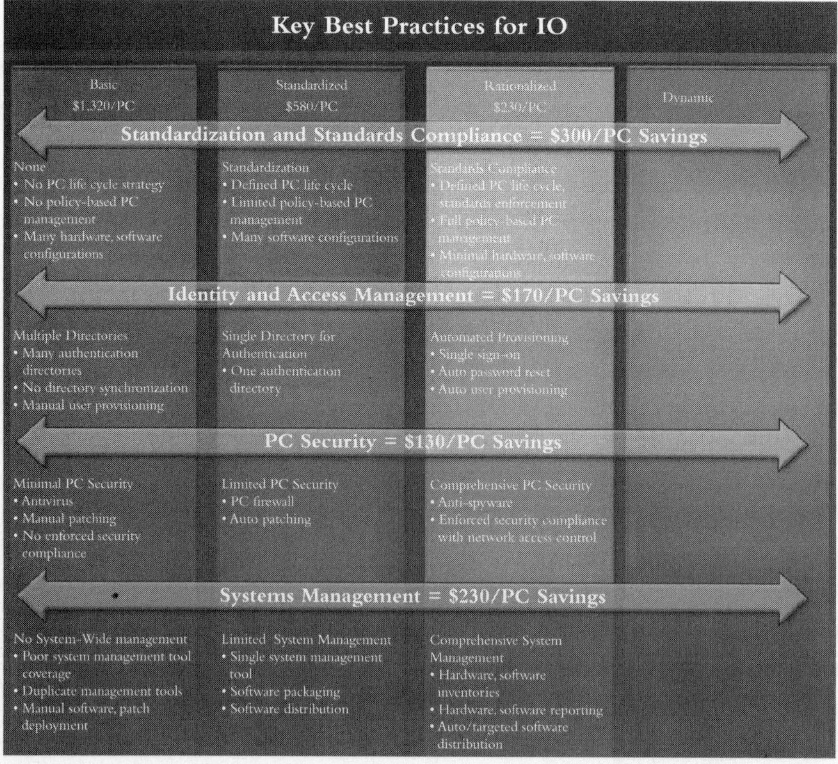

Figure 7.2 IT Maturity Cost Savings

Dramatic cost savings come from moving from an unmanaged environment toward a Dynamic environment. Security improves from highly vulnerable in a Basic infrastructure to comprehensive and proactive in a more mature infrastructure. IT Infrastructure Management changes from highly manual and reactive to highly automated and proactive. Processes move from fragmented or nonexistent to optimized and repeatable. You can see how the costs go down and your ability to use technology to improve business agility and deliver business value simultaneously increases as you move from the Basic state up the continuum toward a Dynamic state.[7]

Control Costs

As a company adopts best practices to improve its optimization level, IT labor costs generally decrease dramatically. On average, companies in the research that were at a Standardized level of Core IO Model had an IT cost structure (per PC per year) that was 56 percent lower than companies at a Basic level. Companies at a Rationalized level had an IT cost structure (per PC per year) that was 60 percent lower than companies at a Standardized level and 83 percent lower than companies at a Basic level.

Where do those savings come from? Outside of the organizational improvements we looked at in Chapter 6, key cost reduction drivers are:

- Reduced IT management costs by moving from Basic to Standardized and Rationalized Core IT Infrastructure.
- Reduction of licensing and maintenance costs by vendor and software consolidation.
- Reduction of employee and IT staff training need by using familiar environments and development tools.
- Improved service levels and reduced help-desk calls are generally achieved when an organization transitions from a Standardized to a Rationalized level of optimization. The number of service-desk calls per PC per year was used as a proxy for service levels within the organizations that were analyzed.

To truly understand the impact these numbers have on your overall IT spending, let's look at the total cost of ownership (shown

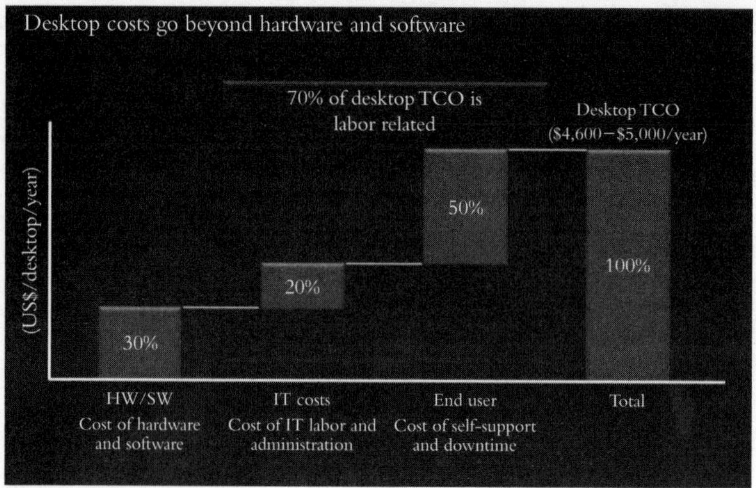

Figure 7.3 Desktop Total Cost of Ownership (TCO)
Source: Adapted from www.informationweek.com/story/showArticle.jhtml?articleID=60401983

in Figure 7.3). Hardware and software typically make up about 30 percent of the overall IT budget. However, when you look at the labor cost, you quickly see it sucks up 70 percent of the budget.[8] Reducing labor costs has a huge impact on the overall budget. In many of the case studies in this book—regardless of the type of business solution a company was improving through IT infrastructure—the companies all said that reduced labor costs was one of their most important results of changes they made.

IDC and other leading research firms typically publish updates to their research every year. They also report cost findings across the entire spectrum of capabilities covered in the IT IO Model. A unified communications (UC) plan is another area where companies can create cost savings through technology. The 2009 Microsoft report "Achieving Cost and Resource Savings with Unified Communications" highlights potential savings exceeding $5 million per year for each 1,000 employees through infrastructure maturity in UC capabilities.[9] A mature UC infrastructure does this by:

- Reducing out-of-pocket costs for communications services, such as telecom and cellular bills and hosted audio and video conferencing, and for related expenses, such as travel and office facilities.

Potential annual savings range from \$2.6 million to over \$8 million per 1,000 employees.

- Consolidating communications infrastructure to lower operating costs by replacing multiple diverse and dispersed legacy products with the integrated functions of the new UC solutions. *Potential annual savings are in the range of \$0.9 million per 1,000 employees.*
- Leveraging human capital by supporting individual productivity, workgroups and collaboration, and enterprise governance. *Potential annual savings range upward of \$2 million per 1,000 employees.*

The report noted that the savings actions had paybacks of less than a year—within a single annual budget cycle—and many have paybacks of less than six months when applied to the high-savings use cases.

OPTIMIZING FOR SIMPLICITY AND AGILITY

Five years ago, it made good sense for IT departments to identify and implement best-of-breed products. Some applications worked well for accounting while other products worked well for product development and other products fit the needs of marketing perfectly. Systems and applications didn't need to share data or capabilities, so it was no big deal. Fast forward to today, and the landscape has changed. An effective and efficient IT infrastructure must be integrated, extensible, and support full employee productivity. In short, everything needs to connect—quality is important, but equally critical is compatibility.

While this is the goal, IT decision makers live in a triangle of conflicting priorities that constrain their efforts. First, they are tasked with reducing the costs of the IT environment. Next, individual capabilities must be improved and developed for specific business requirements. And last but not least, they are responsible for helping the organization realize the maximum benefits of the IT infrastructure.

Roland Zeitler, Information Technology Strategist for Microsoft's Global Accounts, agrees with his customers: "Spending money is only increasing costs, if the benefit and the capability are not increased. Investments on the other hand drive the organization's ability to succeed with increased capability and economic impact." This section is a reflection of the work he and other strategists have done from within Microsoft with some of the largest companies worldwide.

In working with global clients over the past several years, Zeitler and his colleagues identified these key cost drivers:

- Lack of integration
- Best-of-breed islands of software and hardware that involve multiple interfaces
- Many third-party suppliers and even more contracts
- Lack of know-how, either through lack of being up to date or not knowing what is available
- No life cycle management of systems and application—especially no end-of-life strategy

While these are areas that drive costs up, they are also the areas where IT teams can pinpoint to reduce costs. Lack of integration and best-of-breed islands of software have created environments that work very well for a few individuals, but the team across the hall might use a different solution for a very similar task. The IT organization is overtaxed maintaining all the different environments. How many different Internet browsers and versions does an organization really need? How many directory systems or document management solutions? Are four different versions of three different media players really business critical, or merely an IT management and security challenge or even nightmare?

Zeitler and his colleagues focused on five different areas that help customers realize tremendous optimization potential (all are now capabilities integrated in the IO Model):

1. Desktop, device, and server management
2. Collaboration and portals
3. Enterprise content management
4. Business intelligence
5. Development environment and business integration

In all of these areas, customers have the choice between many great products that often provide functionality far beyond what they actually need. However, many of these point solutions often come with not-so-hidden costs. Not only do the different point solutions have to be implemented and maintained, but companies can't realize true benefits unless the different solutions are integrated to work together. Often such integration and customization can take months and armies of consultants. Before making technology decisions, it is far more effective if companies first identify key business capability requirements and then clearly define the infrastructure tool decisions necessary to support the business. This strategy has a direct positive impact on the short-term costs of the IT environment and also creates infrastructures that support business and technology agility.

Through technology, platform, and often vendor consolidation, customers are seeing across-the-board benefits in:

- Reduction of interfaces
- Reduction of applications and tools
- Consolidation of IT vendors
- Consolidation of maintenance agreements
- More empowerment to the IT team
- Average of 25 percent reduction in IT cost of delivering at or above current service and capability levels

Zeitler has worked with many leading manufacturing companies and he shared the next example of what this information looks like in an actual organization. The company wants to protect its competitive advantage, so while I can share the story and most of the facts, I can't disclose the company by name.

This company has a long tradition of innovation. When the business and IT leadership planned their next strategic moves, it became clear that the IT environment had great potential to support both the current and, more important, the future business requirements. However, while IT was clearly seen as a key enabler of the business, more and more of its budget was sucked up in maintaining existing capabilities. There was no money to expand and build new capabilities. Tight supply chain management and a modular platform with interoperable components was a key for success in the industry so the concept of consolidating and building an IT platform that mimicked these manufacturing capabilities made sense to the organization's decision makers.

As the IT and business leaders developed a strategy, they targeted areas that would ensure future agility of the IT platform for the business. However, the solutions would have to—at the same time—reduce software life cycle management costs, evaluation and testing costs, system integration costs, and licensing and maintenance fees.

Consolidation was the first goal. The organization did an inventory across geographies and business functions of existing IT products, tools, capabilities, and workloads. The initial inventory cataloged:

- Vertical applications, such as facility or logistic management tools
- Utilized technologies, such as radio-frequency identification (RFID), storage area networks, or XEON processors
- Utilized standards within IT, such as ABAP, C#, or iSCSI
- Software products
- Customer-specific solutions and solution scenarios

If you are in charge of an IT infrastructure of any size, you are familiar with the difficulty in creating an inventory in an organization that does not have a Standardized IT infrastructure. A rule of thumb to estimate the number of different software applications for larger organizations is to take the number of employees of an organization and divide it by 10. Take the resulting number as a proxy for the number of different applications and versions in use in an organization at any given time. For banks and insurance companies, though, that ratio can easily be 1 to 1.

As the second step, the organization used the Microsoft Infrastructure Optimization Model to identify current and targeted IT capabilities. Figure 7.4 shows the final step in the process: The actual workloads necessary for the organizations business functions were matched to those IT capabilities.

After completing the inventory, the IT team identified redundancies. Figure 7.5 shows as an example the typical IT infrastructure workload for back-end servers and the required functionalities. The company—with a relatively well-managed IT infrastructure—looked like most others. The organization had two or three different products for each function that were not only redundant but were paid for and often under costly maintenance agreements.

Capability	Workload
Business Intelligence	Data warehousing, performance, project management, reporting and analysis, scorecard management
Collaboration and Portals	Automated provisioning and access, business-process planning, desktop integration, enabling, enterprise search, web
Desktop, Device, and Server Management	Consolidation and branch offices, imaging and testing, monitoring, configuration management and capacity planning, operating system and applications distribution and patch management, security, data protection and security
Development and Business Integration	Application integration, application life cycle, development tools, run time and platform, work flow
Enterprise Content Management	Ad hoc work flow and forms, backend and LOB data integration, documents and records management, policy-based retention, auditing and archiving, web content management
Identity, Access, and Networking	Authentification and authorization, configuration, and policy enforcement, directory services, networking services, provisioning and syncronization
Information Worker Client	Access, communication, mobility, productivity, security
Unified Communications	Conferencing and online, instant messaging and presence, mail policies, retention, compliance, journaling protection and archiving, messaging, calendaring, client access, voice integration

Figure 7.4 Workloads for Specific Capacity Improvements

In the third project phase, the IT and business-planning teams analyzed the business case across the targeted capabilities as well as the technical, political, and business requirements. It became clear that sometimes a redundancy could not be avoided, but in many areas duplications were completely unnecessary.

Figure 7.6 from the actual business case shows the cost savings across the different business units. These are not the actual numbers that went out in the company's investor report but do reflect the type and scale of savings realized based on similar projects and organizations.

The final calculation for this organization outlined a 25 percent savings potential, in line with usual projects in this area. The actual implementation surpassed that number as fewer business teams could justify why a point solution really was needed when confronted

Component	Functionality	Common Providers	# of Redundancies
Windows Server, System Center, Forefront, Identity Manager, ISA Server	File sharing	NetApps	2
	Web service	Linux, Apache	2
	Virtualization and management	XEN, VMWare, Citrix,	3
	Network services	Linux, Cisco, Juniper, Bluecoat	2
	Provisioning, identity management, single sign-on	DirX, iPlanet, Siteminder	3
	Configuration	Nagios, Apache	2
	Monitoring	Nagios, Tivoli	2
	Backup/restore	Veritas, Symantec	1
	Virus and spam	Symatec, McAfee, Eleven	3

Figure 7.5 IT Redundancies by Functionality

with the cost impact. When calculating the potential cost reduction for your organization, don't forget that this specific company started on a relatively high level of understanding and standardization. If your organization is more in a Basic maturity stage, the savings

Operating Cost Total		€20,000,000.00	Assessed Redundancy	Reduced Redundancy	
Support	24%	€4,800,000.00	2.03	1.5	€3,200,000.00
Management	18%	€3,600,000.00	2.03	1.7	€2,117,000.00
Hardware/Software	11%	€2,200,000.00	2.03	1.5	€1,466,000.00
Development	7%	€1,400,000.00	2.03	1	€1,400,000.00
Communcation	2%	€400,000.00	1.00	1	€400,000.00
End User	18%	€3,600,000.00	2.03	1.6	€2,250,000.00
Downtime	20%	€4,000,000.00	2.03	1	€4,000,000.00
Without Redundancy		€10,055,172.41		Adjusted Budget	€14,834,313.73
				Business Case	€5,165,686.27

Figure 7.6 Cost Savings across Business Units

potential often is significantly higher. What would your organization be able to accomplish with a more effective IT environment and 25 percent of the current IT budget available for reinvestment into the business?

OFF-THE-SHELF SOLUTIONS VERSUS CUSTOMIZATION

Is the most cost-efficient solution the best strategy to solve an IT issue, or is a strategy of using a few specialized vendors preferable? The best is the enemy of the good. Or is it? Unfortunately, there is no black-and-white answer. The answer will depend on your viewpoint. A simple point solution to a specific problem—there are always a myriad of different products out there—might solve not only the actual problem but include functionality far beyond the actual need of the organization at that moment. Well, having more is better, isn't it? Again, it depends. Even if employees don't use certain software functionality, you still need to maintain the software, pay for licensing, and provide IT support. A limit in functionality actually might be preferred once you look at the big picture.

Let's add these points to the larger viewpoint:

- A heterogeneous environment is more difficult and costly to maintain.
- Integrated systems often provide big-picture synergies. Think of it as 1 + 1 = 3.
- Consistent management tools across the system cost less to support and maintain.
- Consistent end user tools have lower training efforts and costs.

Also, it is important to look at the vendor's road map—and its likelihood to actually deliver against it. While one well-integrated product might not have all the features we desire today, it might be on track to have most of those missing features relatively soon. And software vendors that have systems in place to provide continuous upgrade patches and processes can get additional features to your IT team without additional effort or cost.

Bloomberg, as I discussed in Chapter 5, has always been at the forefront of offering the most-up-to-date technologies, and its employees use the very same systems its customers use. The focus on innovative technology creates strategic relationships with technology leaders. This allows Bloomberg to exchange ideas and directions that impact the tools it offers to its customers. Bloomberg's partnership with Microsoft is one of those relationships.

One result of this customer-centric innovation process is revolutionizing how customers can access and process the more than 20,000 different data sources provided by the Bloomberg service. The Bloomberg team leveraged Microsoft Excel, a tool most of its customers already used, to dramatically simplify and enrich the experience of accessing and analyzing extensive amounts of data. Previously, users had to know which of the more than 20,000 individual data fields they wanted to combine and utilize for a specific analytic task. The data was presented in a horizontal fashion and generically for every user role and type independent of their desired task. Any field and any data could be imported, a fact that overwhelmed many less experienced users.

The Bloomberg development teams under Stefanos Daskalakis and Martin Volerich knew that while Bloomberg customers access information through the BLOOMBERG PROFESSIONAL service, commonly known as the Bloomberg terminal, many users also imported the data into their own customized Office Excel worksheets, which provide more customized analysis. Importing relevant information required memorizing numerous specific field names in order to pull the correct data. Considering the amount of available data, that was a challenge in and of itself.

By grouping fields together for a specific analysis task—such as an earnings estimate analysis or prediction of a company's dividend—end users could create their customized worksheets and insights more quickly.

The development team created a tool—called the Navigation Pane—within the Bloomberg Excel Add-in, which ships with the BLOOMBERG PROFESSIONAL service. The Navigation Pane solves the workflow needs of Excel users based on their primary data needs by automating and extending how data is presented and unlocks new analytic capabilities with a few mouse clicks.

With the new Navigation Pane, those fields are grouped together in a way that makes sense and supports vertical approaches for users, making it much easier to create an earnings or a fundamental analysis template. While all the different data fields are still available to users, the more than 20,000 fields are now much more accessible and are presented to users as predefined groups, specific to the kind of analysis users are interested in. This makes users' lives easier and sparked the next move: providing customers a Rationalized content creation experience in the way data is presented to the users.

Previously, there was a Standardized generic template library from which users could download spreadsheets prebuilt by Bloomberg. Now, with the Navigation Pane, if users click on data item they are interested in, they get only those spreadsheets relevant for their particular task. These task-oriented prepopulated spreadsheets integrate the key variables and data points as a starting point. Users can drill down further by customizing or incorporating additional data points using the drag-and-drop technology within the Navigation Pane. Formulas are then automatically created for users in the spreadsheet.

Fast brains and fast data together are a powerful competitive advantage. And more smart people can now leverage more information. The Navigation Pane improvements and prepopulated analytic tools, leveraging standard and familiar environments, open up critical data to a wider number of users. More users can reach into the data without using advanced features and needing in-depth knowledge of spreadsheet tools. Based on Bloomberg's focus on customers, feedback was translated into tools, and users gained a tool that was concise and tailored to their needs.

Since rolling out the new Navigation Pane, Bloomberg has received ecstatic feedback from customers. Simplicity and ease of use win here, too, as far more Bloomberg customers are now able to derive deeper, more complete, and faster analysis in their areas of responsibilities, gaining a real competitive advantage through the combination of technology for analysis and content creation with information sources. Building on the success of leveraging standard and user familiar platforms to build on, the Bloomberg Product and R&D teams continue to improve the infrastructure and offerings. Through their increased outreach engagements with strategic technology partners, they have raised the awareness level of what is possible if not every component is developed from scratch but synergetic capabilities are unlocked and leveraged.

BUILDING YOUR A TEAM

Business value is generated by what organizations do with IT rather than by the technology itself.[10] If this is true, then IT teams need the expertise to see and articulate the business value their infrastructure brings to the table. Your progressive IT team moves beyond being the technical experts to agents of change driving business transformation. Keeping these highly valuable players on your team and keeping them motivated and equipped is challenging, to say the least. Look at the issues your IT team faces:[11]

- **Runaway user requests**. User requests continue to mount and grow exponentially once the service availability is discovered.
- **Lack of internal coordination of solutions**. There are multiple IT solutions and experiences, but expertise is not being properly leveraged, creating overlapping services and mushrooming solutions.
- **High cost and unstructured ongoing support**. There is dependency on external support; challenges are not being handled adequately, requiring third-party help at higher costs.
- **Unclear business return on IT investment**. There is little or no oversight on benefits/value-add of IT investment to the business; lack of measurement.
- **Little impact on existing schedules and milestones**. A coordinating function that stringently prioritizes portfolio decisions and has oversight on running projects either does not exist or does not work properly as a decision broker.
- **Lack of focused coordination with vendors, suppliers, or partners**. Insight on resources available does not exist or is not leveraged to advantage.

With the increasing importance of team and collaborative work, innovative organizations are forming competence centers to manage shared business infrastructures such as enterprise resource management and business intelligence. An Information Worker Competence Center (IWCC) is a coordinating function providing strategic oversight and decision levers across its portfolio of programs. As an administrative entity, it logically groups "people with interrelated disciplines, domains of knowledge, experiences and skills . . . generally focusing on crucial expertise for the business."[12] An IWCC becomes, therefore, the focal point to turn to for information work–related topics.

Your technology experts—those valuable resources you need to keep—are at the core of the competence center. They are the ones providing strategic oversight and decision levers across your portfolio of programs. They work *upward* with the business goals of the company, *inward* managing the resources and projects, and *outward* networking with other institutions and liaising with its external delivery partners.

The IT team—the core of the competence center—helps drive the innovation and infrastructure by playing the role of change agents who:

- Define training and coaching principles.
- Define and deliver project/solution related training and coaching activities.
- Contribute to the marketing program.
- Apply success measures and reporting.
- Act as the quality assurance entity for the project.
- Have a continued end user improvement plan in place.
- Contribute to a knowledge management repository.
- Supervise change management processes and measures.
- Create online forums where users can support each other and ask questions.
- Create opportunities for face-to-face learning in unstructured or semistructured environments, such as blogs, lunch and learns, or after-hours discussions

Without a strong core of IT players, organizations struggle to implement change.

Involving Key Stakeholders

Throughout this book, I highlight the work done by Microsoft Netherlands and its focus on the "New Way of Working."[13] Its own organization transformation was based on a very savvy strategy: Involve key stakeholders to drive change. The very first step the IT team took was to secure an executive sponsor with enough credibility, influence, and skills to get commitments from the management team members and the rest of the organization. At Microsoft Netherlands, the General Manager, Theo Rinsema, took on this role and stayed personally involved through the process.

Other stakeholders were selected based on functions or skills that were needed to implement the initiative. Each stakeholder also had a strong personal interest and passion in seeing the project completed successfully. Figure 7.7 shows a typical stakeholder team, along with each member's responsibilities.

ROLE	RESPONSIBILITY
General Manager (overall)	Act as the executive sponsor, the public spokesperson, and the customer meetings lead.
Real Estate & Facilities (place)	Provide workplace advantage design, lead local tours, and handle public relations/ executive engagement with press and peers.
Human Resources (people)	Hold change management workshops and ensure compliance with local HR policies for flex time or activity-based working.
Microsoft IT (technology)	Ensure unified communications technology roll-out and training.
Public Relations (communication)	Provide internal and external communications plan.
Training and Readiness Lead (overall)	Ensure internal and partner training delivery.
Business Marketing Organization (marketing)	Provide business productivity IO marketing, executive engagement, and lead generation.
Solution Sales Professionals (technology and sales)	Provide unified communications subject matter expertise and deliver New Way of Working pitch.
Microsoft Services Strategy and Information Worker Consulatants (technology)	Deliver the IMPACT model (see Chapter 6) to customers while providing internal support.
Account Technical Unit (sales)	Get trained, facilitate customer meetings, and drive enterprise agreements.

Figure 7.7 New Ways of Working V-Team Members and Responsibilities

This figure comes directly from the Microsoft Netherlands team's experience and has been utilized as a best practice across many other Dutch and international organizations. Although the list of roles and responsibilities presented in the figure is comprehensive, it is not exhaustive. Your stakeholder team may need other leaders who reflect your organization's requirements.

Including external partners is often critical to the success of your team. Most companies do not have expertise in areas such as interior design, building offices, and cultural change. Additionally, external partners can bring a broader view, both during and after the project. Involving consulting firms that specialize in end-to-end approaches for implementing new working concepts can also be beneficial. These firms often understand the synergies among people, place, and technology issues *and* understand the politics involved with change.

Next Level of Team Players

The transformation was to affect people, the space in which they worked, and the technology infrastructure. With the scope of change that Microsoft Netherlands envisioned, the team chose to extend its reach deeper into specific areas by creating subteams. In addition, the organization also wanted to position itself as a leader in the new way to work so it included sales and marketing in the mix to help the team continually think about how this change could help drive interest and sales. Figure 7.8 shows how they chose to structure their subteams and the tasks assigned to each team. You will notice that the figure reflects the expected amount of time this project would require from team members. Microsoft Netherlands initially made the mistake of not providing team owners with dedicated time for the initiative. As a result, the associated tasks were added to their existing workloads. Lesson learned—not an approach we would recommend today. Instead, ensure that team members are allotted the time it takes to do their team job and are rewarded for their contribution to the company's future.

Subteams work independently, but their progress, data, and decisions need to be checked regularly with the other teams. Most important, subteam participants need to be aware of interdependencies among different teams and establish lines of communication early in the project. Another unpleasant lesson the Dutch colleagues learned was that the

SUB TEAM	RESPONSIBILITIES AND TASKS	GROUP MEMBERS AND AVERAGE TIME SPENT PER WEEK
People	Focusing on development, deployment, and implementation for the mental readiness-of employees; empowering people; addressing change management and communication.	• Human Resources Lead (Owner): 40% • 1 Human Resources Employee: 30% • 1 Training and Readiness Employee: 15% • 1 PR/Communications Employee: 10% Note: At Microsoft Netherlands, ownership of the people subteam was a special assignment for the Communications Manager who spent 30% of her time on culture and mental readiness and was the architect behind our first phase.
Place	Thinking about and implementing physical solutions for the new office building and its interior and facilities, including meeting rooms, audio/visuals, parking, reception, catering, entrance, and security.	• Real Estate and Facilities Lead (Owner): 50% • 1 Real Estate and Facilities Employee: 40% • 1 Real Estate Manager: 15% • Microsoft IT (for audio/visuals, wireless connections, self-service tooling, etc): 30% • 1 PR/Communications Employee: 10%
Technology	Developing and implementing (new) technologies with a focus on the actual usage of the technology instead of executing the technical implementation.	• Microsoft IT Lead (Owner): 40% • 2 Microsoft Services Consultants: 30% • 1 UC Solutions Sales Professional : 10% • 1 Training and Readiness Employee: 15% • 1 PR/Communications Employee: 10%
Marketing and Sales	Increasing the subsidiary's capability to credibly "tell and sell" its own solution to drive product sales, in addition to the New Way of Working initiative at customer sites.	• Business Marketing Organization (Owner): 30% • Specialist Team Unit Manager: 20% • UC Solution Sales Professional: 15% • Account Technical Unit: 15% • 1 Partner Tranining Employee: 30%

Figure 7.8 Phase I Implementation Team Roles, Membership, and Responsibilities

teams wasted time and energy on clashes between overly enthusiastic people who were more or less working from their own vision of the initiative. These participants were good at speaking their minds but not as successful when listening to others. Differing opinions often led to heated and emotional debates.

Rinsema, in his GM role, decided that he would not interrupt these arguments. He wanted to listen to everyone and to keep everyone on board. Rinsema would never push his own ideas or overrule others. Whenever ideas got too far off track, he would say, "They need to have a Zen training facility in their new office." Rinsema then added, "Come on, they are Microsoft. They are down-to-earth, pragmatic, thinking people. Arguing doesn't work here."

At Microsoft Netherlands, Gonnie Been, Manager Communications, took on the role of shaping the New Way of Working subteam focused on people issues. "The development of mental readiness has to be organic," she said. "In my mind, empowering people—giving them the freedom to flourish—results in a win-win situation. The individual is a happier person, and the company profits from an intrinsically motivated, more effective worker who will always look for the next challenge."

Over the last years, organized visits to the Microsoft office in Schiphol have become a "must" for organizational designers and executives rethinking the potential for their organizations. Hundreds of visitors are hosted every month. If you are changing planes in Amsterdam during business hours and have enough time for a visit, stop by. The Microsoft office is a ten-minute walk past the airport hotel.

ONGOING UPGRADES: MOVING FROM "OLD" TO "ALWAYS FRESH"

Improving the core infrastructure capabilities and processes in your organization means software deployments and upgrades can happen at far lower costs, with much higher velocity. With a Rationalized or Dynamic IT, managing, integrating, and deploying a new component is much cheaper, faster, and easier. If the U.S. Army can upgrade more than 400,000 PCs worldwide in less than a year, your organization can do it too.

Organizations now have the choice to either improve or build a capability in house and on premises or simply to buy the capability as a service from a specialized provider. Adding business capabilities to the organization's IT arsenal has never been this easy or cost effective.

Having been responsible for five years with helping customers deploy productivity infrastructures, I was able to discuss with them their technology migration expectations, challenges, and results. While the process can be daunting, deployment tools have vastly improved over the past ten years.

To be clear, even the upgrade of a simple browser creates a variety of technical, compatibility, and end user challenges that shouldn't be underestimated. Upgraded management best practices and tools have come into their own and are readily available. However, more often than not, business leaders are not familiar with the improvements that started in 2001 and do not realize how they could positively impact their environments. When you are assessing the maturity of your IT infrastructure, you have to understand how your organization deploys and manages the IT infrastructure.

What you might find is resistance to change: Think "penny wise, pound foolish." End users don't want to change. Employees don't see the value in doing things differently or do not want to give up their own favorite, and quickly outdated, tools. IT members who want to maintain control use the it-is-very-technical-and-complicated facade to avoid giving you a straight answer. But this is where you have them all beat. While it may seem daunting to give up the old ways of managing software, you have joined the other business leaders who thought the same way. They have been surprised at how smoothly it goes once they get started and are more than happy about both the reduced costs and the required IT support.

ADOPTION MADE EASIER: MOVING DATA, TRAINING PEOPLE

There is a difference between deployment and adoption, and it is critical to understand the difference. "Deployment" is often used as the technical term for software distribution and installation. Deployment starts with planning and installing the IT infrastructure—the hardware, software, and cloudware necessary to support your solutions. The more mature your IT infrastructure is, the more efficient and cost effective the deployment will be. We looked earlier at the IDC data showing 90 percent cost reduction when maturing the IT infrastructure to Rationalized or Dynamic. Figure 7.9 provides a snapshot of what deployment looks like at each maturity level.

Adoption can, but does not necessarily have to, follow the deployment of a new technology or functionality or capability. "Adoption" in our context means the organization has embraced the change and is

Level 1 Basic	Level 2 Standardized	Level 3 Rationalized	Level 4 Dynamic
Basic IT infrastructure is characterized by manual, localized processes, minimal central control, nonexistent or nonenforced IT policies and standards regarding security, backup, image management and deployment, compliance, and other common IT standards. Generally all patches, software deployments, and services are provided with high touch and high cost.	The Standardized infrastructure introduces controls through the use of standards and policies to manage desktops and servers, how machines are introduced to the network, the use of Active Directory to manage resources, security policies, and access control. Generally all patches, software deployments, and desktop services are provided through medium touch with medium to high cost.	The Rationalized infrastructure is where the costs involved in managing desktops and servers are at their lowest and processes and policies have matured to begin playing a large role in supporting and expanding the business. The use of Zero-Touch Deployment* minimizes cost, time to deploy, and technical challenges.	Customers with a Dynamic infrastructure are fully aware of the strategic value their infrastructure provides in helping them run their business efficiently and staying ahead of competitors. Processes are fully automated, often incorporated into the technology itself, allowing IT to be aligned and managed according to the business needs.

*Zero-Touch Deployment is a fully automated desktop deployment in which up to tens-of-thousands PCs are updated or upgraded to a newer software version remotely and without actually physically touching the PC. With this methodology organizations are upgrading thousands of PCs over a weekend at costs of only several $ per PC. In contrast, a manual PC upgrade can cost as much as hundreds or even over $1,000 per PC.

Figure 7.9 Deployment at Different Maturity Levels

Source: Microsoft Corporation, Microsoft Infrastructure Optimization Journey, 2005.

using the new capabilities, and the business is seeing positive change. An organization can deploy new solutions and capabilities, but doing so doesn't mean that employees or business partners will adopt them. And if employees do not embrace the change, you have not only wasted time and resources, but chances are high that you are falling behind your competitors who are leveraging new capabilities. It's the difference between purchasing, deploying, and using technology as opposed to truly owning it. Your new optimized desktops and their management infrastructure enable more sophisticated distribution and security methods. However, efficient deployment does not guarantee maximum productivity gain. Employee acceptance and adaptation have to be part of the optimization plan.

I would like to look at Microsoft Netherlands one last time because its deployment plan leveraged the documented insights from the earlier decade and considered both the mental and technical readiness required for the transformation initiative. The organization believed that employees at all levels needed to internalize the vision, which would make it meaningful to them on a personal level. Employees needed to understand that the changes and tools would improve how, where, and when they worked. Microsoft Netherlands felt that if it had a solid process for change management and strong leadership in place, it could transform a company's culture in six months. It also believed that the process would be iterative—trial and error would be part of the process as employees embraced the concepts and made them their own. For a full explanation of their process, read the Microsoft whitepaper "*A New Way of Working: The 7 Factors for Success, Based on Microsoft Netherlands Experience.*"[14]

Here is a summary of some of the high-level findings and goals from the Microsoft Netherlands, especially three best practices focused on people and cultural issues during a transition.

1. **Analyze employees' work styles and patterns to identify areas for improvement**. To integrate technology effectively with its business, Microsoft Netherlands developed methods to analyze its workforce and gain insight into the current status of employees. This workforce analysis is a useful tool in aligning employees' abilities with the business vision. The analysis gathered information on tasks and activities as well as perceptions about the workplace. Based on the analysis, Microsoft Netherlands could identify individuals who were already prepared to engage in their jobs effectively and, more important, those who needed coaching to determine more efficient ways to work and more effective alignment with company goals. Your organization might have its own expertise in the area, but if not, don't hesitate to bring in specialist outside help to help with this critical analysis.
2. **Pinpoint early adopters and start a pilot**. Because they are willing to change and innovate, early adopters are likely good candidates for departmental pilot leads or leaders for broader parts of the initiative. Their enthusiasm for change is invaluable, and they often provide valuable feedback and assessments to improve deployment and training plans. Identifying and

recruiting early adopters should be a priority. I talk more about early adopters, change agents, and motivation in Chapter 8.

3. **Develop a "guided discovery" rollout**. Cultural change does not work using a top-down approach, although management leadership is still vital. Empowering people to discover how they can use the new capabilities to improve their work life means higher acceptance levels. Microsoft Netherlands found that personal discovery—permission to engage with tools, space, and other people in ways that are comfortable and productive for their own work styles—gives individuals an ownership stake in the initiative. They will experiment and make mistakes, but they will also have the coaching of their peers and managers to help direct them. This is what is meant by "guided discovery."

The organization constantly explored innovative ways to engage employees in its transformation. Managers wanted to promote more transparency and involvement so they gave up their offices and started sitting among their coworkers at a different place each day. Although the organizational structure remained, everyone shared the same type of space.

Assigning a brief homework was another approach to adaptation. Microsoft Netherlands created a short self-evaluation, similar to those found in lifestyle magazines, and sent it via email to all employees. Employees had to take the test to be admitted to an upcoming company wide team event. The questionnaire was a combination mini-personality test and work style test. The results were used to create groups of like-minded people who would attend the offsite together. Four distinct profiles emerged: Entrepreneurs, Researchers, Idealists, and Diplomats. Entrepreneurs, for instance, were found to be overly busy, fast thinkers, and strong communicators. Short messages are the best way to communicate with them, so a five-minute voicemail with an introduction to the new program and details of what the subsidiary expected from them was devised. Researchers, however, were given a memory stick with several documents from which they could retrieve information that met their individual needs.

To be clear, we don't advocate simply replicating the categorization that worked for a sales-focused subsidiary in every work environment. What we do recommend is to understand that your employees have different communication and learning preferences, often based on a combination of job function and working styles. Define and sort your employees by different profiles into several categories, and then determine what kind of communication styles and tools are most appropriate for these categories. The outreach and acceptance will be much smoother. In our case, the self-evaluation was tied to the offsite because business leaders felt if employees spent a full day learning about, discussing, and realizing the potential of the New Way of Working initiative, they would be more likely to feel that the program was beneficial to them personally. Smart planning meant it was a fun day with good food, conversation, and interaction. Employees did not sit in a meeting room for hours on end listening to a talking head.

Over the years, more and more research has been done on how to accelerate change and technology and process adoption in organizations. Pick those that work best in your environment in order to boost adoption rates in your organization. Don't overlook this critical final step in rolling out new capabilities to your organization. You have to plan this part of the process as completely as your infrastructure capability improvement prioritization and your capability deployment plans.

NOTES

1. www.ivi.nuim.ie.
2. Al Gillen and Randy Perry, "Windows Client Operational Costs: Trending Toward a More Mature and Cost-Effective Infrastructure," IDC, June 2009.
3. Microsoft, "Cable Operator Delivers Applications Dynamically to Keep Users Productive," 2009.
4. Microsoft, "The Road to Desktop Optimization," 2008.
5. Microsoft, *Microsoft Security Intelligence Report*, vol. 7, 2009. The *SIR* is published twice per year. These reports focus on data and trends observed in the first and second halves of each calendar year. Past reports and related resources are available for download at www.microsoft.com/sir.
6. Microsoft, "IT Company Claims 100 Percent Secure and Clean Network Using New Forefront Security Services," 2010.
7. Al Gillen, Randy Perry, Seana Dowling, Tim Grieser, "Optimizing Infrastructure: The Relationship between IT Labor Costs and Best Practices for Systems Management Server," IDC, 2007.
8. Leading analyst firm, December 2005. Note: Excludes server and network costs for centrally managed services.

9. Microsoft, "Achieving Cost and Resource Savings with Unified Communications," 2009.
10. IT Governance Institute, "Enterprise Value: Governance of IT Investments," 2006, p. 10.
11. Simone Ruppertz-Rausch, "Information Worker Competence Center—Achieving Business Success with Your Collaboration Infrastructure" (May 2009).
12. Gartner 2002 (IGG-08072002-03).
13. Microsoft, "A New Way of Working: The 7 Factors for Success, Based on Microsoft Netherlands Experience," 2009.
14. Ibid.

CHAPTER 8

OPTIMIZING YOUR WORKFORCE: LEVERAGING THE NEW WITH THE OLD

Many people think that IT companies are naturally the fastest adopters of technologies. While that is not necessarily correct for all IT development companies, Microsoft is proud to embrace (its own) technology early. Employees get to be early adopters way before the software goes out the door; often most of the workforce is migrated to a new Exchange, Windows, or Office version more than a year before the products are released into the market. By "eating their own dog food" and working closely with actual customers participating in beta programs, Microsoft ensures that its products are used and tested in a real environment well before shipping to customers.

This access to early technology innovations means that the average Microsoft workspace is usually more advanced than you would find at most companies. Always looking for a new edge, Bill Gates published an internal study in the early 2000s. One point the study made was that the average productivity of an employee can be increased by 25 percent simply by adding a second screen to the workplace. Multiple monitors immediately started springing up on desks all over the Microsoft campus. Those departments with bigger budgets skipped the multiple small-screen tactics and went with one very-large-screen monitor. To some, size mattered.

It makes sense that the IT industry and IT service providers have the most advanced and mature business infrastructures. IT is their business, so they should darn well have the biggest and best IT toys. But what about the customers who are outsourcing their IT infrastructure to third parties?

We analyzed the maturity data for customers who had outsourced their IT infrastructure and compared them to their peers by size and country as well as across their own industry. We discovered an astonishing trend. While IT third-party developers are early and major adopters of new technologies, their customers—in general—are slower than their geographical and industry peers. Of course, there are exceptions. However, those companies that take in-house ownership of their IT infrastructure are operating on a higher maturity level compared to organizations that outsource core IT functions.

A commitment to be on the leading edge of technology has given many companies a competitive edge in their industry. Every once in a while, one of these companies impresses even the most experienced Microsoft executives. Microsoft Vice President Gurdeep Singh Pall is responsible for the technical side of Microsoft's Unified Communications business. He has been with the company in executive positions well over a decade and has seen Microsoft change from a PC-focused organization to one that leads the way in helping develop enterprise infrastructure.

Which company made him stop and take notice? Was it another IT company? Was it some Internet start-up in the Silicon Valley? No. It was Bloomberg L.P. in the heart of Manhattan. The company provides financial tools such as analytics and equity trading platforms, as well as data services and news to financial companies and organizations around the world via the BLOOMBERG PROFESSIONAL service. Bloomberg is also known for its unique company culture and office space: part trading room, part newsroom, and part technology research and development—all in perpetual motion.

When Gurdeep visited Bloomberg the last few times, he was very impressed by its design and adoption of technology through the Bloomberg Workspace for employees. He explained, "[They are] getting and realizing the impact on results of smart technology use." Bloomberg's physical and technological work environment was described by Paul Goldberger[1] as

> truly designed for the electronic age . . . a dazzling work environment. In the workspace, large, flat-panel monitors hang from the ceilings, flashing constantly updated numbers: how many customer-service people are working at that moment, how many calls they have answered, how long it's taking to answer the average call that day. Other screens display the latest news, market happenings, and other information.

Founder Michael Bloomberg famously insisted on an open workspace, with no closed offices, even for himself, to limit physical boundaries that could be in the way of an employee with a great idea to discuss with a colleague or a senior manager. Every Bloomberg employee who comes up with an idea of making a product or service offering more customer focused is literally expected to walk up to the leadership team to effect change immediately.

In this open and transparent work environment, employees are leveraging the latest individual productivity, communications, and collaboration tools to foster customer-centric innovation and creativity. The combination of culture, tools, and physical setup ensures that the enormous amount of information relevant to the employees and their clients' businesses can be accessed, absorbed, integrated, and improved as efficiently as possible. Keeping workplaces up-to-date also requires having proactive control of the underlying architecture and IT management environment. In this Dynamic environment, the IT department has shifted resources from maintaining the status quo to becoming a business enabler and business driver for the organization.

Why did Bloomberg make these investments in technology, environment, and culture? Bloomberg executives were very clear on the necessity of this workplace environment for a simple reason: "Having the best employees deliver the best solutions for their customers."

In the business of collecting and distributing knowledge and information, it is critical to attract the brightest and best people to work for the organization. Those people want the best tools, and it is Bloomberg's strategy to deliver them. The leadership team is convinced that the strong, motivated, and creative workforce is the key reason why Bloomberg is able to stay ahead in the knowledge business and why its customers and clients can stay competitive in their businesses utilizing the solutions Bloomberg offers.

TECHNOLOGY IMMIGRANTS AND DIGITAL NATIVES

While some people (mostly us geeks) salivate when they hear "computer" or "upgrade" or "Internet" in a sentence, many others panic. A company can dedicate resources and dollars to optimize its technology infrastructures and then see the entire project flop—not because the integrated platform and innovative collaboration tools don't work but because employees don't use them.

Much has been written about the challenges of making sure employees who care little for or fear technology are comfortable embracing IT tools. Many books cover dealing with different generations and technology experiences. Building on this academic foundation, we will be looking specifically at how technology immigrants—those who did not grow up using PCs—can embrace new technologies and innovations. We will also focus on the "digital native"—those workers who have grown up wired to technology wherever they go.

There is a new kind of generational gap forming in the accelerated world of social computing: microgenerations. Where traditional gaps were every 15 or so years, these new gaps are narrowing to less than 10, possibly even getting down to 5. Technology is driving this rapid change. One of the main drivers is social tools that are evolving at a blistering pace and are connecting people in ways and scales never before seen in human history.

"People two, three or four years apart are having completely different experiences of technology," Lee Rainie, Director of the Pew Research Center's Internet and American Life Project, recently told the *New York Times*. "College students scratch their heads at what their high school siblings are doing, and they scratch their heads at their younger siblings. It has sped up generational differences."

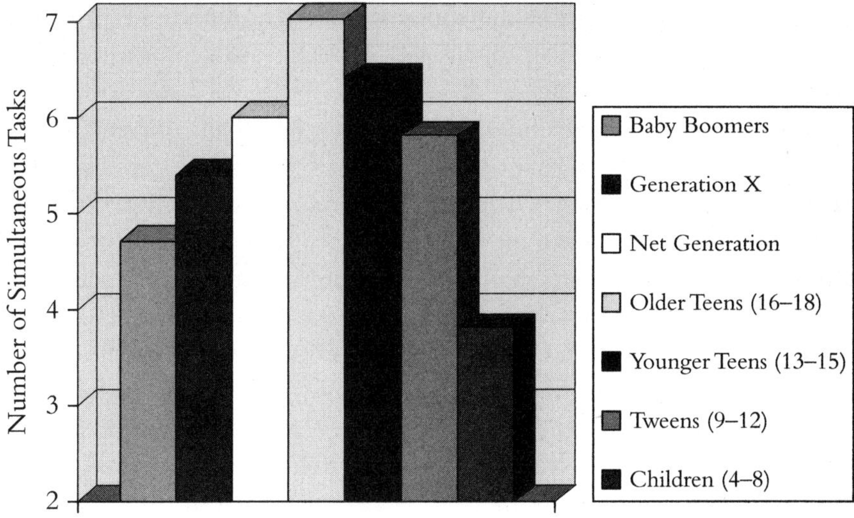

Figure 8.1 Multitasking by Generation

According to Mizuku Ito, of the University of California Humanities Research Institute, younger children will make less of a distinction between online (virtual) friends and real friends and will be pickier about what they decide to adopt from popular culture. And according to Larry Rosen, professor at California State University-Dominguez Hills, the number of simultaneous tasks that each generation can handle is increasing (see Figure 8.1).[2]

Younger employees are going to bring a whole new set of skills and expectations to the workforce. That has been true for the PC generation, the email generation, the instant messaging wave of people, and now the social networking citizens. And very likely it will be true for whatever technology and generation comes next. While I don't know what the new tool in ten years will be, I am sure the speed of innovation and adoption will continue to increase and span more platforms, more geographies, and more people. Savvy IT and business leaders need to consider, plan, and implement the foundation for the current and the future needs today. As they look at how their current infrastructures will need to become even more flexible to support the next generation of workers, the focus on and need for simplification and manageability in combination with capability improvements will only accelerate.

Rosen also points out that the tools up-and-coming generations use to communicate are going to impact organizational communications infrastructures.

Another interesting trend is the increasing use of all communication tools, including email, instant messages, chats, telephone calls, and text messages. All told, 5- to 8-year-olds communicate "electronically" a half hour a day; the figure increases to nearly two and a half hours for 9- to 12-year-olds, more than six hours for 13- to 15-year-olds, and a whopping eight and a half hours a day for 16- to 18-year-olds. In addition, teenagers are now spending more time sending text messages from their cell phones than actually talking on them. According to a 2009 national survey by Nielsen Mobile, U.S. teens send or receive an average of 2,899 text messages a month compared to making or receiving only 191 cell phone calls. A Harris Interactive national survey of teens has even shown that 47 percent of the 2,089 nationally sampled teens could compose text messages blindfolded.[3]

But even before these kids make it into the workforce, social media and networking are influencing business practices and affecting the bottom line. A study by Wetpaint and the Altimeter Group confirms that deep engagement with consumers through social media channels correlates to better financial performance. The study showed significant positive financial results for the companies who had the greatest breadth and depth of social media engagement. These social media mavens, on average, grew company revenues by 18 percent over a 12-month period while the least engaged companies saw revenues sink 6 percent on average over the same time period.[4] Companies will look to IT departments to make sure the organization has an understanding of and a presence on social media sites.

It is important to understand that not only young people adopt new technologies. If the value is clear for the older demographics, they quickly adopt a technology. Most people of all generations are now familiar with email and online banking, but social networking also has become prevalent. MySpace was adopted mostly by the younger generation, but Facebook is on a broader adoption trend.

Facebook began in the student community, but it soon branched out into cross-generation communication and information sharing as well as into commercial space. From 2009 to 2010, the strongest growth in the Facebook user community was in the 35-and-older age group. By spring 2010, the number of 55-and-older Facebook users had reached nearly the number of teenagers. However, the older group has an astonishing growth rate of more than 10 times faster than the teen group. A niche technology in 2008, Facebook crossed the chasm in 2009 and became mainstream in 2010. Today social networking technologies are used by many employees outside of work, and more and more members of all generations are expecting to use this new way of communication and information sharing in the workplace too.

GETTING EVERYONE ACROSS THE CHASM

Throughout this book, I've talked about how agility—the capability of rapidly and cost efficiently adapting to change—is a necessary tool for organizational innovation. IT teams not only have to design a mature and flexible IT infrastructure to support this innovation; they have to get the individuals and the organization itself to embrace and to use it. And that doesn't mean use it eventually. It means using it now.

Figure 8.2 gives a quick snapshot of the typical adoption curve IT teams face. This particular curve looks at social computing—a fast-growing area, especially within consumer product companies. The

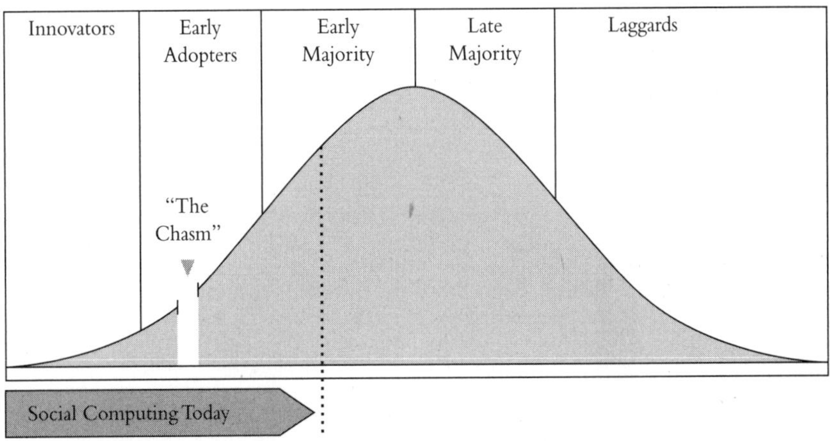

Figure 8.2 Technology Adoption Curve

Source: Forrester, "Technology Adoption Affects Social Computing Adoption and Brand Affinity," 2007.

Innovators and Early Adopters are on one side of the chasm. The challenge is getting the Early Majority, Late Majority, and, last but not least, the Laggards across the chasm.

Ways to motivate the 80 percent on the other side of the chasm can come in several forms. In the book *Influencer: The Power to Change Anything*,[5] the authors maintain that successful change is about clarifying measurable results, finding vital behaviors, and analyzing six sources of influence (see Figure 8.3). Change efforts fail because people either overlook sources of influence or they miss vital behaviors.

IT teams can learn valuable strategies from their thinking. The foundation of the approach is thinking about change in terms of motivation and ability. It's asking the questions: "Can they do it, and is it worth it?" Then IT teams need to add the layer of personal, social, and structural perspective. Here is a simple way to look at it. If you don't deal with personal motivation—What is this worth to them?—your influence will fail. If you don't provide solid training—Can they do it?—your influence will fail. If you don't enlist help and influence of others, you miss the key factor of social ability: If an entire department is making a change, it makes it much harder for a few dissenters to dig their heals in against the

	Motivation	Ability
Personal	1 Make the Undesirable Desirable	2 Over-Invest in Skill Building
Social	3 Harness Peer Pressure	4 Find Strength In Numbers
Structural	5 Design Rewards and Demand Accountability	6 Change the Environment

Figure 8.3 Six Sources of Influence

Source: Kerry Patterson, Joseph Grenny, David Maxfield, Ron McMillan, and Al Switzler, *Influencer: The Power to Change Anything* (New York: McGraw-Hill, 2007), p. 78.

change. If you don't make it worth their time and energy or help them understand why this is important to the company's bottom line, your influence will be limited. And, more important, if you do not have the infrastructure to support the change, you might as well go home.

SOCIAL NETWORKING: A TOOL FROM HOME GOES TO WORK

Change is a process, and IT teams need to be able to accept success and quickly learn from failure. Since some initial efforts will fail, it is important to leverage the lessons learned in an iterative fashion. This means that when something looks like it is stuck or going south, don't be afraid to make a quick change to see if it alters the direction. Facebook has been a perfect example of the process. Its success is in trying, failing, and adjusting quickly rather than trying to be perfect out of the gate.

While Facebook is a great tool for the public, enterprise social computing has to be a bit more structured. Employees need to get a job done, not just share information for a social purpose. To that end, the policies, motivations, and roles have to be constructed in such a way as to enable those employees to work better, faster, and, it is hoped, cheaper.

Why this focus on enterprise social computing? Hard return on investment/cost savings are not the main reason a company embraces social computing. Many studies have shown that this is not the primary (or even tertiary) benefit. Rather, the benefits are around capturing and sharing valuable knowledge, increasing the ease of finding/communicating with colleagues, driving innovation through the unstructured work paradigm, and attracting and retaining talent of the newer generations.

Employees who have experienced the productivity- and work environment–enhancing effects of social networking cannot imagine going back to a working world without it. For them it is like having to live and work without email or a cell phone. A large investment bank in South Africa learned this lesson the hard way.

Even in the midst of the largest financial crisis of nearly a century, the competition for talent is still on. The financial sector, in particular, works hard to attract new talent by providing the latest and greatest technology. Doing this falls on the shoulders of the IT department. If it is not proactively providing this technology, employees—even in these tough economic times—will vote with their feet by leaving to go to an organization that is more technologically savvy. They don't want to work for an organization that focuses on putting out IT fires; they want a company that gives them the tools to be successful.

Sarah Mocke is a senior architect in our South African Services organization with more than a decade of experience helping customers realize their potential. She got pulled into a situation at an organization where the pattern of putting out small fires had led to a full-fledged three-alarm fire. And how hot the fire was burning became very clear when she met with the IT leaders who were in complete panic mode.

The bank was experiencing a tremendous brain drain. Over a few months, the entire actuary workforce—who represented over 1,000 years of experience—left the bank to join their competitors. The business leaders of the bank put the blame squarely on the IT leadership.

During exit interviews, it became blatantly clear that the actuaries were leaving because the company did not provide the IT tools they expected and needed to be successful. The most glaring hole was the lack of an internal social networking structure. The lack of a networking infrastructure meant actuaries could not efficiently create and share business knowledge. Furthermore, they felt unproductive, underutilized, and disconnected.

Broad layoffs across the organization made it clear to many of these employees that they could not count on their employer's loyalty toward them. And studies show that employee loyalty toward companies is diminishing dramatically at the same time. Today's employees look at their work experience and culture in the short and medium term instead of the long term. The bank saw how these two trends come together adversely. Its employees left because they thought they could be more productive, more impactful, and have more fun in their daily roles and responsibilities with competing organizations.

Until the bank's business leadership confronted the IT team, the team was completely unaware of the demand or need for social networking. But even worse, it also was completely unprepared to address the challenge by building the infrastructure and tools necessary to enable the capability in a reasonable time. It was a tough spot to be in, especially with the pressure of executive leadership on the team's back.

Luckily, the established relationship between IT and the Microsoft team paid off. The bank's IT leaders reached out to Microsoft contacts for advice. Sarah and her team were brought in to design a solution based on the latest technology and standard software components. Finding and acquiring such talent—either internally or externally—is a huge challenge for many organizations. The ability to design business-oriented technology infrastructure on standard components with quick turnaround times is a talent in strong demand and in short supply.

In this particular case, the Microsoft and partner team is working with the customer to establish the social networking infrastructure based on SharePoint 2010. The bank will have the technical ability to create what its employees were seeking. The IT team still leaves the bank leadership with the task of actually building a functional internal social network of individuals and replenishing the loss of talent. But at least the infrastructure is there. The brain drain has slowed, and the investment bank can stay competitive in the talent and knowledge management battles.

SECTOR INFLUENCE ON CHANGE

It is not only the employee or corporate culture that sets the tone of technology acceptance and change. Different business sectors adopt change at different rates for different reasons. For example, for the financial services sector, speed is usually a defining success factor. Companies continually try to seize opportunities faster than their competitors—constantly shifting or adjusting strategies to meet the needs of regulators, evaluating global business opportunities, enticing new customers, and attracting new talent. Our data analysis and the work of the research teams have clearly shown that Agile companies come out ahead. These firms know they can realize benefits quickly if they introduce new capabilities that allow more connections and collaboration among various business units and the customers they serve.

As part of the analytic work to derive insights from the infrastructure assessment data by capability and to allow customers to utilize their own assessment and general industry data for benchmarking, Mathias Wunderer, the director of Infrastructure Optimization strategy, and his analytic team realized that an intuitive way for the visualization of multivariable data sources is the format of a radar chart. This chart, which is sometimes called a star chart, star plot, or Kiviat diagram, allows graphical presentation of many variables starting from the same central point. Because of the multitude of Infrastructure Optimization (IO) capabilities represented, the resulting graph by industry or customer resembles a spider's cobweb (and is sometimes called a web or spider chart).

As we outlined earlier, benchmarking within an industry is important to identify direct competitive threads as well as opportunities. The radar chart visually shows the position of an organization against a comparison group, such as an industry or geographical area.

The comparison across industries to see what is the norm in a segment of the market we traditionally haven't considered as a benchmarking point can be very interesting. We can see our position and optimization potential and learn from the optimization and business impact potential from other sectors.

During our drill down into specific industries with Wunderer and his team, we looked at the industry average and how technology leaders in one industry benchmark against the technology leaders in a different industry. The results were eye opening and provide excellent guidance for readers to benchmark their own organization against.

Figure 8.4 visually shows you how a company can benchmark against not only its sector but against sector leaders. The image looks very different depending on the sector you use. For example, leading automotive companies traditionally live in the Basic to Standardized region for most capabilities. However, top companies in the finance sector can call far more mature capability status their own.

As discussed earlier in detail, the measurable impact of agility on business success was made extremely and painfully clear in the financial sector. Some Wall Street firms chose to adopt technology as fast as possible with the right controls and governance in place. These firms view IT as an important part of their winning strategy. Other financial services firms chose to just "keep the lights on." They let others lead in technology adoption. Sometimes they made a conscious decision, and

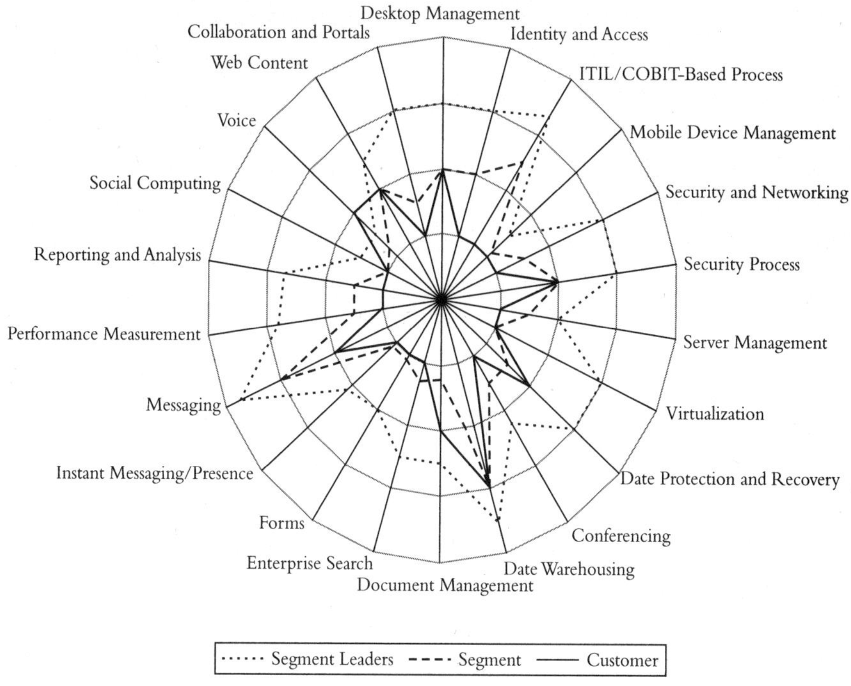

Figure 8.4 Company IO Compared to Sector and Sector Leaders

sometimes they made a we-always-did-it-this-way decision to spend their budget and resources on *maintaining* services. Many of these non-Agile firms have (or had) incredibly talented and savvy employees, but their Basic IT infrastructure limited their ability to truly collaborate and apply technology to solve business problems. Many of the slow adopters became nonadopters just before they went out of business.

Not all sectors move as fast as the financial industry. But the data shows clearly that even in industries that have a conservative reputation, some organizations get Agile and carve themselves a competitive advantage. Government, oil and gas, publishing, and manufacturing—all conservative sectors—are applying technology to improve common business processes. But there is a reason these sectors have moved more slowly and given IT more scrutiny. Just a few months before the disastrous sinking of the Deepwater Horizon in the Gulf of Mexico, one major oil/gas firm IT executive told me that while innovation in his industry is important, if someone makes a mistake in implementation, "an oil rig could blow up in the middle of the ocean." In his industry, even modest innovation without the right controls can introduce unanticipated results. The security and stability that comes with proven fine-tuned processes, repeated thousands of times, outweighs the ability for innovation of an organization. But even such a conservative approach is not fail-safe, as we have unfortunately seen far too often. And in the response to such a disaster, if man-made or natural, we can see the agility of an organization clearly again. Finding the right balance between organizational agility and efficient and repeatable processes holds true across all industries, although not with the same life-or-death consequences. Careful analysis and evaluation are key parts of a successful migration project.

Sometimes manufacturing firms face a similar problem. A firm manufacturing jet engines or night-vision goggles, for example, does not rush into change in its core business. IT teams in these organizations must balance employee drive to use technology to improve their work with the absolutely necessary goal of producing high-quality, predictable products. These companies can focus on improving the processes that *surround* the critical path product work. For example, the way design information is communicated, analyzed, and stored is often easy and quick to modernize with direct business results. It doesn't affect the actual product or production process in the short term. but it helps designers and businesses get the correct information into the correct hands more quickly.

Government entities also have traditionally taken a very conservative approach to the use of technology. The risks to national security or the overhead and costs associated with adopting new platforms without a solid and well-thought-out business case slow many projects. Even in the face of obvious business benefits, the politics and perceived complexity involved have affected the pace of innovation in many government entities. Today the situation is changing somewhat, and some U.S. government sectors are adopting new and innovative technologies faster than ever before—some even faster than commercial industries.

Military leaders look at the importance of a Dynamic IT infrastructure with two goals in mind. A very senior official in the U.S. intelligence community commented that in today's world, the availability of accurate, reliable information is critical for decision making. Agility in the field and in the supporting technologies is not a nice to have; it is a must-have. It is interesting to note that the Internet was used heavily by the military before the rest of us got hooked on it. For example, look at peer-to-peer file-sharing technology. For many of us, we think of file sharing as music and video files shared over Napster or BitTorrent. The U.S. military has used distributed file sharing over the last decade to share intelligence and field data. Many consulting organizations need an easy system to keep distributed consultants informed and in sync. They picked up on the system used by the U.S. military, which has been one of the largest users of the secure and encrypted file-sharing Groove technology.

But military leaders have looked beyond immediate benefits of improved intelligence. They also see technology as an innovative recruiting tool. Today's military has to appeal to the younger audience to attract new recruits and retain talent. Take a look at any defense-related public Web site and you see links to video, audio, multimedia, social networking tools, and very appealing and fresh content.

Because content and information rule in social media and networking, they are creating major changes in the publishing industry. These firms certainly are interested in making sure they have unique and excellent content, but their use of technology to distribute content was bumpy at first. Not so long ago, our discussions with IT professionals about the merits of improved database mining, up-to-date desktop operating systems, and improved email and presentation software was met with resistance. Many media executives and their IT teams didn't necessarily see the business value. And until the business value is proven or a business unit takes the initiative to do something innovative, adoption of new technology happens at a slower pace. By now it has become clear to all that the media industry is in dire need of changing its view of IT business value based on global economic conditions, increased competition, and the need to deliver content over nontraditional means. The good news is that such change is possible.

The media industry today is in process of a massive change. The Internet and the way information is controlled and exchanged have challenged the traditional business model of distributing news and financing journalism via advertising. Posting a small ad in the local newspaper to sell a car, find a mate, or rent a house seems antiquated. Craigslist, Match.com, and eBay have changed the way we buy and sell, date, and rent. These modes are so much more efficiently and Agile. Why would we ever go back to the "old way" of advertising information? With traditional advertising revenue disappearing, how can the actual journalistic content creation be financed and capitalized on?

In the United States, nearly one-third of journalists have lost their jobs in the last years, and newspapers are closing in many cities. But some media companies are growing. How? One of the clearest explanations I have seen was from Mathias Döpfner, CEO of Axel Springer, in an interview with Charlie Rose on PBS. Döpfner stated that by focusing on the consumer experience and leveraging the strong consumer base as content providers, his corporation had actually grown, both in profits and in employees, over the last years. Key for his company has been embracing new media, especially mobile devices. Mobile device users are familiar with paying for usage and consumption. Axel Springer has found that consumers will pay for exclusive content that is easy or entertaining for them to consume. Döpfner sees the iPad and similar devices, such as Amazon's Kindle, as additional distribution channels and, from a cost perspective, they are superior delivery channels to his consumers.

But one of the most interesting places to look right now for innovation and future visions is in the pharmaceutical industry. *Sanofi-Aventis* is the world's third-largest pharmaceutical company. It primarily develops and markets prescription pharmaceutical products but also makes over-the-counter medications. It has 100,000 employees working in 100 countries across five continents.[6] And it is one of the most innovative and forward-thinking enterprises around.

In late 2008 Chris Viehbacher came on board as Chief Executive Officer and launched a transformation initiative aimed at broadening the company's portfolio beyond traditional pharmaceuticals. "The problem with a business model based on blockbuster drug development is that it's highly cyclic and very expensive," Viehbacher explains. "Pharmaceutical companies spend billions of dollars and many years developing a drug that can either be very successful or be shot down during testing. Even if a drug is successful, it's a gamble whether we make our investment back before the patents expire. We want to get out of this peak-and-valley cycle and diversify our business into vaccines, branded generics, and more over-the-counter medications, in addition to pharmaceuticals, to create a basis for more sustainable growth."

To execute such a far-reaching transformation, Sanofi-Aventis planned on giving employees the most up-to-date software so they could collaborate, innovate, and cross-pollinate ideas more quickly and easily. To achieve this vision, the company chose a set of Microsoft products and services that includes Windows 7 Enterprise, Windows Server 2008, Microsoft System Center Configuration Manager 2007, and Windows Internet Explorer 8. By upgrading its 100,000 client computers to Windows 7 Enterprise, Sanofi-Aventis gained a modern, stable desktop environment that the company can build on for years to come. Standardizing on the most current operating system will help the company achieve its business-transformation goals by giving users and IT staff alike a foundation for the latest productivity and communications software. "We would struggle to deliver the new services and innovations that our CEO Chris Viehbacher envisions on an old-technology platform," says Daryl Corum, Senior Director of Client Engineering Services at Sanofi-Aventis. "To take the business in new directions, our employees need to be able to take advantage of the latest communications, collaboration, and social networking technologies," Corum says. "Our IT staff, too, needs to be more agile and able to plug in all the new applications and innovations that the future will bring."

Users have seen significantly improved performance with Windows 7, particularly during computer start-up and shutdown, which were previously causes for complaints. Faster computers mean fewer interruptions throughout the workday and a greater ability to work more productively and creatively. "Our business transformation initiative is all about equipping employees to collaborate more, use new social networking technologies, and innovate faster," Corum says. "When we are trying to accelerate the overall pace of business, we can't tolerate slow underlying technologies." This is a prime example of a company striving to build a Dynamic infrastructure that not only supports business goals but also enables and drives these goals.

OLD DOGS, NEW KIDS, AND THE NAYSAYERS

I've talked a lot about the people in charge of the IT infrastructure; now it's time to look at the different employees who plug into and use it. We often associate the use of new technologies with the incoming younger generation. However, many members of the older generations—which covers all of us born before 1975—are not apprehensive about embracing new technologies. Many Baby Boomers are avid users of Facebook or MySpace, using these tools to stay in touch with their families. They are also getting comfortable with video-chat and instant messaging.

While they are not leading the charge in new technology adoption, the experienced members of our workforce are the ones who actually carry the decades of experience and business intelligence that are critical to company success. The challenge is getting the experience and knowledge out of their heads and into the broader corporate culture. Social networking and presence technology can help unlock this knowledge for broader leverage in an organization, but you may need more directed efforts actually to get the old dogs and new kids on the same page.

One of my favorite concepts in the work environment is structured and targeted peer mentoring. By systematically creating and fostering peer mentoring relationships between a tech-savvy newcomer and a senior but less "modern" employee, both employees and the organization usually win big. Benefits are often immediate, especially when structured around an actual project. It is also one of the best ways to foster the transfer of knowledge, experience, and productivity potential.

So, you have developed a great peer mentoring program, dedicated resources and dollars to optimize its technology infrastructures, and are blessed with strategic and smart organizational leadership. But you still have parts of the employee base—and leadership—who are reluctant at best or rabidly negative about change. This is not unique to technology changes. It is discussed in literature on organizational leadership and change management. You may want to do a detailed search on specific tactics that fit your organization.

One of the best places to view the convergence of old dogs, new kids, and naysayers are in certain government organizations. Exacerbating the challenges of a diverse employee population is the issue of reconciling huge numbers of forms and data on aging technology infrastructures. In developed economies, governments face the challenge of replacing legacy infrastructure assets and systems. In developing or rebuilding economies, governments face the challenge of building or establishing systems for the first time.

As if insufficient IT infrastructures aren't bad enough to deal with, significant workforce skills shortages compound matters. Beginning in 2005, the number of retirees—the old dogs—in Europe is expected to increase by up to 30 percent each year, and this retirement rate is already affecting the national pool of skilled IT people.[7] Agencies not only face the challenge of reducing the complexity in the IT environment and the total cost of ownership; they also have to contend with a shrinking pool of skilled workers. Research also points out issues upstream in the education system. European countries already have difficulty generating a sufficient level of enthusiasm for computer sciences among prospective students—our new kids. U.K., Dutch, and German technical universities showed a drop in student numbers of between 5 and 20 percent between 2001 and 2005, with some drops as steep as 40 percent. European governments are thus likely to struggle simply to meet the bare minimum of IT workers that will be needed by the industrial and commercial sectors.

Registries—such as land registries, business registries, registries of births, deaths, and marriages—and forms—if you have been in a government office lately, you know what I'm talking about—are the backbone of most government organizations. The quantity of data is staggering, and the amount of data handled manually is almost too much to imagine. You have the Bermuda triangle of bad IT infrastructure—data sitting in silos, systems that are incapable of handing any type of work flow, and a workforce that is unable or unwilling to work from anywhere except a cubicle in the government office. It's not that government agencies don't want to be Agile and transparent; they often just lack the tools, budget, and leadership necessary to drive change.

Budgets are not going to change. One research paper on government workforce issues points out that governments are sharply focused on the converging economic costs of aging populations, red tape, tax avoidance, and benefits fraud. These converging forces will have widespread impact on budgets. For the first time, more of the populations will be old rather than young, requiring a broader range of services over a longer period paid for by a smaller taxpayer base. In addition, escalating tax avoidance and benefits fraud add to the pressure to protect the revenue base.[8]

If budgets can't change, then government agencies will need to look at tools and leadership to impact their issues. For an example of how sound leadership in government affects change, we can look at the local authority in the state of Hessen in Germany. Hessen has a population of about six million people and in addition to traditional government and clerical workers, also police, teachers and, e.g., social service workers are employed by the state. Like many government agencies, it was under pressure to improve services, manage the issues based on urban transitions (demographic change), and, of course, reduce costs. An integrated IT infrastructure would be the necessary foundation. Yet, like other government authorities, Hessen has innumerable departments with various activities within the state, each of which has its own business systems and applications designed specifically to deal with its needs. When Viprocom, a leading information systems consulting group, first met with the leadership team in Hessen, it calculated something like over 400 different applications and user interfaces used by 65,000 employees.

It wasn't just the infrastructure that was overly complex. The forms and processes were equally impenetrable. For example, in Germany there is a regulation that requires employers to submit an application if they want employees to work on Sundays or national holidays. The Sunday labor approval process included over 11 steps with up to 7 employees working on it at different locations. This involved assessing of approval rules, editing and managing the notice, and controlling the respective invoice receipt, all of which required multiple specialized applications. The overall process was both labor intensive and time consuming, and with several system discontinuities and changes in responsibility, there was a high risk of failure.[9]

This is a system that was crying out for intervention. Working with Accenture, Microsoft, and Viprocom, the department deployed a government workplace modernization concept that would standardize and unify the work environment. The hub of the solution was the Viprocom Office Business Gateway (OBG.net). The platform was designed to improve workforce performance, help employees respond to citizen demands quickly, and, at the same time, reduce costs—all using applications already owned by the department. Employees were able to work with software programs they already knew, which made adoption easier and quicker. Since the programs were fully integrated with each other, employees never had to leave one application or system and log onto a new one to only have to log back onto the original one. One study of the Frauenhofer Institute showed that by using OBG.net, time spent handling administrative processes was reduced by as much as 60 percent.[10]

NOTES

1. Paul Goldberger, "Towers of Babble," *New Yorker*, August 6, 2007.
2. Larry Rosen, http://drlarryrosenmemyspaceandiblog.blogspot.com/.
3. Ibid.
4. "Deep Brand Engagement Correlates with Financial Performance," *The Altimeter*, July 20, 2009.
5. Kerry Patterson, Joseph Grenny, David Maxfield, Ron McMillan, and Al Switzler, *Influencer: The Power to Change Anything* (New York: McGraw-Hill, 2007).
6. Microsoft, "Sanofi-Aventis Upgrades Desktop Software to Aid with Business Transformation," 2010.
7. Richard Peynot, "Europe's Looming IT Skills Deficit," Forrester July 6, 2005.
8. Microsoft, "The New World of Government Work," 2006.
9. Viprocom analysis report for customer.
10. Jens Fromm and Josephine Hofmann, "Wirtschaftlichkeit und Interoperabilität des Modernen Verwaltungsarbeitsplatz. (MVAP) an Musterprozessen im Arbeitsschutz Wiesbaden," Fraunhofer Institute, 2009.

CHAPTER 9

STARTING OVER TO STAY AHEAD

As we have seen, Agile organizations, more often than not, eventually triumph over organizations that are unable to adapt as quickly and efficiently. If we take responsibility for the future of our organization, taking the steps necessary for improving our agility must be a core element of our strategy.

In the first section of this book, we took a good look at ourselves. As Sun Tzu explained in his *Art of War* over 2,600 years ago:

> So it is said that if you know your enemies and know yourself, you can win a hundred battles without a single loss.
>
> If you only know yourself, but not your opponent, you may win or may lose.
>
> If you know neither yourself nor your enemy, you will always endanger yourself.

An organization that has assessed their own strengths and weaknesses has identified capabilities necessary to sustain and to grow in the environment and benchmarked its processes, costs, and infrastructure capabilities against the leading organizations. Those insights, coupled with key business goals, prioritize the investments and execution focus to be taken.

We discussed how to leverage synergies between IT and business process improvements and how to use the capability improvement project to grow a sustainable, Agile organization. We looked at the typical challenges faced in such a change process and how to overcome them.

So we arrived, didn't we?

Well, competition is a journey. A competitive advantage today is likely to become a common business practice sooner rather than later. If we don't continue to innovate and to stretch our organizations, we fall behind quickly—even if we are a leader today. Organizations that truly change their DNA into a continuous self-innovating organism continue their assessments on a regular basis. They will look back at their accomplishments and celebrate and recognize how far they have come. And then they reassess the situation. As the world changes, what capabilities do organizations need going forward? What is the updated priority list? And how can we leverage the latest improvements in process and IT to stay competitive?

I know that starting over is about the last thing you want to do now. You have assessed, designed, deployed, and gained new agility with a more mature IT infrastructure. You have reduced costs while improving efficiencies in the overall business. New capabilities increase system security and employee productivity. Your IT team can now design and deliver services and capabilities that provide greater business value, fortifying and strengthening your organization's competitive position through technology-driven business innovation.

So why am I asking—actually telling—you to start over? Technology continues to evolve. Hackers dream up new ways to attack your system. Customer wants and needs change. New competitors come onto the playing field, and old ones continue to innovate. You get the picture. However, you don't truly start over. Your Infrastructure Optimization (IO) Model provides the stepping-off point for further innovation. Your now-improved capability position in your IO Model informs your next steps and is the foundation for further growth.

Throughout the book, we've looked at customers who started with little or no real IT infrastructure—like the government office in Hesse, Germany—to companies with a strong foundation of IT expertise—like Bloomberg or BMW. Bloomberg isn't waiting around for others to catch up but continuously focuses on how their employees can be more effective in bringing better solutions to their customers. They continue to analyze, compare, learn, innovate, and build. Even with their Dynamic IT infrastructure, they continue to find new opportunities to innovate their services. And they have the infrastructure in place that supports rapid development and deployment.

New advances in user interfaces, devices, and mobile technology will contribute to push productivity capabilities. If you have put a solid unified communications strategy in place, you have the infrastructure to add new capabilities and ensure security across various communication channels. We have seen how advance business intelligence solutions let financial institutions differentiate themselves from competitors and how modern collaboration platforms can save thousands of lives in a disaster situation. Other industries can learn from these knowledge and innovation entrepreneurs and employ the same types of solutions to gain a competitive edge in their business sector. However, deploying and, more important, maintaining, integrating, and managing the solutions to unlock their full potential and the lowest costs require a mature IT infrastructure of people, tools, and processes. All the data we have seen and the stories we have heard are clear in one message: If you have invested in maturing your IT infrastructure, you are very likely going to win over the competitors that have not. They just can't keep up in business-critical areas as customer engagement or insight, innovation or knowledge management, or simply with their less effective cost structure and ability to adjust process and for business changes.

During the course of this book, we looked at the reason why your organization must be an Agile one if it is going to be around and relevant for your customers in the future. We looked at the different ways to understand and prioritize technology capabilities for maximum business impact—either to defend against competition or to grow and expand an organization's impact. If we learn fast, we can develop a competitive advantage. If we learn slowly, we will play catch-up with our competition. And if we don't learn, we will be out of the game sooner or later.

Studying examples across industries, organizational sizes, and initial capability maturity levels, I found it encouraging that if leaders have the will to push the self-critical assessments, organizations can turn around rather quickly. Sometime, with the right leadership, organizations that were so far behind their competition that they had nothing to lose take the challenge of optimizing their IT infrastructure and rebuild from the ground up. If those organizations truly have learned and leveraged the ecosystem of platform technologies, they could rebuild a very capable organization in surprisingly little time. Working jointly with those motivated and self-critical leaders has been a highlight of my professional life. Helping these truly Agile leaders to be successful through sharing experiences, coaching, joint learning, or hands-on strategy development and implementation planning is rewarding and invigorating. For me, it demonstrates the potential the organizations and we as society have and actually can realize.

It is said that it is relatively easy to identify the right ladder to climb up when you are standing on the ground and hardest when you are already up the wrong ladder. Nobody likes to climb down before they begin. Sometimes it is too late for an organization to make changes. Markets change so quickly that the lack of capabilities, agility, and competitiveness becomes blatantly clear, and organizations simply disappear.

But, hey, let's not get to that point, okay? You bought the book, and that's a good sign! You are willing to learn. And in addition to the examples here, many of your peers in similar situation are willing to share their experiences. Remember that simplicity wins; complexity in the IT environment makes only your IT services provider happy. It doesn't help you run your business. The IO Model has—in only five years—become a tremendous asset for all of us. Designed originally to help explain the value of technology to a business, the model and the data have become so much more. Experiencing and helping organizations through the capability optimization journey to unleash their potential was a game changer for me and my personal career direction.

The world is changing: often for the better, and surely increasingly fast across many dimensions. Especially in the IT environment, most of the change will benefit you and your business; you just have to ride the wave and not be pulled under it. Every part of your business can and likely is (and should be) impacted by technology.

Granted, leveraging technology to create an Agile organization is not always easy, but it also is not that hard either. I truly believe that this book provides you the guidance to take the steps and drive the discussion between the business and the IT leadership on business and IT capabilities. If necessary, don't hesitate to bring in consultants who understand business and technology. They are excellent resources to facilitate and help lead your business through the discussions and process.

Peer networking with good consultants and partners can help you to ask critical questions.

Don't be scared by change, technology, or buzzwords. Not moving hurts more in the long run.

Get going! Embrace technology—early and fast. Continuously leverage insights and improve your business processes. Maintaining the status quo is ultimately organizational death.

Get your new folks and young employees to show you and your leaders their stuff. And yes, even if some of your IT folks joke about it, keep reading the technology section in the news and airplane magazine.

In the end, we are responsible for our own success. Are we Agile and on the edge? Or are we members of the club of laggards? It is not the buzzwords we use to define ourselves but the actions we take every day that define us.

As Eleanor Roosevelt summarized nearly a century ago:

> One's philosophy is not best expressed in words; it is expressed in the choices one makes. In the long run, we shape our lives and we shape ourselves. The process never ends until we die. And the choices we make are ultimately our own responsibility.

INDEX